D1631970

1 331990 001 1F

ONE-ACT PLAYS
FOR THE
AMATEUR THEATRE

ONE-ACT PLAYS
FOR THE
AMATEUR THEATRE

CHOSEN BY

MAX H. FULLER

EDITOR OF
"TEN SELECTED ONE-ACT PLAYS"
"MORE SELECTED ONE-ACT PLAYS"

AUTHOR OF
"CHOOSING AND PRODUCING A PLAY"

GEORGE G. HARRAP AND CO. LTD
LONDON   SYDNEY   TORONTO   BOMBAY

First published 1949
by GEORGE G. HARRAP & CO. LTD
182 High Holborn, London, W.C.1

Dewey Decimal classification: 822·08

*Composed in Baskerville type and printed by the Pitman Press, Bath
Made in Great Britain*

FOREWORD

IT will be noted from the contents that several leading playwrights have contributed to this collection of one-act plays; it is important that such outstanding authors should write shorter plays for the amateur theatre, for the amateur, no less than the professional, needs plays of the highest quality; indeed, the professional actor can often 'save' a poor play, the amateur seldom, if ever.

This does not mean that only the well-known playwrights can write good one-act plays: gems from unknown authors turn up now and again, but they are so rare that the amateur theatre is almost starved of new material worth producing. Thus, unless our best playwrights can be attracted to write in this particular medium, there is likely to be a continued dearth of good, new, actable material.

This collection will, I hope, help in some small way to meet the demand for such material. With the exception of two, all the plays are published for the first time: they are all actable; and they should suit all tastes.

Several of the plays have either been broadcast or televised, but, except in two instances, all were written primarily for the stage. It does not follow, however, that plays written specially for broadcasting cannot, as some critics suggest, be successfully adapted for the stage: certain radio plays, it is true, are exclusively radiogenic, but many need very little adjustment for stage purposes.

Now that the interest in dramatic work is so widespread, perhaps other of our leading playwrights

will have time to turn a kindly eye on the amateur
theatre; and, after all, the greater the stimulus the
amateur gets, the larger will be the audiences in the
professional theatres, and the more discriminating will
these audiences become.

M. H. F.

ACKNOWLEDGMENTS

THE compiler desires to express his thanks to Mr Denis Johnston (formerly Television Programme Director at Alexandra Palace); Mr Geoffrey Whitworth (formerly Director of the British Drama League); the author and Messrs Constable and Co., Ltd, for *Paradise Enow*; and the authors for *The Rose and Crown, Remember Cæsar, The Dark, The Man who thought for Himself, The Creel of Trout, Malvolio, The Advantages of Paternity, Moggy the Cat-burglar, We were Strangers, Song in the Wind, Operation 'Cold Cure'*, and *Bicycle Belles*.

CONTENTS

THE ROSE AND CROWN

by

J. B. PRIESTLEY

CHARACTERS

MR STONE
MRS REED
PERCY RANDLE
IVY RANDLE
MA PECK
HARRY TULLY
A STRANGER

The action takes place in the Public Bar of the Rose and Crown, a small public house in North-east London. The time is an evening in early autumn.

Applications regarding amateur performances of this play should be addressed to the agent, A. D. Peters, 10 Buckingham Street, London, W.C.2.

THE ROSE AND CROWN

*The scene is the Public Bar of a small public house in poorish
district of North-east London. If an actual set is used, then it
should show a dingy and rather cheerless room, with perhaps
one curtained window and the usual advertisements, preferably
faded in colour, on the walls. The door is centre up stage, and
so long as it is practicable it can either be a simple single door
or the familiar swing doors. The actual bar is not seen, being
on the fourth wall. What is seen, just inside the setting line,
is the counter of the bar, cut through the middle, so to speak,
and quite solidly built. It should be about 12 feet wide. As
no landlord can be seen—though the actors have to play, very
carefully, as if he were there—the business of receiving drinks
and paying for them must be imaginary business; but if the
producer prefers the actors to have glasses in their hands—and
this is better—then the bar counter must be built fairly solidly
to the ground, and these glasses must be produced cunningly by
the actors from shelves, invisible to the audience, fastened on to
the up-stage side of the bar.*

*But for a simple production no actual set is necessary, only
the door at back and the bar counter, with drab curtains as
walls.*

*The lighting is fairly strong but should have a dreary effect.
It is absolutely essential that there should be at least one strong
F.O.H. spot. Ideally the play should be lit from the front.*

At rise of curtain the stage is empty for a moment, and then
STONE *enters. He is a grumpy, middle-aged man, fattish,
shabby but not too shabby. He can smoke an unpleasant little
pipe. He carries an evening paper. Like the others who follow,
he must go through the pantomime of ordering the drink, etc.,
very carefully, and it is primarily his business to create the
illusion of the invisible landlord,* FRED.

STONE [*grumpily, at counter*]. . . . And good-evening to
you, Fred, if you want to call it a good evening. . . .

Pint of brown . . . [*He glances at his paper, then goes through business of receiving and paying for his drink, then taking a pull at it. He looks suspiciously at his paper again.*] What? No, I 'aven't seen Charlie lately, and I don't know that I want to . . . well, 'e doesn't amuse *me*. . . . All right, Fred, it takes all sorts to make a world. I wish some of 'em 'ud make me a few two-inch lead pipes. . . . No, not for love nor money. Drive yer barmy. [*He has now settled down, staring gloomily down at his paper, towards right end of bar.*] Two planes crash. I'm not surprised. There'll be plenty more before so long, you'll see. Cars too. You watch it. Just blue murder, that's all—blue murder. No proper precautions—that's the trouble—no proper precautions. . . . [*As* FRED *apparently tries to tell him a story*] If it's the one about the bookie who stayed with the widow at Doncaster, I've 'eard it.

> [*He stares at his paper again.* MRS REED *now enters. She is a thin, middle-aged woman, loquacious and mournful.*

MRS REED. Good-evenin', Fred. Good-evenin', Mr Stone.

STONE [*shortly*]. Evenin'.

MRS REED [*to* LANDLORD]. I'll take a drop o' stout, Fred—Guinness if you 'ave it. I feel that tired some o' these nights—properly worn-out, you might say—that I don't feel like eatin' nothing—an' only a nice drop o' stout will sit on my stomach. I went out to my sister's last night—the one that's married to a painter an' decorator with a nice business of 'is own—at least it *was* a nice business once—an' she give us rissoles—an' nice an' tasty they seemed at the time—but when I got 'ome my inside felt 'eavy as lead an' burnin' like fire. [*She has now gone through the business of receiving and paying for her drink. Her story is broken off because Stone stares disapprovingly at her and makes a tut-tutting sound. She stares aggressively at him now.*] 'Ow d'you mean—*t-t-t-t*?

STONE [*heavily*]. I mean—I've got enough troubles of me own, Mrs Reed—without you servin' up your rissoles an' your inside——

MRS REED [*on her dignity*]. Oh—well, if it comes to that, Mr Stone—I've got plenty o' troubles of *my* own—an' one of 'em is that you won't come an' put a new pipe in my sink——

STONE [*indignantly*]. If I've told you once, Mrs Reed, I've told you a dozen times—I can't put a new pipe in till I get a new pipe. That stands to reason, doesn't it?

MRS REED [*very dubiously*]. Does it?

STONE [*exasperated*]. Look—I spend all day tryin' to argue with people like you——

MRS REED. Not with me, you don't. I've something better to do——

STONE. I said, "People like you." An' when I can take 'alf an hour off of an evening, like this, I want to give it all a rest, see? But I can't put a new pipe in for you if I 'aven't got a new pipe to put in, can I? Is that reasonable—or isn't it?

MRS REED [*darkly*]. I don't know. What I *do* know is that Mrs Ferguson, three doors down, 'as 'ad a whole bathroom put in—double-yew and all——

STONE. Well, I don't know anything about that—she isn't a customer of mine——

MRS REED. No, that's easy to see. Black Market, I expect. It all goes together. 'Aving her 'air waved every five minutes an' nipping into the Saloon Bar of the White Horse for gins an' limes—I've 'eard about 'er——

STONE [*grumpily, trying to read*]. Well, I 'aven't, an' I don't want to.

> [*He reads.* MRS REED *stares at him indignantly, and then looks bored. It is obvious that the* LANDLORD *is no longer in this bar.* MRS REED *tries again.*

MRS REED. 'Ave you read where it says that woman

in Moseley Terrace gassed herself 'cos 'er 'usband wen'
an' sold the pianner to go bettin' at the dogs? [STONE
*merely grunts, without looking at her. After another moment
during which* MRS REED *gives up any attempt to interes.*
STONE, PERCY *and* IVY RANDLE *enter. They are a young*
married couple. He is tallish, thin, pessimistic. She is small
and slight, fearful and rather wistful. MRS REED *looks at*
them with interest, and then calls officiously for the LAND-
LORD.] Fred—Fred!

> [*We see* FRED *enter by the answering stares of* MRS
> REED *and the* RANDLES.

PERCY [*as if replying to Fred*]. No, I don't think it *is*
a very nice night.

IVY [*in a tiny voice*]. It's turned quite cold.

PERCY. What yer 'avin', Ivy? Bitter or mild?

IVY. Mild, I think, Percy.

PERCY [*to* FRED]. 'Alf of bitter, 'alf of mild. [*Goes
through business of getting drinks and paying, while* IVY *and*
MRS REED *exchange tentative mournful smiles*.] Well, here
you are, Ivy. Now drink it, don't sip it.

IVY [*to Mrs Reed*]. He always says that to me, an' I
know I never do drink it—I always sip it. I don't
think I like beer really—I just come in to keep Percy
company—what I really enjoy is a nice glass of port
wine.

PERCY [*with sad raillery*]. You an' your port wine!

MRS REED. I used to like a small port now and then
meself—but now, look at the price, even when you can
get it.

IVY. That's right.

PERCY. Isn't much of it about these days.

STONE [*heavily*]. There's plenty o' port wine about, if
you keep your eyes open.

MRS REED [*aggressively*]. Oh—is there? News to me.

PERCY. Same 'ere.

STONE. Well, there is—only it's muck. Like a lot of
other things now—it's muck.   [*Returns to his paper.*

MRS REED [*to Ivy*]. 'Aven't I seen you at Magby's— greengrocer's at the corner?

IVY. I expect you 'ave. Though I've only just started going there.

MRS REED [*gloomily*]. You want to watch 'im.

PERCY. Isn't that just what I said, Ivy?

IVY. Yes, you did, Percy. [*To Mrs Reed*] My 'usband said just the same thing. "You'll 'ave to watch 'im," he said.

MRS REED. He doesn't try it on with me any more— he knows better.

STONE [*looking up, aggressively*]. Try what on?

MRS REED. Never you mind. I'm not talking to you, Mr Stone. [*To Ivy*] But you watch 'im.

STONE [*heavily*]. 'Ave you people ever 'eard of the lor of slander?

MRS REED. Go on. Nobody's gettin' slandered.

IVY [*alarmed*]. Oo—I never said anything, did I? Did I, Percy?

STONE. I didn't say you did. But *she* did. And *'e* did. An' what I say is that there's such a thing as the lor of slander. I'm a tradesman an' shopkeeper myself——

MRS REED. That's right—an' you're all in a click, if you ask me.

PERCY [*gloomily*]. I wouldn't be surprised.

IVY [*frightened whisper*]. Shut up, Percy.

PERCY. Why should I?

MRS REED. Don't you.

PERCY. This—er—gentleman 'ere says 'e's a tradesman an' shopkeeper. Well, I an' my wife are customers, that's what I say. That used to be something, one time, to be a customer.

MRS REED. Yes, when they couldn't afford to treat you like dirt.

STONE [*rather violently*]. Nobody wants to treat anybody like dirt except when they behave like dirt——

MRS REED [*angrily*]. Who behaves like dirt? That's

B

casting aspersions, that is, an' it's personal, an' not called for. Dirt indeed! If you'd attend to my sink like I've asked you to do——

STONE [*cutting in*]. There it goes again. That's just what I mean. Customers! They won't listen to reason, just won't listen to reason. I suppose you think I can grow new lead pipes in the back garden like sticks of flamin' rhubarb!

IVY [*hopefully*]. I can't touch rhubarb. Never could.

STONE [*in despair*]. Am I askin' you to touch rhubarb?

PERCY. That's right. You're off the argument there, Ivy. It's like I told you. You will get off the argument.

MRS REED. Well, who wants to get on to the argument? Argument! Argument! There's too much argument nowadays.

IVY. That's what I keep tellin' Percy.

> [STONE *wags his head angrily and makes a loud tut-tutting sound, then retires to his paper.* MRS REED *makes a face at him, for* IVY's *benefit.* IVY *giggles and tries to suppress it.* PERCY *looks at her severely.*

MRS REED. I'm like that about tomatoes.

IVY. Are you reelly?

MRS REED. It come over me quite sudden too. One day, you might say, I properly enjoyed a tomato. Next day, as you might say, I couldn't face one. An' I been like that ever since. But I've 'ad a lot of trouble with my inside—delicate.

IVY. My 'usband's sister's just the same. Isn't she, Percy?

PERCY. Been like it ever since she was a kiddie, Doris has. An' it doesn't make for 'appiness, does it?

MRS REED. 'Appiness? Don't make me laugh. Look —I wouldn't know it if I saw it now.

STONE. Don't worry. You won't see it.

MRS REED [*ignoring him*]. I'll tell you straight—what with one thing an' another—if I was asked right out if life was worth living—d'you know what I'd say. I'd say No. Honestly I would.

IVY. Percy says the same thing sometimes. Don't you, Percy?

PERCY. Now an' again. I'm not like some chaps— I notice things an' try an' think a bit. And then—as Ivy says—it gets me down. Yes, I'll admit it. It gets me down.

STONE [*grimly*]. If it gets you down now, what are you going to be like at my age? You 'aven't 'ardly started yet. You wait!

PERCY. It may be as bad for me as it is for you. There needn't be any waiting about it.

STONE [*grimmer still*]. You'll see. Just wait till you 'ave to try an' run a business with everybody screamin' at you—an' you've got a family that's grabbin' everything you earn—an' your 'air's fallin' out an' your teeth's droppin' out—an' you get varicose veins an' lumbago——

IVY [*proudly*]. Percy has very responsible work at the warehouse —an' he has to 'elp to keep 'is mother—an' he gets terrible 'eadaches. Don't you, Percy?

PERCY. Cruel. That's the only word for 'em. Cruel. An' there's no cure. 'Ad 'em all me life.

MRS REED [*sighing*]. Oh—well—if it isn't one thing it's always another.

IVY. That's right. Though I suppose it's a long road that 'as no turning.

STONE. Well, what if it is? Where does that get you?

PERCY [*with dignity*]. My wife was just passin' a remark, that's all. No need to pick on 'er like that.

MRS REED. Take no notice of 'im. Got out of the wrong side of the bed this morning.

STONE. 'Ow do you know?

MRS REED. That's personal an' uncalled for again, if you ask me.

PERCY. Quite so. Ungentlemanly.

STONE [*disgusted*]. Oh—turn it up.

> [*He stares at his paper. The others relapse into a gloomy silence.* MA PECK *now enters. She is an untidy old woman who looks a bitter and disreputable character.* MRS REED *sees her as she advances slowly.*

MRS REED. I understood Fred Norton 'ere was tryin' to keep a respectable house.

MA PECK [*arriving at bar*]. Did you pass a remark to me, Mrs What's-it?

MRS REED [*with dignity*]. No, I didn't. Not to you. I was speaking to this lady 'ere.

MA PECK [*with mock refinement*]. Oh—to this lady 'ere —was you? Charming weather we're 'aving—except that the nights is drawin' in rather. *Grrrr!* [*Bangs on the bar counter and shouts.*] Hoy—what's your name! Fred! [*She goes through business of watching him enter bar, and grins.*] Now then—just look after an old woman who's 'ad more than 'er share of trouble. I want a glass of brown with a nice drop o' gin in it. . . . Go on, of course you've some gin. . . . Don't worry, you won't see too much of me this time, 'cos I can only afford one go, an' I don't see any o' this lot paying for a few more for me.

MRS REED. The last time anybody did, you was 'ad up in Court.

STONE [*nastily*]. And not for the first time neither.

MA PECK. Well, they'll never 'ave you for bein' drunk an' disorderly. You're too mean—even to yerself. Stone by name, an' stone by nature. And her father was just the same.

STONE. Now—look 'ere——

> [*But it is obvious that the* LANDLORD *has protested too, and* MA *listens and replies to him, having now got her drink.*

MA PECK [*to* LANDLORD]. All right, Fred boy. Not another word, I promise. I'll be good. [*She drinks, and obviously enjoys her drink.*] I'm only a daft old woman that's buried everybody that ever cared anything for her—an' with one foot in the grave. [*To the shrinking* IVY] You'll come to it, dearie, if you live long enough —you'll come to it. [*As they are silent and look glum*] 'Ere I come in 'ere to be cheered up a bit. What's the matter with you lot? You're young an' got yer 'ealth an' strength, 'aven't yer?

PERCY [*with dignity*]. We've got our troubles same as you. In fact, we was just talking about 'em.

IVY [*warning him*]. Percy!

MA PECK. Percy! So Percy's got 'is little troubles, 'as 'e? Poor Percy!

PERCY. All right, Ma. Not so much of it.

MA PECK. Ma! Listen, Percy, I've buried five men —two 'usbands an' three sons—that would 'ave eaten you for breakfast—yes, an' then asked for some 'addock. Ask Mr Stone there—'e knows. [*She looks at* STONE, *who keeps his eyes on his paper.*] Well, what's in the paper?

STONE [*growling*]. A lot o' dam' bad news, as usual.

MA PECK. I dare say. But it's my bad news that worries me—not theirs. [*To* IVY] What do you say, Ducks?

IVY. Yes, that's right.

MA PECK. That's right, is it? Well, I'll bet you don't 'ave much trouble with Percy 'ere—unless 'e doesn't always wipe 'is nice little shoes clean when 'e comes in. When I was your age, Dearie, I was married to a sergeant in the Marines, an' when '*e* came 'ome— something 'appened—one way or the other—upstairs or down—an' you knew you'd got a man in the 'ouse. [*She sprawls mournfully on the bar, almost talking to herself.*] Oh—Gawd—what's the use o' talkin'? Nobody knows any more, an' nobody cares. An' why the 'ell should they? Old Ma Peck! She ought to be quietly pushin' the daisies up somewhere like the rest o' the Pecks. [*She turns to the others.*] You an' your troubles! Just wait till you're old an' alone an' nobody wants you any more—an' you're awake night after night—an' every bone in your rotten old carcase is aching! [*Almost mumbling to herself*] An' then when you come in to enjoy a drink an' some lively company—same as there used to be—you find nothin' but a handful o' long-faced, scowling bloody dummies. Oh—Gawd's bitter truth—but I wish I was dead an' done with it.

> [*There is a gloomy silence. This is broken by the entrance, brisk and hearty, of* HARRY TULLY. *He is any age between thirty-five and fifty, decently though not well dressed, and a healthy, jovial, matey fellow.*

HARRY. Evening, everybody! Thickening a bit outside to-night, but a nice smell of autumn about it. Always reminds me of when I was a lad. Don't know why, but it does. Good evening, Mr Stone. How's business?

STONE. Evening. An' business is the same as usual these days—rotten!

HARRY. Go on! You're not doing so bad. I know. How are you, Mrs Reed?

MRS REED. About the same. It's my inside.

HARRY. Hard luck. But you're looking better. Now where's Fred?

MA PECK [*suddenly looking up*]. I know you—Harry Tully.

HARRY. That's right. And I know you, Ma. Enjoying yourself?

MA PECK. Miserable as hell, Harry boy. This lot act as if they'd be better dead, an' I feel it.

HARRY. Well, have one with me, Ma.

MA PECK. That's a good boy. Now, don't go, Harry.

HARRY. I'm not going, I've only just arrived. Pull yourself together, Ma. Then you can tell me some of them funny stories that Mr Stone's been telling you.

MA PECK. What—'*im*? If he had a funny story, he wouldn't part with it. This is Percy, Harry.

HARRY. How are you, Percy? This the wife?

IVY [*shyly*]. Yes.

HARRY. Pleased to meet you. Hoy, Fred. Don't keep the customers waiting. [*He obviously sees* FRED *enter.*] How's it going, Fred? . . . That's right. It might be better, but it might easily be a hundred times worse. Remember that night we all jumped for it under the bar counter. And the night we pulled Meaty an' his missis an' the kids out of the back of the shop. It's Bob's your uncle now compared with them days. Well, a pint of half-and-half for me, Fred, and a small brown with a drop of gin for Ma here. . . . Go on, Fred, you can find a drop for old Ma. . . . That's right, Fred. Oh—and what about Mrs Percy here—one for the bride, eh? All right to you, eh, Percy?

PERCY. Oh—certainly—what would you like, Ivy?

IVY [*shyly*]. There isn't any port wine, is there—just a little glass?

HARRY. Yes, every time. Fred's got some port wine somewhere, haven't you, Fred. . . . Right you are, then. In a minute we'll settle down and make our miserable souls happy. Eh, Ma?

MA PECK. You're a good boy, Harry.

HARRY. Don't you believe it. What do you say, Mrs Reed? You've heard a thing or two about me, haven't you?

STONE [*grimly*]. If she hasn't, *I* have.

MA PECK. Nobody ever believed a plumber yet, and we're not going to start now.

HARRY. O-oh! Well, it served you right for talking out of turn. Good old Ma! Now here we are. Thanks, Fred. [*Pantomime of taking drinks, handing them to* MA *and* IVY, *paying for them, then taking his own drinks.*] All right, Fred. You pop off. I know you're busy in the other bar.

[*They watch* FRED *go, then* HARRY *holds up his glass and* MA *and* IVY *hold up theirs.*

MA PECK. All the best, Harry boy!

HARRY. And to you, Ma!

IVY [*shyly*]. All the best!

HARRY [*very heartily*]. Same to you, my dear, and may we all live a hundred years.

> [*As they drink the* STRANGER *enters quietly. He is not extraordinary and yet not quite ordinary. He is a plumpish, middle-aged man with a rather pale clean-shaven face, dressed in dark clothes. The others ignore him, and he remains in the background for the moment.*

STONE. What for?

HARRY. How do you mean—what for?

STONE. I mean—why do you want to live a hundred years?

HARRY. Oh—I see. Just a saying, that's all. Still, it'ud be all right to me. To enjoy life, y'know——

MA PECK. Don't talk to this lot about enjoying life. They wouldn't know what you mean.

MRS REED. Well, just before he came in you were carrying on—as if you wished you was dead.

MA PECK. Well, so I did, and so would you in my place. As for you, you're dead already, only you don't know it.

HARRY. Now, Ma. Mrs Reed's all right in her own way, and we're all friends here. I must tell you, I had a good laugh to-day——

STONE [*cutting in, almost angrily*]. Just a minute, Harry Tully. Before you start on the good laugh, I want you to answer just one question for my benefit.

HARRY [*cheerfully*]. Go on, I'll buy it.

STONE. What have *you* got to be so cheerful about?

HARRY. Well, what have you got to be so miserable about?

STONE. Do you want me to tell you?

HARRY. No, I've heard it before.

STONE [*almost angry again*]. You're no better off than

the rest of us. You're in the same old mess-up we're all in. If you're doing as well as I'm doing, I'd be surprised——

HARRY. So would I.

STONE. Well, what's the idea then?

PERCY. If you ask me—and I read a piece about it in a magazine—it's something to do with glands——

IVY [*shocked*]. Percy, don't be rude.

PERCY. It's not rude—it's scientific. Glands.

HARRY. Can't say. I don't read magazines. But what I say is this—we're alive and kicking, aren't we? All right then.

PERCY. Yes, but where does that get you?

STONE. Nowhere. He doesn't know what he's talking about.

STRANGER [*politely, advancing*]. Excuse me!

> [*He has a quiet, apologetic, but curiously authoritative tone. They all stare at him.*

STONE. What's the matter?

STRANGER. You must excuse me for interrupting you, but I'm here on business, you know, and I'm afraid I'll have to get on with it, if you don't mind.

HARRY. Well, we're not stopping you. Do you want to see the landlord—Fred?

STRANGER. Oh—no, that's not necessary. One of you will do very well. In fact, now it'll have to be one of you.

STONE. Look here, if you're trying to sell us something, you can leave me out now. I've been had before.

STRANGER. No, no. I'm not trying to sell you anything.

> [*He looks at them for a moment.* IVY *clutches her husband's arm.*

IVY [*in a whisper*]. Percy—I'm frightened.

PERCY [*who is not so sure*]. It's all right, Ivy. [*With all his courage, staring at the* STRANGER] 'Ere—what's the idea? Nobody asked you to come in 'ere.

STRANGER. Quite so. But, don't forget, this is a public house.

HARRY. Certainly. Got as much right here as we have. But if you've got anything to say, I think I'd get on with it, chum.

STRANGER. That's what I said myself, if you remember, when I apologized for interrupting you. And now I'll explain——

MRS REED [*cutting in, sharply*]. You needn't do any explaining to me. I don't see why you should come botherin' us—it isn't supposed to be allowed in most bars—an' I'm goin' to 'ave a word with the landlord, Fred Norton.

STRANGER [*still apologetically*]. I'm afraid you can't now. We shall have to get our little bit of business done before Fred can come in again.

MRS REED. Don't be silly. 'Ave 'im 'ere in a tick. [*She raps on the counter and turns to call* FRED. *The call dies in her throat as she stares in amazement. She points to where we have imagined* FRED *to enter from the other bar.*] Look— it's all walled up—or something——

[*The others stare in amazement, and then* IVY *gives a frightened scream.*

IVY. It's a marble slab—like a cemetery——
[*She turns to cling to* PERCY.

STONE [*who is farthest away*]. Go on—it can't be.

HARRY [*quietly*]. It is, though.
[*They all turn now and stare at the* STRANGER, *who looks at them with a little apologetic smile.*

MA PECK. I knew you was a rum sort o' sausage from the start.

STRANGER. Now, Ma Peck——

MA PECK [*cutting in, sharply*]. Who give yer my name?

STRANGER. I know all your names. I have to—in my business. [*He points to each one as he recites their names.*] Edward Stone. Harry Tully. Percy Randle.

Ivy Randle. Bertha Reed. Kathleen Peck—commonly known as Ma Peck. All right, eh?

IVY [*urgently*]. Percy, let's go.

PERCY. Hold on a minute, then we'll go.

STRANGER [*smiling apologetically*]. You can't go until I've finished.

STONE. I'll go when I like.

STRANGER. I don't think so.

MA PECK. He's a busy—a 'tec—that's what 'e is.

HARRY. No, he isn't. Well, tell us what it's all about.

STRANGER. Quite simple, really. Every day people die, don't they? Not the same number every day, of course, but we have to keep up a certain average. No doubt you've wondered how it's done—who picks out the ones who are going to die. Now it's all right saying "Death went to that house" or "Death struck down this man," but of course it's obvious Death couldn't do it all by himself. There's got to be some sort of organization, like any other business. Well—to cut a long story short—I'm the representative for the Number Two North-eastern District of London—— [*He produces a large black-edged card or two and hands them to the others, who stare at them and pass them on, then stare at him in wondering silence. He continues smoothly, still in an easy and rather apologetic strain.*] Now my quota for to-day was eleven, for my district, and I worked off eight early this morning, which is the best time of course, and then I chose two more this afternoon—but I had some trouble about a little boy—nice kid just turned four—and I got a bit mixed up and thought I'd finished for the day. So I was on my way home when I suddenly remembered I was one short of my quota, so I looked in here. Of course I could have picked out one of you in the usual way, but I thought it would make a nice change and that you'd appreciate it if for once I let you decide which one of you it should be.

IVY [*gasping*]. To die—to-night? . . .

STRANGER. That's it. Don't forget, you've all got to die sometime. It isn't as if some died and some didn't —that would be a horrible idea. As it is, it's only a matter of one of you obliging the rest of you and me by taking an earlier turn.

STONE. I don't believe a word of it, but I've 'eard quite enough—and I'm going.

STRANGER. I told you—nobody can go now until I've finished.

STONE. You try an' stop me.

STRANGER. Well, you try and go. After all, you can't do a job like this without having a bit of author-ity. And nobody can say I haven't been trying to make it all easy and pleasant for everybody. I had to block up that bar, of course, because we have to settle it among ourselves without being interrupted.

STONE. That door isn't blocked up, and now I'm going straight through it.

> [*He marches towards the door, then suddenly stops and cries out with pain, twisting and wriggling with it.*

STONE [*groaning*]. It's this damned back o' mine. Can't move a step farther.

STRANGER. It hits you where you're weakest. We know, of course. Now, anybody else like to try—so as not to waste much more time?

MRS REED [*shivering and desperate*]. Yes, I'm going.

STRANGER [*coolly*]. It'll get you in the stomach, I imagine. Just try—and see.

> [*MRS REED runs for it, but within three or four paces of the door is stopped as if by a blow at her stomach, and she too cries out in pain and bends almost double. Care must be taken not to overplay this little scene.*

MA PECK [*muttering*]. Hell's Judas!—but if he isn't the devil 'imself—he's tellin' us nothin' less than the truth.

[STONE *has now sullenly returned to his place and shakily finished his drink.* MRS REED, *softly whimpering, comes back too. All stare wonderingly at the* STRANGER.

STRANGER. Well, that's that. And now the question is—which one is it to be?

STONE. All right, that's easy.

[*He points dramatically at* MA PECK.

MA PECK [*aghast*]. What—me?

STONE. Yes, you. [*He turns eagerly to the* STRANGER.] Just before you come in—an' just before Harry Tully 'ere stood 'er another drink—she was complainin' an' moanin' about being old an' alone an' saying she wished she was dead an' done with it——

PERCY. That's right. I heard her.

MA PECK [*indignantly*]. There you are—pick on a poor old woman who's never done nobody any 'arm an' just because she 'asn't the price of another drink just talks daft for a minute——

MRS REED [*cutting in*]. But we all 'eard you—sayin' you'd nobody left an' you ought to be pushin' the daisies up——

MA PECK [*furiously cutting in*]. Go on, you! That's just my silly talk—but what about you, eh? always goin' on about your terrible inside—an' never gettin' a bit o' pleasure out of anything. What 'ave you got to live for, I'd like to know?

MRS REED [*angrily*]. I'm twenty-five years younger than you—an' you said yerself you'd one foot in the grave——

MA PECK. Yes, but the other foot's alive all right—an' for two pins I'd use it to kick——

HARRY. Now, now, Ma—that's no way to carry on. Let's take it easy.

MA PECK [*almost tearfully*]. All right, Harry, you're a good boy. But don't let 'em put it on me—a poor old woman who 'asn't seen a priest nor the inside of a church for thirty years—and isn't fit to die yet. [*To the* STRANGER] It's got to be to-night, 'asn't it?

STRANGER [*prominently looking at his watch*]. Yes, and soon too. I can't give you more than another quarter of an hour. He'll be here then for one of you.

PERCY [*uneasily*]. Who's he?

STRANGER. We needn't go into that. One of my superiors. It's a big organization.

PERCY [*uneasily*]. I see. Well——

IVY [*urgently*]. Percy—don't interfere.

PERCY. I was only goin' to say it's got to be one of them three.

[*Indicates* MA PECK, MRS REED, *and* STONE.

MRS REED. Oh—'as it—what's the matter with you?

STONE. Just what I was goin' to say. Who told us life wasn't worth living?

PERCY [*hastily*]. She did—Mrs Reed. She said if she was asked right out, she would say No—it wasn't worth living——

MRS REED [*cutting in*]. And then your wife said that was what you was always saying——

IVY [*desperately*]. I didn't say *always*—I only said *sometimes*—honestly I did.

STONE. He said it got 'im down. We 'eard 'im.

IVY [*desperately*]. It's only 'is way of talking. I know 'im. An' he's young—an' we've only just got married —an' got a nice little 'ome together——

STONE. He doesn't seem to be enjoying it much.

IVY. He does—he loves it reelly—it's only his way of talkin'. [*With the sudden boldness of the shy*] You talked a lot worse than he did—tellin' us just to wait till we got older——

STONE. That's just a manner of speakin'. I've got a business. I've got responsibilities. It'll make a lot o' difference to people if I suddenly pop off. What does it matter to one of you youngsters? Save yourselves a lot o' worry.

PERCY. Well, you can save yourself some now, can't
ou?

STONE. Talk sense.

MRS REED. Well, 'e is talkin' sense. You was easily
he worst of the lot, Ted Stone—grumble, grumble,
rumble——

STONE [*almost shouting*]. All right, I grumble. But I
ust want to go on grumbling—see?

MRS REED. Well, you're not the only one. An' anyhow
Ma Peck ought to go—she's got nothin' to live for——

MA PECK [*almost screaming*]. I've more than you ever
ad—yer miserable selfish basket——!

STRANGER [*with sudden authority*]. Quiet! [*There is a
udden complete silence. They look at him.*] I'm disappointed in you. And if I'd known this would lead
o such an undignified wrangling scene, I'd have chosen
ome other method. I thought it would be easy for one
of you to volunteer.

STONE [*sullenly*]. I don't see what put that silly idea
nto your 'ead.

MRS REED. Neither do I.

STRANGER. I think you're forgetting, aren't you?
All right, then.

> [*He regards them gravely and with authority, and
> then makes a great anti-clockwise movement
> with one hand. This should be accompanied
> by a ratchety sound, as of a gigantic watch
> being wound.*

HARRY. What are you doing?

STRANGER. Putting the clock back. Now, then, listen
to yourselves.

> [*The scene that follows is played exactly as before,
> except that the actors suggest a certain hypno-
> tized effect.*

HARRY [*as before*]. . . . And may we all live a
hundred years.

STONE. What for?

HARRY. How do you mean—what for?

STONE. I mean—why do you want to live a hundred years?

HARRY. Oh—I see. Just a saying, that's all. Still, it'ud be all right to me. To enjoy life, y'know——

MA PECK. Don't talk to this lot about enjoying life. They wouldn't know what you mean.

MRS REED. Well, just before he came in you were carrying on—as if you wished you was dead.

MA PECK. Well, so I did, and so would you in my place. As for you, you're dead already, only you don't know it.

HARRY. Now, Ma. Mrs Reed's all right in her own way, and we're all friends here. I must tell you, I had a good laugh to-day——

STONE [cutting in, almost angrily]. Just a minute, Harry Tully. Before you start on the good laugh, I want you to answer just one question for my benefit.

HARRY [cheerfully]. Go on. I'll buy it.

STONE. What have you got to be so cheerful about?

HARRY. Well, what have you got to be so miserable about?

STONE. Do you want me to tell you?

HARRY. No, I've heard it before.

STONE [almost angry again]. You're no better off than the rest of us. You're in the same old mess-up we're all in. If you're doing as well as I'm doing, I'd be surprised——

HARRY. So would I.

STONE. Well, what's the idea then?

PERCY. If you ask me—and I read a piece about it in a magazine—it's something to do with glands——

IVY [shocked]. Percy, don't be rude.

PERCY. It's not rude—it's scientific. Glands.

HARRY. Can't say. I don't read magazines. But what I say is this—we're alive and kicking, aren't we? All right then.

PERCY. Yes, but where does that get you?

STONE. Nowhere. He doesn't know what he's talking about.

STRANGER. Excuse me! And then that's where I came in. Well, you heard yourselves. [*He looks at them gravely, then looks at his watch.*] I can give you five more minutes. After that, if you can't settle who's to go, then it'll be my choice.

IVY [*bravely*]. He's right. We're all in it but him— Mr Tully. That's how we talked. As if it didn't matter if we were all dead. [*She hesitates a moment, then looks anxiously at the* STRANGER.] Could it be two—instead of just one? I mean, if it was Percy an' me together, I wouldn't mind so much——

PERCY [*indignantly*]. Now just a minute, Ivy. What d'yer want to go pushing us forward for?

STRANGER. It can't be two. Only one.

MRS REED [*frightened*]. Don't look at me like that.

HARRY [*to* STRANGER]. All right. Don't let's have any more argument.

IVY [*astonished*]. D'you mean *you're* offering to go——?

HARRY [*easily*]. Yes. Why not?

IVY. But you're just the one——

HARRY. I know, but what of it? I've enjoyed my life—and we've all to die some time——

IVY [*protesting*]. It isn't right——

PERCY. Shut up, Ivy.

IVY [*sturdily*]. I won't shut up. I say—it just isn't *right* that he should be the one. No, Percy—I'll feel *ashamed* all my life——

HARRY [*smiling at her*]. Now don't start that, Ivy. Just cheer up—and make him a bit more cheerful, too. And look at *him* now.

[*They look, and the* STRANGER *is smiling cheerfully.*

HARRY. He's got what he wanted, and I believe he knew it was going to be me all the time.

IVY. Did you?

C

STRANGER. Just a moment. [*He produces from his inside pocket a small white hand-telephone, and proceeds to talk into it.*] Yes, sir. Number Two District North-east London here. All set, sir. Yes, sir, that's right. Harry Tully. [*Puts away telephone, and smiles at* IVY *and* HARRY.] Yes, I'd a good idea who it would be. If you're frightened of Life, you don't live properly, and then you don't like Life. But that doesn't mean you want to die. You're still more frightened of Death. So I guessed Harry, who'd enjoyed life, would be just the one who'd be ready to go.

IVY. And I still say—it isn't *right* and I feel ashamed—and if it wasn't for 'aving to look after Percy——

HARRY. Just forget it, Ivy. And you'll make a man of him yet. [*Looks round at them.*] Well, Mr Stone, Mrs Reed, better not let our friend overhear you next time——

STONE. You don't catch me coming 'ere ever again.

STRANGER [*grimly*]. You would be surprised the places I get into, though.

HARRY. And Ma—look after yourself——

MA PECK [*muttering*]. God bless yer—Harry. Always said you was a good lad——

HARRY. Percy, look after the wife here. You're lucky. She's worth ten of you——

IVY [*shyly*]. I'm not. But—thank you—for saying it to him. An' I'll never forget you—never—never——
[*She kisses him quickly and lightly, then crying quietly rests against Percy's shoulder. He puts a protective arm round her, looking at the others rather defiantly.*

HARRY. That's the way, boy. Keep on like that. [*He looks at the* STRANGER.] Well, I suppose we're all set for the big jump. Good-bye—the old Rose and Crown.

STRANGER [*gravely*]. And if Life is a rose, then Death is a crown. [*He lifts his voice, looking towards corner where entrance to other bar is presumed to be.*] All right, sir.

*[They all stare towards that corner, and then all but
HARRY, who remains at the bar—and of course
the STRANGER, who is farther up stage—draw
back looking frightened. The light from front
should now be stronger and direct on HARRY,
who looks frightened, too, watching something,
somebody, come in. But then he stops looking
frightened and slowly smiles as if this were an
old friend. Then he nods slowly, with the
others behind him still looking terrified and
awe-struck, and the STRANGER nodding and
smiling, as the curtain slowly descends.*

REMEMBER CÆSAR

by

GORDON DAVIOT

CHARACTERS

RICHARD, LORD WESTON (*a judge*)
LADY WESTON (*his wife*)
MR ROGER CHETWYND (*his clerk*)

Period: *Reign of Charles II*, 1660–85

Applications regarding amateur performances of this play should be addressed to the agents, Messrs Pearn, Pollinger, and Higham, Ltd, 39–40 Bedford Street, London, W.C.2.

REMEMBER CÆSAR

A room in the house of Richard, Lord Weston, on a spring morning in the reign of Charles II. Lord Weston (until his late elevation to the bench, Sir Richard) is not wealthy, and the room is a combination of study and withdrawing-room. Up right is the door to the landing (it is a first-floor room), in the rear wall a large casement window looking out to the front of the house, in the left wall the fireplace, and down from it another window through which one can see the trees in the garden. Up stage of the fireplace a cupboard in the wall. Hanging on the walls and over the fireplace are family portraits.

Lord Weston is seated by the fireplace, a table of books and papers beside him. He is engaged in filling his pipe. And talking.

Down right, where the light from the side-window falls across his small writing-table, is seated Mr Roger Chetwynd, a thin, earnest, absent-minded, and conscientious youth. So conscientious is he that his mind, even when absent, is absent on his employer's business. He has begun by listening to his master's lecture, but the lure of his work has been gradually too much for him, and he is now blissfully copying from one paper on to another while the measured words flow over him, his lips forming the phrases while he writes.

WESTON. . . . And furthermore [*he pauses to arrange the tobacco*] it is not alone a question of duty; there is your own success in the world to be considered. It is not your intention to be a secretary all your life, is it? No. Very well. Diligence and a respect for detail should be your care. I did not become Lord Weston by twiddling my thumbs and hoping for favours. I won my honours by hard work and zealous service. Men who were at Corpus Christi with me are to-day copying documents for a living, while I—let us not

39

mince matters—am the best-known, and certainly the most impartial, judge in England, and a favoured servant of his gracious majesty, Charles the Second. That, I submit, my good Roger, is an example to be studied. It is not only unbecoming in you to ask for a half-holiday, but it is greatly unlike you. I fear——
[*He has turned towards his secretary, and discovers his misplaced diligence. After a pause, coldly*] Can it be, Mr Chetwynd, that you have not been listening to my discourse?

ROGER [*brought to the surface by the cessation of the word-music*]. What, my lord? Oh, no. Yes, certainly, sir, I am listening.

WESTON. What was I talking of?

ROGER. Yourself, sir. [*Amending*] I mean, of your rise to success, my lord.

[*It is apparent that it is an oft-heard tale.*]

WESTON. We were talking of your extraordinary request for a half-holiday, when you had one only last month. On that occasion, if I remember well, your parents came to town and you must needs go gadding. Would it be straining courtesy too far if I were to inquire what prompts this new demand for heedless leisure?

ROGER. I thought perhaps if you did not need me this afternoon, my lord, I might personally interview the clerk of the Awards Committee, and find out why he has not sent that document.

WESTON [*a little taken aback*]. Oh. Oh, indeed.

ROGER. The lack of it greatly hinders my work, you see. And at this most interesting point——

[*His glance goes longingly to his desk.*]

WESTON. That, of course, is a different matter. I see no reason [*he looks for a spill for his pipe first on the table and then, rising, by the fire*] why you should not take a walk to Mr Clay's in the afternoon if the weather is fine. I am relieved that your thoughts are on sober matters, as befits a rising young man. Diligence, courage, and attention to detail: these are the three—— Where are the spills? These are what bring a man to success and endow him with dignity—— No tapers and no spills, as usual! [*Looking on the table for a scrap of paper and finally feeling in his pockets*] Without an orderly mind no man can hope [*Roger has gone back to his work*] to excel in any of the learned professions. [*He has found a scrap of paper, rather crushed, in his pocket and smooths it out, uninterestedly, to make a rough spill.*] Detail, my good Roger, attention to detail. That is the beginning of greatness. That is the—— [*reading automatically and with some difficulty what is written on the scrap of paper*] "Remember Cæsar." [*Repeating, with vague interest*] "Remember Cæsar." [*He turns the paper back and forth, at a loss. And then a new idea occurs to him, a rather horrible idea. To* ROGER] What is the date to-day? [*As* ROGER, *buried again in his work, does not answer*] Roger! I said, what day of the month is it?

ROGER [*hardly pausing*]. It is the fifteenth, my lord.

WESTON. The fifteenth! The fifteenth of March. The Ides of March! [*Looking at the paper again; in a horrified whisper*] "Remember Cæsar!" [*Louder*] So they want to kill me, do they? They want to kill me? [*ROGER comes to the surface, surprised.*] That is what it is to be a judge over men [*all his pompousness is dissolving in agitation*], an instrument of justice. Sooner or later revenge lies await in the byways. And the juster a judge has been, the more fearless [*he waves the paper in the astonished* ROGER'*s face*], so much greater will be the hate that pursues——

ROGER. What is it, my lord? What is it?

WESTON. My death warrant if I am not careful. What cases have we had lately? The treason affair— I refused to be bribed! [*The boast gives him a passing comfort.*] The piracy—both sides hate me for that! Or there was that footpad——

ROGER. Is it a threat, the paper? Where did it come from?

WESTON. It was in my pocket. Some one must have—— Yes, now I remember. A man brushed against me yesterday as I was leaving the Courts. A small, evil-looking fellow, very sly.

ROGER. What does it say, the paper?

WESTON [*much too occupied with his own fate to attend to his secretary's curiosity*]. Just at the door, it was, and he didn't wait for apology. I remember. Well, I can only thank them for the warning. I may die before my time, but it will not be to-day if I can help it. Go downstairs at once, Roger, and lock and bar all the doors. Lock, bar, and chain them. And ask my wife to come to me at once. At once. Stop! Are there any strangers in the house? Workmen or such?

ROGER. Only Joel the gardener, my lord; he is cleaning the windows on the landing.

[*He indicates with his head that Joel is just outside.*

WESTON. Send him away at once. Tell him to leave everything and go, and lock the door behind him. And the windows—see that all the windows, too, are closed.

> [ROGER *goes with speed. One can hear him begin his order to* JOEL *before he shuts the door:* Joel, his lordship says that you must . . . *and the whistling which has become audible through the opened door dies away.* WESTON, *left alone, peers cautiously from each window in turn. Then his mind, temporarily relieved, goes to the cupboard and is greatly exercised again. He stares at it fearfully for a moment or two, and then puts his fear to the test. He takes a pistol from the drawer of his desk.*

WESTON [*facing the cupboard with levelled pistol*]. Come out! Come out, I say. [*There is silence.*] Drop your weapon and come out, or I shall shoot you now.

[*As there is still silence he forces himself to close in
on the cupboard door, and, standing to the side,
pulls it quickly open. It is empty. As soon as
his relief abates he is ashamed, and hastily
returns the pistol to its drawer.*

[*Enter, bright and purposeful,* LADY WESTON. *A
charming creature. One knows at a glance that
she is an excellent housewife, but to the last
one is never sure how much intelligence and
sweet malice there lies behind her practical
simplicity.*

LADY WESTON [*looking back as she comes in*]. I do wish
that Joel wouldn't leave pails of water on the landing !
What is it, Richard? It's baking morning.

WESTON [*going to her and taking her hand in his re-
assuringly*]. My dear, don't be alarmed——

LADY WESTON. I'm not. But the surest way to make
me is to pat my hand and tell me not to be.

WESTON. My dear, your husband's life is in grave
danger.

LADY WESTON. The last time it was in danger you
had been eating game pie. What is it this time?

WESTON [*annihilating her flippancy with one broadside*].
Assassination !

LADY WESTON. Well, well ! You always wanted to
be a great man and now you have got your wish !

WESTON. What do you mean?

LADY WESTON. They don't assassinate nobodies.

WESTON [*showing her the paper*]. Read that, and see if
you can laugh.

LADY WESTON. I'm not laughing. [*Trying to read the
writing*] What a dreadful scrawl.

WESTON. Yes, the venomous scribbling of an illiterate.

LADY WESTON [*deciphering*]. "Remember Cæsar." Is
it a riddle?

WESTON. It is a death warrant. Do you know what
day this is?

LADY WESTON. Thursday.

WESTON. What day of the month.

LADY WESTON. About the twelfth, I should guess.

WESTON [*with meaning*]. It is the fifteenth. The fifteenth of March.

LADY WESTON. Lawdamussy! Your good sister's birthday! And we haven't sent her as much as a lily!

WESTON. I have deplored before, Frances, the incurable lightness of your mind. On the fifteenth of March Cæsar was murdered in the Forum.

LADY WESTON. Yes, of course. I remember. They couldn't stand his airs any longer.

WESTON [*reprovingly*]. He was a great man.

LADY WESTON [*kindly*]. Yes, my dear, I am sure he was. [*Looking again at the scrap of paper*] And is some one thinking of murdering you?

WESTON. Obviously.

LADY WESTON. I wonder some one hasn't done it long ago. [*Before the look of wonder can grow in his eye*] A great many people must hate judges. And you are a strict judge, they say.

WESTON. It is the law that is strict. I am a judge, my good Frances, not a juggler. I have never twisted the law to please the mob, and I shall not please them by dying on the day of their choice.

LADY WESTON. No, of course not. You shall not go out of the house to-day. A nice light dinner and a good glass of——

WESTON. I have sent Roger to barricade all the doors, and I think it would be wise to close the ground-floor shutters, and see that they are not opened for any——

LADY WESTON. Is it the French and the Dutch together you are expecting! And this is the morning Mr Gammon's boy comes with the groceries. How am I to——

WESTON. My dear, is a little pepper more to you than your husband's life?

LADY WESTON. It isn't a little pepper, it's a great deal of flour. And you would be the first to complain if the bread were short, or the gravy thin. [*Giving him back the paper*] How do you know that the little paper was meant for you?

WESTON. Because it was in my pocket. I found it there when I was looking for something to light my pipe. [*With meaning*] There were no spills.

LADY WESTON. No spills. What, again? Richard, you smoke far too much.

WESTON [*continuing hastily*]. It was slipped into my pocket by a man who brushed against me yesterday. A dark, lean fellow with an evil face.

LADY WESTON. I don't think he was very evil.

WESTON. What do you know about it?

LADY WESTON. It was kind of him to warn you. And wasn't it a mercy that the spills were finished and that no one had made any more! If there had been even one there you would never have seen the paper. You would have gone for your noon walk down the Strand and some one would have stuck you like a goose on a spit, and I should have been a widow before dinner-time——

WESTON [*sinking into a chair*]. Stop, Frances, stop. It upsets me to——

[*Enter* ROGER, *a little out of breath after his flying tour round the house.*

WESTON. Ah, Roger. Have you seen to it all? Every door barred, every window shut, all workmen out——

ROGER [*a little embarrassed*]. Every door except the kitchen one, my lord.

WESTON [*angry*]. And why not the kitchen one?

ROGER [*stammering*]. The cook seemed to think—— That is, she said——

WESTON. Well, speak, man, what did she say, and

how does what the cook thinks affect my order to bar the kitchen door?

ROGER [*in a rush*]. The cook said she was a respectable woman and had never been behind bars in her life and she wasn't going to begin at her age, and she was quite capable of dealing with anyone who came to the kitchen door——

LADY WESTON. Never mind, Roger, I shall speak to Cook——

WESTON [*interrupting her, furious*]. Is the woman mad? Did you tell her that her master might be killed in her very presence if the door were not——

ROGER. I did, my lord, I did. She said there would be a killing there and then if I did not leave her kitchen. She is a very formidable woman, my lord, and there was the matter of a rolling-pin . . . I thought it best to desist.

LADY WESTON. Be calm, Richard. It is only that the cook's temper is apt to be uncertain in the morning. I know how to coax her into a better humour——

WESTON. Coax! Since when have my servants to be coaxed! She shall leave my house this very hour.

LADY WESTON. Oh, nonsense, Richard! All cooks are strange-tempered. It comes from standing over hot stoves and breathing in pepper. I shall see——

WESTON. This very hour! If her silly mind is so careless of her master's safety, she has no right to his roof. Tell her to pack her things and leave the house at once, and see that the door is barred after her.

LADY WESTON. And who will cook your pet dishes when I go to stay with Sibylla? Be calm, Richard. The kitchen door will be locked, and cook will see to the barring of it herself, and be proud of her handiwork, I promise you. That is what a mistress is for, to sweep up after the master. I shall also see that all the downstairs windows are shuttered as you suggest. We can always haul the groceries through an upper window. That will be entertaining for poor old Lady Gascoigne, anyhow; glooming there in her window. She has had no amusement out of this street since the dog-fight on Ash Wednesday. [*As she is going, pausing*] Would you like me to block up the chimneys, perhaps?

WESTON [*controlling himself*]. I think that so frivolous a suggestion at so anxious a time is in poor taste, Frances, and unworthy of you——

LADY WESTON. Did it appear frivolous to you? How strange! I had thought it odd to shutter the walls and yet leave openings in the roof that one could drive a coach and horses through. However!

> [*She comes back into the room, takes two candelabra from various places about the room, and goes to the door.*

WESTON. What do you want with these?

LADY WESTON. If we are to be in darkness below we shall want all the candles we can gather. [*Exit.*

WESTON. The aptness of the female mind to busy itself about irrelevant and inconsiderable minutiæ is a source of endless wonder to me. [*Almost without noticing what he is doing he moves over to the fireplace and sticks his head into the chimney to view the width of it. As he withdraws it he becomes aware of* ROGER, *standing watching.*] I see no reason now why you should not resume your work, Roger.

ROGER. Oh, my lord, it is beyond my power to work while you are in danger. Is there not something I could do?

WESTON [*mightily flattered*]. Nonsense, my good Roger, nonsense! Nothing is going to happen to me.

ROGER. I could perhaps go and warn the authorities, and so prevent——

WESTON [*very brave*]. No, no, no. Am I to spend the rest of my life with a guard at my heels? A pretty figure I should cut! Go on with your work and——
[*His eye has lighted on a package which is lying on a chair*

against the right wall. The box is oblong—roughly 18 × 10 × 4 *inches—and tied with cord.*] [*Sharply*] What is this?

ROGER. That came for you this morning, sir.

WESTON. What is it?

ROGER [*with the faint beginnings of doubt in his voice*]. I don't know, my lord. A man came with it and said that it was important that you should have it to-day.

WESTON. And you didn't ask what it was! You fool!

ROGER [*humbly*]. It didn't seem to be my business. I never do ask about the contents of your lordship's—— I showed your lordship the package when it came, and you said to leave it there.

WESTON [*peering with growing uneasiness at the thing*]. The man who brought it, what did he look like? Was he small? Dark?

ROGER [*who obviously had taken no notice*]. I think he was smallish. But as to dark—his hat was pulled over his face. I think, I think he appeared to have a mole on his chin, but I would not—— It may have been just a——

WESTON. A mole? [*His imagination at work*] A mole! Yes. Yes. That man had a mole. The man who brushed against me. On the right side of his jaw. I can see it as if he were standing here. We must get rid of this. At once.

ROGER. Do you think it is some infernal machine, sir? What shall we do with it?

WESTON [*indicating the side-window*]. Open the window, and I shall throw it as far into the garden as I can.

ROGER. But it may explode, sir, if we throw it.

WESTON. What is certain is that it will explode if we do not! How long has it been lying here?

ROGER. It came about nine o'clock, my lord.

WESTON [*in an agony*]. Nearly three hours ago! Open the window, Roger.

ROGER. No, sir. You open the window. Let me

handle the thing. My life is nothing. Yours is of great value to England.

WESTON. No, Roger, no. You are young. I have had my life. There are still great things for you to do in the world. You must live, and write my life for posterity. Do as I say. I promise you I shall exercise the greatest care. [*As* ROGER *rushes to the window*] No. Wait! A better idea. The gardener's pail. It is still on the landing!

ROGER. Yes! Yes, of course!

> [*He is out of the room and back in a moment with the wooden pail of water, which still has the wet cleaning-rag hung over its edge.*

WESTON. Stand back. [*He picks up the parcel gingerly.*] We do not know what satanic thing may happen. [*He inserts the parcel lengthwise into the pail at full stretch of his arm, his head averted, his eyes watching from their extreme corners.*] There is not enough water! Not enough to cover it.

ROGER. I'll get some. I shall not be a moment.

WESTON. No. Don't go. The flowers!

> [*He indicates a bowl of daffodils.*

ROGER. Of course! [*He pulls the daffodils from their setting, throwing them on the desk in his agitation, and pours the water into the pail.*] Ah! That has done it!

WESTON [*dismayed, as he takes his hand from the package*]. Now it is going to float! It must be wet through, or it is no use.

ROGER. We must put something heavy on top, to keep it down.

WESTON. Yes, yes. Get something.

ROGER. What shall I get?

WESTON. Good God, boy! Have you no ideas once the pen is out of your hand? Anything, anything that is heavy and that will fit into the pail. Books, anything!

ROGER [*to whom books are objects of reverence, if not awe*]. Books, sir? But they'll get very wet, won't they?

D

WESTON. In the name of Heaven bring the first six books off the shelf!

ROGER [*snatching the books and bringing them*]. I suppose it cannot be helped. Such beautiful bindings too!

> [*He picks the wet cloth off the edge of the pail, dropping it on the carpet, and plunges the books into the water, which very naturally overflows at this new incursion.*

WESTON [*letting go his hold on the package and sitting back on his heels with a sigh of relief*]. Ah! Well and truly drowned.

> [*He mops his forehead, and* ROGER *collapses into the nearest chair.*

> [*Enter* LADY WESTON, *with a tray on which is a glass of wine and some biscuits.*

LADY WESTON [*seeing their strange occupation*]. Lawda-mussy, Richard! what have you got in the pail?

WESTON. A package that came this morning. The man who brought it was the same fellow that knocked against me yesterday and slipped that paper into my pocket. They thought I would open it, the fools! [*He is beginning to feel better.*] But we have been one too many for them!

LADY WESTON [*in wild dismay*]. But how stupid! You are just making a mess of the beautiful, brand-new——

WESTON [*interrupting her angrily*]. Frances! [*The thunder of her name quenches her speech.*] What does your "beautiful brand-new" carpet matter when your husband's life is at stake? You shock me.

LADY WESTON [*who had not been going to say 'carpet'*]. Carpet? [*After a pause, mildly*] No, of course not, my dear. I should never dream of weighing your safety against even the finest product of Asia. Come and sit down and have a glass of wine. [*She puts the tray on his desk, gathering up the scattered daffodils as she does so.*] You know how the doctor disapproves of excitement for you.

WESTON. Perhaps the doctor has never had an infernal machine handed in at his door of a spring morning.

[LADY WESTON *picks up the cloth from the floor, mops the spilt water, and pauses to look curiously at the contents of the pail as they catch her eye.*

ROGER [*who has been staring at the pail in absorbed fascination*]. I am afraid we have made a little mess. Please let me do that.

LADY WESTON [*in mild conversational tones*]. That looks like Mr Spencer in the water.

ROGER. Yes, it is. The thing floated, you see. And time was all-important. So it was imperative to take whatever was nearest to weight it down.

LADY WESTON. I see. [*Handing him the wet cloth and the flowers*] Would you be kind enough to take these downstairs? [*She adds the empty flower-bowl to his load.*] One of the maids will fill it for you.

WESTON. Have the kitchen wenches decided that the door of their domain may at last be bolted?

LADY WESTON. Oh, they are all very happy. Cook thinks she knows how to make bullets by dropping hot lead into cold water, or something of the sort. And the kitchen-maid thinks that she will stay in London after all.

WESTON. Stay in London?

LADY WESTON [*indicating his tray; he is already sipping the wine*]. Try the biscuits. They are Sibylla's recipe. Yes, she was leaving because she found London so quiet after the country.

WESTON [*through his biscuit*]. Ridiculous!

LADY WESTON. In the country, she said, if there wasn't a calving, there was a wedding, and if there wasn't a wedding there was a wake. It was never dull. A pleasant girl. I am glad London is being livelier for her.

WESTON. My household seem to treat my danger as a sort of raree-show.

LADY WESTON. No, dear, no. All maids like a little to-do. It makes life important for them.

WESTON. A little to-do! My funeral, I hope, will be even more exciting for them. You must have a wake to please the kitchen-maid.

LADY WESTON [*not listening to him; contemplative, her eyes on the portrait which hangs opposite the side-window*]. Do you think we had better remove the portrait of Great-aunt Cicely from the wall?

WESTON. In the name of Heaven, why?

LADY WESTON. She is in the direct line of shots coming through that window.

WESTON. And why should any shots come through the window, may I ask?

LADY WESTON [*mildly objecting to the tone*]. I was merely taking thought for your property, my dear Richard. And anyone sitting in the ilex-tree out there would be in a——

WESTON [*on his feet*]. Frances! What made you think of the ilex-tree?

LADY WESTON. That is where I would shoot you from. I mean, if I were going to shoot you. The leaves are thick enough to hide anyone sitting there, and yet not enough to obscure their view.

WESTON. Come away from that window.

LADY WESTON. What?

WESTON. Come away from that window!

LADY WESTON [*moving to him*]. No one is going to shoot *me*.

WESTON [*running out of the room, and calling to* ROGER *from the landing*]. Roger! Roger!

ROGER [*very distant*]. My lord?

WESTON. Has the gardener gone away yet?

ROGER. No, my lord. He is eating his dinner outside the kitchen window.

WESTON. Tell him to sit under the ilex-tree until I give him leave to move.

ROGER. The ilex-tree? Yes, my lord.

[WESTON *comes back and goes to the drawer of the table where his pistol is kept.*

LADY WESTON. What are you looking for, Richard? [*As he takes out the pistol*] Oh, Richard, dear, be careful. That is a very dangerous weapon.

WESTON [*grimly important*]. I know it!

LADY WESTON. It is so rusty that it is liable to do anything. [*As her husband proceeds to load the weapon*] You know that you haven't used it since you were shooting dancing balls off the fountain. That was the year after we were married. The butcher's son blew half his scalp off the other week, trying to fire a rusty pistol. He has no hair left except a few red tufts over the right ear. His father says the only hope for him is to become a gentleman so that he can wear a wig.

WESTON. There is nothing wrong with my pistol but a little dust.

LADY WESTON. Well, I think it is a poor way to foil an assassin.

WESTON. What is?

LADY WESTON. Blowing oneself up.

[*Enter* ROGER *with the bowl of daffodils.*

WESTON [*looking round at him as he comes*]. Ah, Roger. Has Joel gone to sit under the tree?

ROGER. Yes, sir. [*Putting down the bowl and making for the side-window*] At least, I gave him your message.

WESTON. Keep away from that window! [*As* ROGER *looks astonished*] There may be some one in the ilex-tree.

ROGER. But do you think they would try to shoot you as well as—as——   [*He indicates the bucket.*

WESTON. Who knows? When you have dealt with the criminal mind as long as I have—— Did you open the door to speak to the gardener?

ROGER. Oh, no, my lord. I spoke through the

shutter. The cook is of the opinion that we should send for the military.

LADY WESTON. Cook is always of opinion that we should send for the military.

WESTON [*snapping the lock of his pistol*]. Now, we shall see whether there is anyone lurking in the tree.

> [*He moves over to the side of the window, peering out with the fraction of an eye.*

LADY WESTON. Richard, if you are going to shoot off that thing, you will please wait until I——

> [*She is interrupted by a loud knocking on the front door down stairs. This is such an unexpected development that all three are momentarily quite still, at a loss. ROGER is the first to recover; he moves over to the window in the rear wall, from which one can see the street.*

ROGER. Some one at the front door.

> [*He is about to open the casement so that he may lean out to inspect the knocker, when LORD WESTON stops him.*

WESTON [*still at the fireplace*]. Don't open that window!

ROGER. But I cannot see otherwise, my lord, who it is.

WESTON. If you put your head out of that window they may shoot without waiting to ask questions.

LADY WESTON. But, Richard, it may be some perfectly innocent visitor.

> [*The knocking is repeated.*

ROGER. If I were to stand on a chair . . .

> [*He brings a chair to the window and stands on it, but he is still not high enough to look down on whoever waits at the front door.*

WESTON. Well? Well? Can you tell who it is?

ROGER. I am still not high enough, my lord.

LADY WESTON. Add the footstool, Roger.

ROGER. Ah, yes, the footstool. The footstool will do it. There!

[ROGER *adds the footstool to the chair, and, aided by* LADY WESTON, *climbs on to the precarious erection.*

LADY WESTON. Now, can you see anyone?

ROGER [*having seen, scrambling down*]. All is well, my lord. [*He throws open the casement and calls to some one below.*] In a moment, my good sir, in a moment! All is well, my lord. It is only Mr Cæsar. [*As this information is succeeded by a blank pause*] Shall I let him in?

WESTON. Who did you say?

ROGER. Mr Cæsar. You remember: the man you met on Tuesday at Hampton, my lord. He was to come to see you this morning about rose-trees. You made a note of it.

WESTON [*taking the crumpled piece of paper from his pocket in a dazed way*]. I made a note? "Remember Cæsar." Is that my writing? Yes, it must be. Dear me!

LADY WESTON [*considering the writing: kindly*]. I shouldn't have said it was the venomous scribbling of an illiterate. You had better go down and let Mr Cæsar in, Roger. Put the pistol away, Richard dear; your visitor might misunderstand it. [*She speaks cheerfully, as to a child; it is obvious from her lack of surprise that excursions and alarms created by her husband over trifles are a normal part of existence for her.*] And if you take Mr Spencer out of the water, I shall send Joel to take away the bucket. Perhaps Mr Brutus would like some cordial?

WESTON. Mr *Cæsar*. [*He moves towards the bucket.*

LADY WESTON. Of course. How could anyone forget a name like that? And now, if you'll forgive me . . . It's my busy morning.

WESTON [*arresting her as she is going out of the door*]. Oh, Frances! What was in the parcel, do you think?

LADY WESTON. That was your new velvet cloak, dear. I did try to tell you, you know. [*Exit.*

[*The curtain comes down on* LORD WESTON *ruefully taking the first dripping book from the water.*

PARADISE ENOW

by

JAMES BRIDIE

CHARACTERS

ALI
HIS WIFE
MISS WATSON (*a missionary*)
AZRAEL (*the Angel of Death*)
MALE ANGEL
MISS ROBINSON ⎫
MISS JONES   ⎪
MISS BROWN   ⎬ *houris*
MISS GIBSON   ⎪
MISS THOMSON ⎭

Paradise Enow first appeared in a miscellany of James Bridie's work under the title *Tedious and Brief*, published by Messrs Constable and Co., Ltd, in 1945.

Copyright 1945 by James Bridie

PARADISE ENOW

A Play in Two Scenes

SCENE I

A booth in front of a hut in Southern Syria. ALI, *the Proprietor, is beating out a design on a copper tray. His* WIFE *is bustling in and out of the hut. She makes two or three appearances and disappearances. At each appearance* ALI *looks apprehensive and stops work. At each disappearance he falls to again. If the Audience thinks this funny it can go on* ad lib. *At last the* WIFE *speaks.*

WIFE. Did you change your djibbah this morning?

ALI. My what, sweetheart?

WIFE. Your djibbah. The garment that so mercifully hides your disgusting contours.

ALI. Oh, that? Yes, Light of my Eyes and Comforter of my Stomach, I did.

WIFE. You had the brass neck to change your djibbah this morning?

ALI. Why, yes.

WIFE. Who told you you could change your djibbah this morning?

ALI. I should like to say that it had been revealed to me in a vision, but, to be strictly truthful . . .

WIFE. You don't know how to be strictly truthful. And don't try to be funny. You're no good at that either.

ALI. O Moon of my delight that knows no wane . . .

WIFE. Do you know that it isn't washing-day till Friday? You know that perfectly well, and yet you go and change your djibbah. Do you expect me to do a washing every day because you're too lazy to remember which day is washing-day and which isn't? Do you

59

think I'm a camel to do a washing every day and cook
your meals and darn your clothes and . . .

ALI. Camels don't darn clothes.

WIFE. Oh, a little bit of natural history now, eh?
Just to give your poor ignorant drudge of a wife a little
information and make yourself feel cosy inside and
superior, eh? Let me tell you I know perfectly well
that camels don't darn clothes. Nor do washings. Nor
cook. They aren't such soft fools. Of course, if it
pleases you to think that I'm a perfect ignoramus . . .

ALI. Ignorama.

WIFE. Will you kindly let me get a word in edgeways?
I can't say the simplest thing but you chip in with some
terribly smart and clever remark to make me feel how
smart you are and that I'm only a poor, weak, stupid
woman with no intelligence and no feelings to be hurt.

ALI. I didn't mean to hurt your feelings.

WIFE. You did. You do it deliberately. You don't
love me at all.

ALI. Yes, I do. I love you very much indeed.

WIFE. That's a deliberate lie. And you are perfectly
well aware that nothing annoys me more than dishonesty. And you needn't pretend to be busy. That's
dishonesty too. Oh, I know you. I know why you put
on a clean djibbah, too. And you know that I know.
You put it on for one reason, and for one reason alone.

ALI. It happened to be there. I thought you meant
me to put it on.

WIFE. You did not. You put it on for the only
reason men have for trying to look respectable. For a
woman. For a low, sordid intrigue. You put it on
because that pig-eating daughter of destruction from
the Farangi Mission House is coming round to-day to
pretend to buy something. The shameless cow!
Walking down the street with a naked face! I don't
know what the police are thinking about. What decent
woman would expose herself like that? But decent

women are no good to you. I've learned that by bitter
experience. And, my goodness gracious, the stew will
be spoiled, and it's all your fault, keeping me here
chattering about camels and missionaries and I don't
know what. Only, you take care. I'm a patient
woman; but I see a lot, if I don't say much, but there
are limits. And you needn't sulk at me. It makes no
impression on me. None at all.

> [*She goes into the hut.* ALI *goes on with his work,
> singing the words of a recent American song to
> a plaintive Eastern air. To him there enters*
> MISS WATSON, *a Lady Missionary, not an ill-
> looking creature, but wearing blue spectacles
> and a solar topi.*

MISS WATSON. Good morning, Ali. What a nice,
bright morning.

ALI. Salaam aleikum.

MISS WATSON. It is so nice to hear you singing at your
work. One of our poets has it that: "You can make
your labour pleasant with a sweet and noble song."

ALI. One of our poets has it that the sight of a
female gazelle gladdens the heart of the ox; warming
his belly and uplifting his spirit.

MISS WATSON. Ali! Come, come. You mustn't say
such things to me, even if you don't mean them.

ALI. If I have offended you I shall cheerfully eat five
handfuls of dust.

MISS WATSON. Oh, you mustn't do that. It would
disagree with you terribly. It's full of bacilli. Besides,
no doubt you only meant to be polite.

ALI. Ah, Hanum, politeness? I am a rough, rude
man. Allah is aware that I was deprived of my senses
by those eyes behind those spectacles, like two dark
plums glowing on a bed of salt. And moreover,
in'sh'Allah, who would not be bereft of reason at the
sight of those magnificent hips, rolling proudly like
two great whales as you make your orderly progress

down this mean and detestable alley-way, gladdening all beholders with . . .

MISS WATSON. Yes . . . Well . . . It's so hot, I don't . . . Stupid of me. . . . Ah, yes. . . . And now I hope you've made a particularly nice ashtray for me. I'm going to send it all the way home to England to a very dear friend of mine. He is, as a matter of fact, the Vicar of my native village. And it must be good, because the Vicar knows a good thing when he sees it.

ALI. That I can well believe. He chooses his women well.

MISS WATSON. Is the ashtray ready?

ALI. Not yet, Hanum. But presently. And you may rest assured that his soul will be cheered in the torments of Hell by the thought of having possessed the beautiful ashtray I shall make for him.

MISS WATSON. My dear Ali! You couldn't be expected to know, of course, but Vicars don't go to Hell.

ALI. No?

MISS WATSON. No.

ALI. Where does he go, then?

MISS WATSON. Why, to Heaven, of course.

ALI. What does he do there?

MISS WATSON. He plays on the harp.

ALI. All the time?

MISS WATSON. Well, most of the time, I should think.

ALI. That must be very dull.

MISS WATSON. Dull? Really!

ALI. The Mussulman's Heaven seems to have certain advantages over yours.

MISS WATSON. No doubt you would think so. But apart from the fact there is no such place, perhaps you will forgive me for saying that it is a most disreputable sort of Paradise.

ALI. I don't think so.

MISS WATSON. No respectable person could afford to

be seen there. Let us change the subject. I don't feel inclined to discuss it.

ALI [*dreamily*]. I don't know what "respectable" means, but I think Paradise will suit me. Ladies are very desirable objects. Take them all together, they seem to have every quality that might be expected to make a man happy. When we are young, at a season chosen by Allah, we go mad and, in our madness, imagine that all those qualities are concentrated in one single being. In the throes of this illusion we then enslave ourselves to that one being for the rest of our lives. We become married men. When we grow sane again we find that we have been mistaken. If we are wealthy we buy more wives. But if we were Solomon, the son of Jewish David, we should never come on the satisfaction of the desire of our hearts. It is almost as if women were human beings like ourselves.

MISS WATSON [*indignantly*]. Of course they are. And a jolly sight better, too.

ALI. . . . Sympathy, imagination, admiration, the delirium of love, the peace of understanding, loyalty, wit, silence, perfection of form and feature, honour, gentleness, dignity, wildness . . . how can they be assembled together in the boundaries of one individual being?

MISS WATSON. I know what you want. A nice little Aberdeen terrier. I had such a sweet one at home. His name was Bubbles. . . .

ALI. My co-religionists are accustomed to refer to you as a shameless she-dog. I have come to be almost of their opinion.

MISS WATSON. Ali, you are a very impudent fellow. I am deeply disappointed in you. I should never think of sending the Vicar an ashtray made by a person who talks in such a licentious, insolent, and improper fashion. Please consider my order cancelled. Good morning. [*Exit* MISS WATSON.

ALI. Among the Houris of Paradise we shall find all these qualities combined . . . at last.

> [*Above his booth there rises the tall figure of* AZRAEL, *the Angel of Death.* ALI *becomes aware of his presence and looks up.*

AZRAEL. Salaam aleikum.

ALI. Salaam aleyk.

AZRAEL. You are Ali, the Coppersmith?

ALI. Yes.

AZRAEL. I am Azrael, the Dark Angel.

ALI. You have come for . . . my wife?

AZRAEL. Not yet. I have come for you.

ALI. In'sh'Allah! To-day?

AZRAEL. To-day.

ALI. And in what manner, Lord?

AZRAEL. A party of Bedawi have at this moment arrived in the town. They are ripe for a little recreation, and are already looting the shops in the Street of the Well. It is written that you are to receive a crack on the head from a club and to pass for ever out of this life.

ALI. Without pain?

AZRAEL. Without pain. It will not be known to you what has struck you down.

ALI. That is very kind of Allah, the Creator, the Disheveller, the Builder up again.

AZRAEL. You are a good man. I thought I'd let you know.

ALI. It was good of you. [*Noise of a riot is heard.*] What is that noise?

AZRAEL. The rioters are approaching.

ALI. The Devil they are? A lot of stinking Bedawi. Disorderly brutes! I'll show the sons of burnt fathers they can't . . . where's my hammer? . . . they can't get away with that sort of thing here. . . . And my tongs. . . . Come on, you flea-bitten fathers of fifty million pi-dogs. . . . Welcome to our Home Town!

[*He rushes out, brandishing his hammer and tongs.*
AZRAEL *spreads his wings over the booth. The
lights dim slowly till the stage is in darkness.
The clamour increases to a roar and then stops
suddenly. An Arab flute is heard playing soft
but gay music. The lights go up on Paradise.*

SCENE II

*Paradise is an indeterminate place, lit with pink light. A
pointed, mosaicked archway at the back leads to further
delights. An orientalized structure like a pay-box is at the
prompt corner. In it sits a young male* ANGEL *in spectacles,
checking names in a ledger. A telephone bell rings.*

ANGEL. Hello. Yes. Speaking. Righto. [*He gets up,
picks up a scroll, and comes out of the box. He goes over to the
archway and calls through it.*] Next for duty. Five will do.
Miss Robinson. [*A* HOURI *enters and comes briskly down
stage.*] Miss Jones. . . . Miss Brown. . . . Miss Gibson.
. . . Miss Thomson. [*As he calls each name another*
HOURI *enters. They group themselves on a pink rock and await
his instructions.*] Let me see. Let me see. Dash it. I'll
have to look up the specification. I thought I had it
here. Excuse me, ladies.   [*He retires into the box.*

MISS JONES [*calling after him*]. Excuse me . . .

ANGEL. Yes, my dear?

MISS JONES. What sort of a gentleman is it?

ANGEL. An accident case. He was killed in some sort
of a street brawl.

MISS BROWN. Oh, good. There's a chance that he's
quite young. Is he quite young, Mr Grierson?

ANGEL. I'm afraid not. Fifty-four and eight-
twelfths. His name is Ali. He was a coppersmith.

MISS JONES. I had hoped we were getting a sailor.

MISS ROBINSON. Never mind. We'll all do our best to
give the poor old lamb a good time.

E

ANGEL. I'm sure you will. Where *is* that specification?

MISS JONES. It's all very well. I hope I don't have to do "delirium of love."

ANGEL. Here it is. [*He comes out of the box with another scroll.*] Mmmm. Let me see. Perfection of form. You've all got that. We can lump a lot of these things together. Loyalty, sympathy—I hope you've all got those. You had jolly well better have, anyhow. Miss Thomson, do you think you can manage gentleness and admiration?

MISS THOMSON. I think so, Mr Grierson.

ANGEL. I wish I could give you silence, Miss Jones, but you'd better have dignity and honour.

MISS JONES. Righto. I don't mind.

ANGEL. Let's see now. Wit . . . wit . . . wit. What about you, Miss Gibson?

MISS GIBSON. Well, really, I can't think of a thing to say.

ANGEL. You don't think you could remember a few old jokes? I shouldn't think he'll know the difference.

MISS GIBSON. Well, I'm not frightfully clever, but if it's only to make him laugh . . .

ANGEL. That's all. Anything would sound funny, coming from you.

MISS GIBSON [*sadly*]. I'll do my best.

ANGEL. I'd give you silence, but Miss Robinson is better at it. Take "the peace of understanding" too, will you, Miss Robinson?

MISS ROBINSON. I'm not quite sure what it means.

ANGEL. Every time he speaks you give him a pop-eyed look and a half-smile. *You* know. That will do for admiration too. What else is there? Wildness and the delirium of love. That'll be you, Miss Brown.

MISS BROWN. Oh, Lord!

[ALI *comes in, a little dazed and extremely embarrassed; hears the tag of conversation and withdraws.*

ANGEL. The other girls will help you out. Team work. That's what's wanted. That's the watchword. All play up for the side.

MISS THOMSON. Poor old Bessie! Never mind, duck. We'll help you.

ANGEL. Now, hurry. Hurry. He may be here at any minute. Get the props. No time to dither about.

> [*The* HOURIS *unearth garlands, drinks, fruit-baskets, incense burners, and other paradisial paraphernalia. One or two of them have simple musical instruments. The* ANGEL *returns to his box.* ALI *re-enters.*

ALI [*to the* ANGEL]. I'm sorry. I've only just arrived, and I didn't know where to go.

ANGEL. That's quite all right. Perfectly all right. Will you register, please? Your thumbprint will do if you can't write. . . . I hope you'll have a very enjoyable time with us. We do our utmost to make our guests feel at home. It's essential, of course. Eternity is a very long time.

ALI. Yes. I suppose it is.

ANGEL. These young ladies will take charge of you now. They have been longing to meet you.

ALI. I don't know . . . about my luggage. . . .

ANGEL. You have no luggage here. This is Paradise.

> [*He disappears.*

MISS JONES [*sotto voce*]. Isn't he awful?

MISS BROWN [*sotto voce*]. We can always make him tight.

MISS THOMSON [*hissing*]. Sing up!

HOURIS [*intoning to an instrumental accompaniment*].
Under the cool perpetual shade
Of the scented acacias
Flow the four rivers of water, of milk, of wine,
And of clarified honey.
Weary Companion of the Right Hand,
Come now, come now into your rest.

Here in the dark green gardens dwell
Your friends from the first,
Waiting for you alone from the times of the long-
dead gods;
Ruddy like rubies and fair like pearls.
Pouring your amber wine with no ache in the
head for its morrow.
Waking long ecstasies with no sorrow or pain in
their train.
Enter now into delight and delights never ending,
for ever.

ALI. Thank you. Thank you. That was very nice.

MISS BROWN. At last you have come, our beloved, our
darling.

ALI. Yes. Thank you.

MISS JONES. Did you have a pleasant journey?

ALI. Well, I hardly know.

MISS GIBSON [*who has been rapidly rehearsing this piece and
is determined to do her duty in the domain of wit*]. Talking
about travel, did you ever hear the one about the two
commercial travellers who went into an hotel . . .

MISS THOMSON. Darling, you will tell us all your
lovely funny story afterwards. Our lord is weary. He
has a sort of weary splendour that sits nobly upon him;
but I know he longs for rest.

MISS ROBINSON. Yes. Rest. Peace.

MISS JONES. His mighty mind must refresh itself at the
fountains of Paradise.

MISS THOMSON. He will awake like a giant in his
strength.

MISS BROWN. Beautiful strong man, lay your head on
my shoulder and rest.

MISS GIBSON. Would you like a little drinkie? Just a
teeny-weeny drinkie after its long, long trip?

MISS JONES. And then we shall bathe in the river and
dress you in silk and cloth of gold.

MISS ROBINSON. Yes.

MISS THOMSON. Will you speak to us, Master, in your deep, golden voice?

MISS ROBINSON. If you wish to be silent, be silent and let your kindly thoughts flow towards us.

MISS JONES. We are the daughters of kings, but we live in the light of your eyes.

MISS BROWN. Rest here, Master, my sweet one, my storehouse of blessings.

ALI. It is very good of you. I appreciate it very much. All this. I wish I had words to thank you. Words used to come easily to me, down on the earth. But somehow . . . now . . . Will you excuse me for a moment? Just one moment?

> [*He disengages himself and approaches the office.*
> *He raps on the desk and waits, throwing an*
> *occasional sickly smile over his shoulder at the*
> HOURIS.

MISS BROWN. Well, what's he going to do now, of all things?

MISS JONES. I don't know. He seems an odd sort of party.

MISS GIBSON. I think if you'd only let me make him laugh. . . .

MISS ROBINSON. Hush. Here's the Angel.

> [*The* ANGEL *appears.*

ANGEL. Well?

ALI. Have you. . . . You don't happen to have any idea when my wife is expected up here?

ANGEL. My dear sir, you don't need to worry about that. She won't trouble you again.

ALI. Never?

ANGEL. Of course not. She goes to another department, you see.

ALI. Is it far away?

ANGEL. Is what far away?

ALI. The . . . the department my wife is going to.

ANGEL. Let me see. Um. Well, it is difficult to say. It is possible that she may go to Hell.

ALI. Oh, dear!

ANGEL. Very few women go to either place. They have no religion, you see. But there is a chance that . . . I observe that she is at this moment in earnest conversation with an infidel Nasarany woman called Watson. Do you happen to know her?

ALI. Yes, yes. What are they talking about?

ANGEL. There is some talk of her embracing the Watson religion. Now I have heard that they have a sort of mixed establishment. . . . I could find out for you, I think.

ALI. Could you? Thank you . . . and, oh, by the way, do you happen to have an instrument called a harp in this . . . in this place?

ANGEL. A what?

ALI. A harp. I was thinking of taking a few lessons.

ANGEL [*after looking at him severely*]. You had better come with me.   [*He leads* ALI *out.*

MISS GIBSON. But I don't understand.

MISS JONES. We had better pack up the garlands and things. The old fool wants his wife.

[*As they are ill-temperedly collecting the garlands, the*

CURTAIN FALLS.

THE DARK

by

J. L. GALLOWAY

CHARACTERS

MORGAN ⎫ *lighthouse-keepers*
QUAYLE ⎭

*The action takes place in the living-room of the
Spine Head Lighthouse.*

Time: *The present*

The Radio Version of this play was first produced on June 10,
1946, with the following cast:

    Morgan   Geoffrey Wincott
    Quayle   Ben Soutten

    Produced by Peter Cresswell

*Applications regarding amateur performances of this
play should be addressed to the agents, Messrs
Raymond Savage, Ltd, Princes House, 39 Jermyn
Street, London, S.W.1.*

THE DARK

*The living-room of Spine Head Lighthouse. The setting is
conventional and should represent a whitewashed room, semi-
circular, with a heavy iron door, centre back, leading out on to
the gallery. There are two small windows on either side of
this door, through which can be seen the intermittent beam
from the lantern above. Part of an ascending spiral staircase
is seen on the right. There is an open fireplace on the left, and
beside it a door leading to the lower parts. The furniture is
plain: a table with two chairs, and a basket-chair by the
fireplace. The room is lit by a swinging lantern and the
firelight.*

*The sound of a storm is heard off, muffled by thick walls
and closed door and windows.*

One of the keepers, QUAYLE, *is sitting by the fire. He is a
big man, unctuous, unimaginative, and self-absorbed.* MORGAN,
*the only other keeper at present in the lighthouse, is exactly the
reverse: a small man, highly strung and imaginative. He is
a cockney. From time to time he sniffs gently, for he is a victim
of chronic catarrh.*

*It is seven weeks since they last saw the relief ship, and the
monotony is beginning to tell.* MORGAN *feels it most, and the
strained note in his voice indicates this. When the curtain rises*
QUAYLE *is sitting by the fire and* MORGAN *is standing at one
of the windows peering out into the darkness.*

MORGAN. Funny stuff . . . darkness. [*He stands
peering in silence for a moment.*] Look at it out there,
Quayle. 'Undreds of miles of it. [QUAYLE, *who is
absorbed in the filling of a pipe, makes no answer.*] You can
almost feel it, can't you? Funny thing, Quayle, I was
never scared of the darkness. I've always loved it.
Ever since I was a kid. . . . Never 'ad much of it
when I was a kid. I suppose that's why. There was a
street-lamp just outside the window of our 'ouse.

QUAYLE [*placidly*]. Stow it, old man. We've heard that tale before, you know.

MORGAN. That's what made me go into this line o' business, I suppose. Queer the way things work out, ain't it? Funny thing that if I 'adn't loved the darkness when I was a kid, Quayle, I'd never 've landed here with you in Spine 'Ead. [*He stands for a moment or two, peering and sniffing.*] Look at it, Quayle. Like black velvet, ain't it? Almost feel as 'ow you could jump into it from the top of the tower and swim in it. Only you'd need to be an angel to do that. And we ain't angels.

QUAYLE [*mildly*]. You'll be one in a minute, old man, if you don't stow that talk.

MORGAN. We've got to talk about something, 'aven't we?

QUAYLE. Well, talk about something else. We've had enough about darkness.

[MORGAN *peers out of the window for a moment in hurt silence.*

MORGAN. When d'you think the relief 'll get out to us, Quayle?

QUAYLE. Can't say. Might be to-morrow. Might not be for another month.

MORGAN. Blimey, another month! 'Ere, go easy, mate! They can't keep us cooped up for another month.

QUAYLE. We haven't got anything to worry about, old man. Plenty of food. Plenty of water. Plenty of coal and light. Think of the poor fellows ashore that haven't got any of those things!

MORGAN. They 'aven't got darkness, neither. Least, not real darkness like this 'ere. [*He peers in silence.*] Funny to think of us perched up 'ere, Quayle, in mid-air. Eighty feet above the water. Nothing but darkness all round us. Can't get out until they come for us. We got to wait and wait and wait. There ain't no escape . . . Like rats in a cage, ain't we, Quayle?

QUAYLE [*comfortably*]. You stow it, old man. You'll have us jumping at our own shadows next.

MORGAN. There ain't nothing to get jumpy about, mate. Least, I 'ope not. But what if they forget us, Quayle? What if they leave us 'ere to rot? Fancy us waiting day after day, Quayle, and them forgotten all about us! I expec' the drinking-water would give out first. Then the food . . . Blimey, wouldn't it be 'orrible if we 'adn't anything to drink, Quayle?

QUAYLE. Here, will you stow it? You chuck it, see? Otherwise we're going to have an argument, you and me. I'm a bit 'ot-tempered at the best of times. And this ain't the best of times.

MORGAN. All right, mate, all right. No offence. [MORGAN *peers into the darkness for a moment, silent except for an occasional sniff.*] Queer the way the beam cuts the darkness, Quayle. Like a knife cutting cheese . . . 'Ell of a big cheese, though. And 'ere we are, like rats in a trap. Inside a cheese . . . Queer, ain't it? [*He peers and sniffs for a little. Presently he begins to mutter to himself.*] Rats in a cage . . . Rats in a cage . . . Rats in a cage . . . Rats in a cage . . . Ever been in the Caledonian Market, Quayle?

QUAYLE. Can't say I have, old man. What about it?

MORGAN. There's a place there where they sell pets. All kinds of animals, see? Dogs and lizards, cats and canaries, gold-fish and such-like. There was a cage with two rats in it. Big brown ones. There was a wheel in it. The rats would take it in turn to go inside the wheel and run like stink.

QUAYLE. What made them do that, old man?

MORGAN. They thought they were going at an 'ell of a lick. Getting somewhere, see? Escaping . . . But they weren't moving at all. It was the wheel that was moving all the time. The 'arder the rats went, the 'arder the wheel went. They never got nowhere. Stayed in the same place the whole time.

QUAYLE. What about it, old man?

MORGAN. It's like us, ain't it? Going round inside the wheel all day long, day after day. Never getting nowhere. Same place the whole time. No escape . . . Until the relief comes.

QUAYLE [*beginning to be irritated*]. Well, your babbling won't bring it any sooner, see? It won't be long now, anyhow. You stow that talk . . . and chuck over my knitting.

[MORGAN *turns from the window and picks up a piece of knitting from the table.*

MORGAN [*sniffing*]. Knitting! 'Ere, catch! [*He throws the knitting.* QUAYLE *catches it.*] Fancy a man knitting.

QUAYLE. There's worse things a man can do than knitting.

MORGAN. Think you was a woman, the way you keep knitting all day long.

QUAYLE. Keeps the hands busy, and that's the main thing in a job like this. Pity you can't find something that would keep that tongue of yours still. Send us both crazy, you will, before you're done.

MORGAN. You lay off my tongue. Can't even talk in this bleeding rat-trap. [*He goes back to the window and peers out sullenly, while* QUAYLE *begins to knit.*] Can't even talk. All a bloke can do is listen to you knitting . . . Click-click-click-click-click . . . Like the noise the wheel made.

QUAYLE. What wheel?

MORGAN. The wheel the rats ran inside of—the rats in the cage.

QUAYLE. You put a sock in them rats!

MORGAN. And you stop that clicking, see? Talk about *me* sending us crazy! What about you? Can't 'ear nothing all day long but that click-click-click-click . . .

[QUAYLE *rises angrily.*

QUAYLE. Hey! That's enough o' that! What about you and your sniffing? Chronic cold in the head, hey? That's what *you* say. But what the hell does it matter? First thing I hear in the morning is you sniffing. Last thing I hear at night is you sniffing. And I hear you sniffing all the perishing day . . . You damn well stop that sniffing, see? Or I'll shove your ugly nose down your throat. [*He stops, surprised at his own violence and the astonished look on* MORGAN's *face.*] Here, hold hard, old man. Can't go parting brass-rags like this . . . Sorry if I got a bit rough.

MORGAN. All right, mate . . . But you gave me a fright, you did. It's just being cooped up like this.

> [QUAYLE *sits down and resumes his knitting.*
> MORGAN *turns once again to the window.*

MORGAN. That's what it is. It's just being cooped up like this . . . Like rats in a cage.

> [QUAYLE *glances at him over his shoulder but says nothing. Presently he lays aside the knitting with an impatient gesture, and takes a handful of mixed letters and scraps of paper from a letter-rack on the wall at the side of the fire-place. He begins to rummage through these in a bored sort of way. After a little he picks out a photograph and stares at it.*

QUAYLE. Here, look at this, old man.

> [MORGAN *turns from the window and looks at the photograph over* QUAYLE's *shoulder.*

MORGAN. Nothing funny about that. Everybody knows girls have legs.

QUAYLE [*chuckles*]. Gone all holy, have you? . . . You didn't used to be like that, old man.

MORGAN. I got engaged to a girl on my last leave.

QUAYLE. What about it?

MORGAN. She's a decent girl. Got a bit of class, see? And somehow I 'aven't got no use for that sort of picture now.

QUAYLE. Pretty poor life you're going to have i
your girl won't let you have a look at another girl in a
bathing costume.

MORGAN. It ain't that. I just don't want to.

QUAYLE. You wait till you're married, old man.
Marriage'll knock all them damn silly ideas out o'
your head.

[*He puts the photograph away and continues rum-
maging through the papers.*

MORGAN [*after a moment*]. Let's 'ave another look at
it, mate.

QUAYLE. Eh?

MORGAN. Let's 'ave another look at it. [QUAYLE
chuckles, picks the photograph out again and passes it to
MORGAN. *Studying the photograph*] Paula Westlake . . .
Saw one of her films last time I was ashore. With my
girl, I was. One I'm going to marry.

QUAYLE. Pretty, isn't she? . . . Paula, I mean.

MORGAN. Not 'arf.

QUAYLE. My favourite film-star, she is. None of the
others is up to her class, old man. Real peach, isn't
she?

MORGAN. Not 'arf. I like 'er squint.

QUAYLE. Squint?

MORGAN. That's right.

QUAYLE. What squint?

MORGAN. 'Er squint.

QUAYLE. She hasn't got a squint.

MORGAN. Garn, Quayle, she 'as so! It's 'er squint
that's so . . . that makes you go all gooseflesh when
you looks at 'er.

QUAYLE. You watch what you're saying, old man.

MORGAN. Well, it's true, ain't it? Next time you go
to one of 'er pictures, Quayle, you keep a look-out for
that squint. Can't miss it. Sometimes it's worse than
others. Sometimes you can't 'ardly see it at all. But
it's there the whole time.

QUAYLE. You put a sock in it. I'm warning you fair and square. You put a sock in it.

MORGAN. Well, it's true, ain't it?

QUAYLE. Blast you! Think I'm going to sit here and let a yellow-livered little blister like you say things like that about Paula Westlake? Hey?

MORGAN. 'Ere! Who the——

QUAYLE. Because I ain't, see? If you don't put a sock in it there's going to be trouble between us.

MORGAN. Who the 'ell are you calling names?

QUAYLE. You, you little scut! Trying to take away a girl's character . . . Behind her back, to . . . You watch your step, see?

MORGAN. Think you was stuck on her, the way you go on.

QUAYLE. What if I am, hey?

MORGAN [*turning back to his window*]. Blooming great pansy, ain't you?

> [QUAYLE *rises angrily and* MORGAN *turns to face him defensively.*

QUAYLE. I've had enough of this. I don't much mind what you say about her, but you ain't going to start saying things about me, see?

MORGAN. 'Ere, take it easy, mate! I didn't mean any 'arm. What I said about 'er. . . . I likes 'er squint, whether she 'as one or not. That's what I've been trying to tell you. . . . And it ain't no use us going up in blue smoke like this.

QUAYLE [*with an effort*]. You're right, old man . . . We're getting all strung up, that's what it is. What the blazes does it matter whether she has a squint or not?

MORGAN. Well, I don't suppose she 'as really, when you come to——

QUAYLE. She's got nice legs, anyhow.

MORGAN. Not 'arf.

QUAYLE. It's what you said, old man. It's being cooped up like this.

MORGAN. That's right. Like rats in a cage. [MORGAN *turns back to his window.* QUAYLE *sits down again, gathers up the papers and begins to go through them again.*] Quayle.

QUAYLE. Eh?

MORGAN. 'Ow long is it since they took Meek ashore?

QUAYLE. Let's see, now, old man . . . It'll be seven weeks . . . day before yesterday.

MORGAN. Seven weeks . . . Seven blinking weeks . . . Seems like seven years, don't it? . . . What was it they said on the wireless, just before the perishing thing conked out? [*He strikes an attitude and parodies the voice of a wireless announcer.*] "Since Keeper Meek was took ashore from Spine 'Ead Lighthouse, suffering from a severe internal complaint, the relief ship 'as been unable to get in touch with the two remaining keepers. But in the absence of any signals to the contrary they are presumed to be fit and well." Like smoke . . .

QUAYLE. Well, ain't we, old man?

MORGAN. Oh, there ain't nothing wrong with us just now. But supposing something did go wrong, Quayle? Supposing one of us took a pain and started to go all blue in the face? . . . I 'ad an aunt once. Squinted something awful, she did. Like Paula Westlake, only worse . . .

QUAYLE. You leave Paula Westlake alone, see?

MORGAN. All right, mate, all right. No offence . . . Well, any'ow, she took a pain and started to go all blue in the face. 'Orrible, it was. 'Er eyes began to stick out, like the rabbits you see 'anging upside down in fishmongers' shops, till you'd 'ave thought they was going to drop right out of 'er 'ead. . . . I expect they did, only she died in 'ospital, so we never found out.

QUAYLE. Well, what about it?

MORGAN. What if that 'appened to one of us, Quayle? What if you began to go all blue in the face? And your eyes began to stick out?

QUAYLE. Here, stow that talk! If you can't talk about anything better'n that you'd better just close your trap.

MORGAN. Them signals to the contrary wouldn't 'elp us very much, seeing as 'ow the relief can't get out to us. . . . I expect they'd signal what I 'ad to do for you, like they do to ships that 'aven't got doctors. Funny thing, Quayle, if I 'ad to tie you down to the table there and start cutting you open with a knife . . .

QUAYLE. Put a sock in it! I'm telling you for the last time. Put a sock in it!

MORGAN. Blimey, I'd 'ate that, Quayle! I wouldn't know 'ow to sew you up again. You'd 'ave to stay all cut up till the relief came. I should 'ate to 'ave to live 'ere, mate, with you all cut up on the table.

QUAYLE. You bloodthirsty little maggot! You'll have the two of us clean barmy if you go on like this. . . . [*He rises from the chair, turning slowly to look at* MORGAN.] Come to think of it, I ain't at all sure that you ain't a bit off your rocker already. You been talking queer all evening . . . all about darkness and cheese and rats and people going blue and such-like. . . . That ain't the kind o' talk for a man that's in his right mind.

MORGAN. 'Ere, Quayle, you chuck it! I ain't barmy, see? Course I ain't barmy.

QUAYLE. High time you talked a bit o' sense then, old man. Or didn't talk at all for a bit.

MORGAN. And why the blazes can't I talk if I want to? And who's going to stop me, any'ow? You ain't, Quayle. You ain't got no right to. You ain't 'Ead Keeper 'ere. Meek's 'Ead Keeper and 'e's ashore getting 'is appendix out. I wish to 'ell 'e wasn't. If Meek was 'ere 'e'd keep you in your place. Been throwing your weight about all night, you 'ave. I wouldn't 'ave you as my boss, not if you was the last man left in the whole blooming world. I'd push you into the sea from the gallery outside first, and that's straight. . . . If anyone's going to be my boss it's going to be a man and not a fat old basket what goes dippy on film stars that squint, and knits all bleeding day . . .

> [QUAYLE *grunts with inarticulate anger, stumbles across the room, and seizes* MORGAN *by the front of his shirt. He thrusts a clenched fist into* MORGAN'S *startled face.*

QUAYLE. Here, you! See this, hey? See this fist, hey? One more word out of you and I'll shove it through your ugly pan, see? You been handing me out nothing but lip all evening and I've had about enough.

MORGAN. Sorry, mate! Sorry! Honest, I am . . . I didn't ought to 'ave spoke like that. It was you saying I'd gone dippy. Gave me a fright, see. No offence, mate.

> [QUAYLE *hesitates, then thrusts* MORGAN *away from him.*

QUAYLE. That's all right, old man. But you put a brake on that tongue of yours.

> [*He sits down again.* MORGAN *turns to the window.*

MORGAN. Week after week . . . Like rats in a cage. [QUAYLE *picks up his knitting, and the click of his needles and the occasional sniff from* MORGAN *are the only sounds heard for some moments above the subdued noise of the storm.*] Week after week . . . Like rats in a cage . . . Round and round . . . Never getting nowhere . . . Same place the whole time . . . No escape . . . My Gawd, Quayle, when's the relief coming?

QUAYLE. Can't say, old man. Depends on the weather. And it ain't looking too good. But they'll come as quick as they can. There ain't nothing for us to worry about, old man.

MORGAN [*after a moment*]. There's a ship out there, Quayle. A tramp, I expect. Outward bound. Funny

to think of her away out there, Quayle. Alone. Miles
from anywhere, with nothing but darkness all round
'er . . . Like a sort of spook, ain't she? . . . Don't
envy the blokes on board of 'er on a night like this . . .
[*He pauses for a moment. Then he bursts out suddenly.*]
Click-click-click-click-click . . . I wish you'd stop that
blasted knitting, Quayle. Can't 'ear myself think with
that noise.

QUAYLE. Things you think aren't worth hearing.
And what about your sniffing? You haven't stopped
that yet.

MORGAN. I can't 'elp sniffing. It's nature. But it
ain't nature for a bloke to knit all the perishing time.

QUAYLE. You mind your own business. What the
blazes does it matter to you whether I knit or not?
And if you haven't got anything better to do than pass
remarks, you'd better 'op up to the lantern and see
that the light's all right.

MORGAN. It ain't my shift.

QUAYLE. You go up and take a look at that light,
see? I've been too soft with you all evening, and I
ain't going to be soft with you any longer . . . Go on,
'op it.

MORGAN. Who do you think you are? You ain't
'Ead Keeper, are you?

QUAYLE. No, I ain't Head Keeper. Meek's Head
Keeper, and Meek's ashore just now. But I'm the
senior hand here, and I'm in charge until the relief
comes, see? . . . Now, you 'op up them stairs double-
quick and don't give me any more of your lip!

MORGAN. Oh, you go to 'ell!

[QUAYLE *rises.*

QUAYLE. All right. You've asked for it. And now
you're going to get it.

MORGAN. Keep your 'ands off me, Quayle!

[QUAYLE *grasps him by the back of the neck.*

QUAYLE. Going to do what I told you?

[MORGAN, *struggling in* QUAYLE'S *grasp, is thrust towards the spiral stair.*

MORGAN. No, I ain't.

QUAYLE. Oh, you ain't, hey? We'll see about that. Come on! 'Op up these stairs. And don't struggle. It won't help you.

MORGAN [*sobbing with helpless anger*]. Blast you, Quayle! You'll pay for this! I'll make you pay for this some'ow——

QUAYLE. You shut your trap or you'll get hurt. [*There is a sudden scuffle and an exchange of blows.*] There! I told you. Gone and got your nose bled . . . Now you 'op up them stairs and see that everything's all right. I'm going down below for five minutes. And when I come back I'll expect you to apologize proper-like for the way you've been carrying on. See?

[QUAYLE *goes, taking with him the lantern.* MORGAN *is left, a dark shadow, crouching at the foot of the spiral stair.*

MORGAN. You've gone, 'ave you? . . . You'd 'it me and leave me lying bleeding like a stuck pig, would you? . . . All right, Quayle, you'll pay for this, you will. By Gawd, you'll pay for this! [*He begins to climb the stair, laughing hysterically.*] I'm going to bust up the light, see? Smash up the mantles and the burners, so that you won't be able to sort 'em. Then we'll 'ave darkness—real darkness at last . . . Darkness! . . . And when the relief comes you'll get merry 'ell. . . . 'Cause you're in charge, see? You're the senior 'and, and you're in charge. . . . But I won't. 'Cause why? . . . 'Cause I won't be 'ere, see? I'm going out to . . . to swim in the darkness, mate. . . . Out there, Quayle. 'Undreds of miles of it. . . . Like black velvet, ain't it? [*He goes out at the top of the stairs. There is silence for a moment, then confused metallic blows and the smashing of glass off. The intermittent beam of the light stops. After a moment* MORGAN *reappears at the head of the stairs and begins to descend slowly.*] Darkness. . . . You can almost feel it, can't you? . . . Funny thing, I've never been scared of the dark. I've always loved it. . . . Ever since I was a kid.

> [MORGAN *is moving towards the door at the back which leads out on to the gallery.* QUAYLE *is heard returning hurriedly from below.*

QUAYLE [*off*]. Morgan! What's up, Morgan?

MORGAN. Going to jump into the darkness, Quayle. . . . Swim in it. . . . From the gallery, see? [*He struggles to open the iron door. As he unfastens the bolts it is blown violently open. The railing of the gallery can be seen through the doorway. The sound of the storm increases.*] Darkness. . . .

> [QUAYLE *enters, without the lantern.* MORGAN *has climbed on to the gallery railing and is swaying there.*

QUAYLE. Here, what was all that noise? . . . Morgan, where are you? . . . Morgan!

MORGAN [*shouting above the noise of the storm*]. Darkness. . . . Look at it out 'ere, Quaylc! Almost feel it, can't you? . . . I'm going to swim in it. . . . And you're going to swing, mate! . . . They'll think you done me in, see? And you'll swing for it!

QUAYLE. Morgan! Come in out o' that, you blasted fool! You'll get blown away!

MORGAN. Going to swim for it, mate! . . . And you're going to swing. . . . Get 'ung. . . . They'll think you done me in, see, and string you up. . . . Good-bye, Mister Quayle, you knitting-needle-clicking——

> [MORGAN *disappears suddenly. The rest of his words are drowned in the roar of the storm.* QUAYLE *stands staring through the empty doorway.*

CURTAIN

MALVOLIO

by

STEPHEN WILLIAMS

CHARACTERS

MALVOLIO (*formerly steward to Olivia, now running an apothecary's shop*)
FABIAN (*formerly servant to Olivia, now helping Malvolio in the shop*)
OLIVIA (*married to Sebastian*)
MARIA (*her waiting-maid*)

The action takes place in Malvolio's shop in Illyria, about three years after the events in Shakespeare's "Twelfth Night."

This play won First Prize in the Poetry Society's Competition for an original one-act play in verse and was first published in *The Poetry Review*, 1946. It was produced in E. Martin Browne's season of New Plays by Poets at the Mercury Theatre, London, on May 27, 1946.

Applications regarding amateur performances of this play should be addressed to the publishers, George G. Harrap and Co., Ltd, 182 High Holborn, London, W.C.1.

MALVOLIO

*Scene: A room adjoining an apothecary's shop, looking out on
the street. A summer evening.* MALVOLIO, *very grave and
dignified, sits writing at a table on which there is a lamp. The*
CLOWN'S *voice is heard in the street as he passes the window.*

CLOWN

O mistress mine, where are you roaming?
O, stay and hear; your true love's coming,
    That can sing both high and low:
Trip no further, pretty sweeting;
Journey's end in lovers meeting,
    Every wise man's son doth know.

MALVOLIO

My grief should know that voice; and the song, too.
Why, 'tis the song that Feste used to sing
Three years ago. How cruel its magic then!
How viciously it used to sting my sense!
Poison in that bee's honey! Is't possible?
After so long—so long. [*Opens window.*] Yes, 'tis the
    Fool,
Galliarding down the street; two women with him,
Who try to silence him. Their hooded gowns
Billow before the breeze like clouds of smoke,
And dissolve too, like smoke-clouds as they fade,
Into the twilight. [*Shuts window.*] Miserable Clown!
Why do you break the prison of the past,
Prise open echoing dungeons in my mind
Which I thought closed for ever? Dungeons—pah!
The stench of one still crawls into my nostrils;
Poisoning the sweet air of this summer night—
Putrid!—but not so putrid as the gibes
Which you and Toby gibbered through the bars,
Like strident monkeys; you, with green eyes of malice,

89

Toby, his nose half eaten with the pox,
His lips still speckled with the drunkard's slime.
Toby! Whom I had thought to make my kinsman!
"O Mistress Mine"—so runs the measure. Nay,
You were my mistress only in those dreams
That stretched my senses like a viol string,
Till the note snapped and hummed out into silence,
Into air that gave it being; then I awoke,
Awoke before the fields of heaven could flower,
And, like a creature in another play,
I cried to dream again.
                 Well, "Mistress Mine,"
You had your triumph; but you could not know
The sacred essence of the dream that dies
Before the light of day disperse its colour,
And therefore dies, and therefore lives for ever;
The flame that flickers out upon the wind
Before it sinks to ashes; and therefore fades,
And therefore shines for ever. In my dreams
I had you. In my dreams I have you still,
Tight prisoned in a prison with no walls,
Stronger than any prison ever built
Because not built at all. [*Enter* FABIAN.] Ah, Fabian;
How goes our trade?

FABIAN

           The world is full of fools.
Is that a proper answer?

MALVOLIO

           'Tis a just one.
And, to tell truth, my conscience sometimes pricks me
That we should thrive on that preposterous birth-rate.
We are thieves, Fabian; we rob the blind.

FABIAN

If I were blind, that's what I should expect.

MALVOLIO

What, robbery?

FABIAN

Nay, 'tis no robbery;
No more than a musician robs a deaf man
By playing him something that he thinks is music;
No more than a clown, who entertains a clod,
Lives by his talents. We live by our talents,
Practising them on fools who have no talents.
Are we then thieves?

MALVOLIO

I was a fool myself once,
And certainly I thought it thievery.

FABIAN

You were a fool? Now, master, recollect:
Have you forgotten then our friendly pact?
That time when you were—shall I say?—distraught,
I took you from the scene of your distress,
And we set up this shop——

MALVOLIO

Yes, I remember.
I vowed I'd put the past out of my mind,
And look into the future. But, Fabian——

FABIAN

Beware now——

MALVOLIO

No, 'tis not the past, my friend,
It is the present: we are doing harm.

FABIAN

Dear Master, tell me: where's the harm we do?
Sell a lame man a draught of coloured water,
He goes home happy, thinking he is cured;

Sell an old lecher herbs to cure his lust,
He goes home happy, thinking he is impotent;
Sell a love-philtre to a desp'rate lover,
He walks in heaven, dreaming she will love him.

MALVOLIO

Fabian, you are a born apothecary!

FABIAN

My mother, sir, had higher hopes for me,
But they, not she, miscarried.

MALVOLIO

                    Then you think
The end of a human life is to be happy?

FABIAN

I'd rather be a happy than a wise man.

MALVOLIO

Not many men are both. Come, close the shutters.
There is a chill wind creeping through the night,
Colder than a dead man's hand.

FABIAN

                    Why, no, 'tis warm;
A summer night, scented and lyrical;
Even a hint of thunder in the air.

MALVOLIO

Then leave the window bare unto the night.
The chill's in me, perhaps; I'm out of humour;
Something turned over in my heart just now,
And shook my body.

FABIAN

                    Shall I go and mix
A taste of your own med'cine?

MALVOLIO

Let me alone;
The jest is out of season.

FABIAN

Pray, forgive me.
The summer night is playing in my blood
A most aspiring music. I'll be gone.
I have to give a lesson to a wench,
But not in music—nor shall I need a philtre.

MALVOLIO

Take care you do not need some other cure
Some three days afterwards——

FABIAN

Nay, never fear:
I know too well the stuff that cure is made of!

MALVOLIO

Forget all that and let it make you happy!
What signifies it that you are not wise?
You go home happy, thinking you are cured.
Sell a young lecher herbs——

FABIAN

Good, good! you've won!
That bout is yours. But wait till I return:
Love will have lighted torches in my brain
To dazzle you with sparks of rhetoric.

MALVOLIO

Good night, then. [*Knock.*] Hark! We shut up shop
    too soon;
Who knocks so late?

FABIAN

[*At window*] Two women, darkly hooded.
They say a woman's work is never done,
Here are two proofs of it. And yet perhaps
They come for play, not work.

MALVOLIO

I'll have no play.
See what they want. [*Exit* FABIAN.] There were two
    with the clown.
One looked like something out of memory;
A shadow, like the shadow that is thrown
Sometimes between the sunlight and my eyes.
I will make sure. [*Goes to window.*] Yes, yes—'tis the
    same two;
Their hooded cloaks still billow to the breeze,
Like clouds of smoke. The second—I was right:
I have held her in my arms so many nights
In lonely, bitter ecstasy. 'Tis she,
Olivia! The night wind is a sculptor,
Blowing the cloak about the moulded form,
Until it stands even like a naked statue
Against the sky. Old heart, are you there still?
Why don't you turn my ribs into a drum,
Thundering and hammering for your lost freedom?
Why don't the heavens split and shower down blood
Upon my open eyes, choke up my mouth,
Drown all my shattered senses in the bliss
That it is death to know? Is time so strong?
Can it be that this ghost is laid for ever?

[*Comes down centre.*

I used to weep when memories
Burned like unnatural stars to keep
The lacerated heart from sleep;
And staged for my reluctant eyes
Farces I played as tragedies.
I used to weep. . . .

I weep no more; for on my grief
Indifferent time has closed the door;
Bringing what memory should deplore,
A bitter, barren, bare relief,
And sighs that wound—they are so brief.
I weep no more. . . .

Alas, poor ghost of bygone years!
I cannot tell which hurts the most:
My memories, a luminous host,
Or this indifference, that hears
Your voice, yet cannot give you tears.
Alas, poor ghost!

[Re-enter FABIAN.

FABIAN

I told them we had done; but—as I said—
A woman's work——

MALVOLIO

I know. Convey them in. *[Exit* FABIAN.
MALVOLIO *puts on mask and turns down lamp.*]
She's coming in now. I can hear her step.
How calm I am! I think I have no heart.
It's still, thank God! It's cold. Time, you're my
    friend:
You have tamed my wild heart. . . . Alas, poor
    ghost!

[Re-enter FABIAN *with* OLIVIA *and* MARIA, *hooded
and masked.*

FABIAN

Here is his worship.

OLIVIA

Maria, wait outside.

MARIA

Take heed, my lady; do not be misled
Into rash acts. My mind is not at rest;
May I not stay with you?

OLIVIA

Do as I bid you.
[FABIAN *takes* MARIA *out, winking at* MALVOLIO *as he goes.*]
The hour is late. Am I importunate?

MALVOLIO

Lady, I have some skill in alchemy,
And what I have I sell. This is a shop;
I'm forced to earn my living by my learning.
But—learning does not stop at closing-time;
My shop may shut; my mind is always open
To learn fresh things. What can I learn from you?

OLIVIA

'Tis you must teach. I come to you for help;
And yet I know not how to start. I fear
To tell you all——

MALVOLIO

But you must tell me all;
Know you not I must learn before I teach?
How can I help you else? Come, cast out fear;
I think I am old enough to be your father.
Look to me as a father. Tell me all.

OLIVIA

I want to rid my conscience of a dream
That saturates it. O you cannot know
What grief is mine! Have you a herb—a herb—
Something to drive this poison from my heart,
Something to kill the memory of love—

Yet not a memory—— No—there was no love;
But now there is. God, must I tell you all?
Three years ago, a man—he was my steward—
Was tricked into believing that I loved him.
I did not love him. No, I did not love him;
My heart was guiltless—do you understand?—
Guiltless as is a child's. I laughed at him
When he, poor wretch, poor bird in amorous
    plumage,
Appeared before me wearing yellow stockings—
A colour I detested—and cross-gartered—
A fashion I abhorred—I laughed at him.
Why do I tell you this?

MALVOLIO

You did great wrong
To laugh at love. But you must tell me all.

OLIVIA

I did great wrong; but not so much to him:
I did not know 'twas love; I thought him mad;
Perhaps he was; madness and love are kin.
No, no, I did great wrong, but to myself:
For now 'tis I am mad. What was my mirth
Is now become my scourge.

MALVOLIO

What do you mean?

OLIVIA

I am the sufferer: the love I spurned
Returns to plague me. For Malvolio,
I know not what befell him. Two days after
He passed out of my life.

MALVOLIO

Was that his name?
Malvolio? On your lips the name is music.

G

OLIVIA

If music be the food of love. . . . It is!
I told you that he passed out of my life.
I lied to you: he passed out of my sight;
Yet every day and every night since then
I see him, see him with the eyes of love,
Eyes that can overleap a thousand miles.
I love him.

MALVOLIO

Why, what rhapsody is this?
You—*love* him?

OLIVIA

O, I know 'tis foul in me;
A wife, a mother; aye, sir, I am both.
My husband—nay, Sebastian's not my husband,
Not in the sight of God, who sees my heart.
No, not my husband, though I bore his child;
There was no love; life should be born of love.
Well—so it was, but not Sebastian's love.
When I looked up into Sebastian's eyes,
I saw Malvolio's; when that child was made,
I thought not of Sebastian.
Now—you know all.
Have pity on me! I want a cure for love,
A cure for love!

MALVOLIO

You are a haunted woman——

OLIVIA

Haunted. Yes, yes; tell me, what can you do?

MALVOLIO

A haunted woman, and upon your heart
There is a plague-spot that you cannot cleanse
Till a new plague afflict it.

OLIVIA

You seem moved;
There is a strange enchantment in your voice
That stirs the past. What? Have we met before?
I think you are a wizard.

MALVOLIO

That's my trade.
I was once a fool, but now I live by fools.

OLIVIA

I am afraid. I cannot see your eyes,
But they possess me. Let me go from here——

MALVOLIO

[*Rising*] You shall not go! The irony of fate
Never entangled helpless human hearts
In such a web of splendid mockery—
Aye, splendid mockery.

OLIVIA

Mockery? What means this?
Why do you bar my way? Maria! Help!
I tell you I must go!

MALVOLIO

You shall not go.
To let this moment pass—why, it would spoil
The most tremendous jest God ever made
To kindle laughter in eternity! [*Distant thunder.*]
Hark! Do you hear him laughing in his thunder,
Splitting the sides of heaven with his mirth?
See how the lightning wrinkles up his face!
Olivia!   [*Tears off the mask and raises the lamp.*

OLIVIA

Malvolio!

MALVOLIO

Yes, Malvolio!
You knew not what befell Malvolio;
This—*this* befell Malvolio. God delivered
His enemy into his hand.

OLIVIA

His enemy?
You would not murder me!

MALVOLIO

Ha! Never fear:
I would not be so merciful.

OLIVIA

O shame!
To have told all this to you—to you—to you!
Shown you my secret heart.

MALVOLIO

I showed you mine

Three years ago.

OLIVIA

Ah! But you were a man;
A man may show his heart; a woman, never.

MALVOLIO

What did I get for showing you my heart?

OLIVIA

O, do not speak of that! Have I not wept
To think what barren weeds sprang from your love?
Love, gentle love, whose children should be flowers,
Whose flowers should be children.

MALVOLIO

Answer me!
What did I get for showing you my heart?

OLIVIA

Pain and disgrace; but not of my creation.
I swear I did not know, I could not know,
That day when I made you my laughing stock,
How God would make me his.

MALVOLIO

Shall I tell you
All that I got for showing you my heart?

OLIVIA

My tears rob me of breath. I cannot speak.

MALVOLIO

They locked me in a madhouse cell,
And made my madness feed their mirth,
Because I thought I could compel
Beauty to rate me at my worth;
Because I deemed my worth could make
Nature obedient to art,
And sometimes dreamed that love might take
Compassion on a hungry heart.

OLIVIA

O, love was deaf and love was blind,
And love saw not the wound it made,
Be merciful! You are repaid
Daily and hourly, and in kind.

MALVOLIO

I did not care; I had discerned
The love that strikes men blind and dumb;
And for one blessed day had turned
Illyria to Elysium.

OLIVIA

Illyria to Elysium!
Then you did glean some happiness?
Some light shone down on your distress,
Some tender thought did sometimes come?

MALVOLIO

They locked me in a madhouse cell,
Because I'd lost my wits, they said.
I breathed the prison's bitter smell,
I ate the prison's bitter bread.
I bore Sir Toby's ribald spleen
When he and Feste mocked my scars,
And scarcely heard the gibes obscene
They hooted through my window-bars.

OLIVIA

Never by me were they designed;
I knew nought of the pranks they played.
Be merciful! You are repaid
Daily and hourly, and in kind.

MALVOLIO

I did not care; for I had burned
With fire that raised me from the scum,
And for one day and night had turned
Illyria to Elysium.

OLIVIA

Elysium! Why, then, you found
Some secret solace in your heart,
Some hope from which you could not part,
Some dream that raised you from the ground?

MALVOLIO

A dream that spanned a night and day,
And healed my heart and made it whole;
That day and night have passed away;

The dream stays ever in my soul.
My faded yellow stockings lie
Beside those garters worn for you;
As if they would persuade the eye
To tell the mind my dream was true.

OLIVIA

Your dream was true! I know it now;
Malvolio, your dream *was* true.
And fate has led me back to you;
I will not question why or how.

MALVOLIO

It was not true. But it was fair;
And never will I kill the lie
That bids me cherish through despair
My deathless rose of memory.

OLIVIA

Your dream *was* true. Malvolio,
I know it now; your deathless rose
Is the undying flower that glows
Here, in my bitter heart. And so?

MALVOLIO

And so it was that once I learned
The love that leaves all senses numb;
And, for all time to be, I turned
Illyria to Elysium.

[A long pause.

OLIVIA

[*Very softly*] Malvolio: need it always be a dream?

MALVOLIO

Always. My dream is my reality.

OLIVIA

Malvolio: what is *my* reality?

MALVOLIO

You have left your reality at home.
Go back to it, and trouble mine no more.

OLIVIA

Go back! I think I never shall go back.
Malvolio: I, too, have seen the rose
That burns within the memory like a star,
Red as the blood of Christ upon the Cross;
I, too, have known the love that strikes men blind
And unseals women's eyes. I, too, have turned
Illyria into Elysium.

MALVOLIO

I will not stay to hear my words blown back,
Like paper in the wind.

OLIVIA

You shall not go!
Shall we not taste the irony of fate?
To let this moment pass—why, it would spoil
The most tremendous jest God ever made!

MALVOLIO

Leave me. I will not hear my dream degraded.

OLIVIA

Have you, then, a monopoly of dreams?
Malvolio: you are my prisoner,
Tight prisoned in a prison without walls,
Stronger than any prison ever built,
Because not built at all. I, too, have known
The dream that dies and therefore lives for ever;
I, too, have yearned that love some day might take
Compassion on a hungry heart. Love did:

It was the love I cherished in my soul
These three years past; the love that grew and
  quickened
Even as a child that leaps within the womb;
The deathless rose of memory that changed
Illyria into Elysium.

MALVOLIO

For you there was no need of such a change;
For you Illyria *was* Elysium.
Do you forget Orsino's headstrong love,
Which you despised, as was your gentle fashion?

OLIVIA

Speak not of him; Viola has that love.

MALVOLIO

Sir Andrew—there was a feast spread for your wit!
A greater fool than I, if such can be;
The boon companion of your uncle Toby.

OLIVIA

Toby is dead.

MALVOLIO

Of drink, I have no doubt.

OLIVIA

It was not well to say you had no doubt.

MALVOLIO

And, to complete the tale, Sebastian,
Whom you trapped into marriage——

OLIVIA

No—no trap;
A sad mistake. I have paid for that mistake.
Daily and hourly I have paid for it.
Be merciful! You are avenged—in kind.

MALVOLIO

Confess, then; there *was* something to avenge?

OLIVIA

Malvolio: I have opened up my heart,
As though a surgeon's knife had cut it out.
What further can I do? You torture me.
I came here desperate for a cure for love—
No more of that. What's in your shop I know not,
What potent arts you may command, I care not;
I want no cure for love: I have found love.
Are you a man? Can you not read my heart?
This is the supreme hour in both our lives;
If we reject it, we kill life itself.

MALVOLIO

Why should we not kill life? What has life brought
To you or me? To you a foolish husband,
To me a love despised, a madhouse cell,
An apothecary's shop——

OLIVIA

A splendid dream
Which has this hour come true.

MALVOLIO

Olivia:
That is mere woman's talk. If dreams came true,
There would be dreams no more. The holy fire
That lifts man's being high above himself,
That paints his mind in pictures, hoists his visions
Upon the wings of music, sets his words
Sailing upon a halcyon stream of verse
Would fall to ashes. How can dreams come true?
And why should dreams come true?

OLIVIA

You are a man;
A man can live by dreams. I am a woman,
And for a woman dreams are not enough.

MALVOLIO

What further do you wish?

OLIVIA

I wish to live;
I cannot live by dreams. Malvolio:
I want your love again, even as that day
You stood within my garden, in your eyes
The light that lit the lovers of all time,
And mirrored the bright sun.

MALVOLIO

You laughed at me.

OLIVIA

O yes, I laughed at you; scourge me with that;
Say it again—again! I thought you mad;
But now I know too well that I was mad.
Now that my eyes are open to the truth
I laugh no more. Malvolio, say you love me—
You love me!

MALVOLIO

No, I will not, cannot love you!
I hate you now because you laugh no more.
You? Who are you? I know you not. I love
The "Fortunate Unhappy," she who laughed
To see that vain, deceived, bedraggled peacock,
Brave in his yellow stockings and cross-garters,
On that June day, ringed round with laughing
    flowers;
Laughed with the music of heaven in her laugh.

She whom I love was haughty, proud, and cruel.
She was a queen enthroned within my being,
She was a star enthroned within my soul,
She was a goddess crowned in Paradise.
I have her still; never can she elude me;
Never can she withhold her queenly presence;
Never can she reject the offerings
I lay before her in the dust of dreams,
Humble, yet deathly proud. I am her slave,
Rejoicing in my servitude. And you—
Wife of Sebastian—mother of his child—
You come to me with love, with mortal love;
You come to break this box of spikenard,
To tear the fabric of this fantasy,
Dig up this buried treasure. O, your love,
Your vanity, your itching lust to shatter
This holy shrine, and raise one to yourself—
Wife of Sebastian—mother of his child !
How can you think that I would change that dream
For this reality?

OLIVIA

Malvolio:
Cast out this dream, shake off this fantasy,
And live, Malvolio. Life calls to us;
Why should we struggle? Why should we resist?
We are caught fast within the toils of life,
Caught in its wheel and whirled round at its
    pleasure—
Its pleasure ! And *our* pleasure—what of that?
Love spreads its golden pasture at our feet
To tread into delight, as the wine-pressers
Tread out the teeming grapes. Immortal longings
Heave up their urgent clamours in our breasts.
Our children: they are crying to be born.
Do you not hear them singing in your blood,
Singing the song that rises above death?

MALVOLIO

I can hear nothing but your voice.

OLIVIA

Behold me:
Is not my hair enticing to your eye,
Soft to your touch? Touch it, Malvolio.
  [*He puts out his hand, shudders, and draws it back.*]
Is not my flesh desirable? 'Tis white,
  [*She draws down her dress, revealing part of her breast.*]
White as the moon when she lies on her back,
Quivering with ardour for the cloud's embrace.
I am your moon; you are my cloud, Malvolio—
Stifle me, cover me with your vast embrace!
See, see, my flesh is white. Touch it, Malvolio,
Touch it! Sebastian kisses my twin breasts
When he bends over me and girdles me
With his strong arms as with a belt of love.
Why should it be Sebastian? Why not you?
Your arms are strong—enfold me with your arms—
Press me to death with love——

MALVOLIO

Ah! Godless harlot!
My hate and not my love shall overpower you.
You have thrown filth upon my memories,
Debased the image of what once you were.
My dream shall live, the reality shall die!
            [*Draws a knife and points it at her breast.*

OLIVIA

[*Inspired*] Look in my eyes, Malvolio, look in my
    eyes!
Why should you heed a dying woman's cries?
E'en though their sharpness make you catch your
    breath;
E'en though they ring in your brain until your death?

Say are you brave, Malvolio, are you brave?
Dare you destroy the truth, your dream to save?
Be strong, Malvolio, summon what strength you can
Against the power that woman has over man.
Look in my eyes, Malvolio, look in my eyes!
Let them not shake your purpose. Are you not wise?
Here is my breast; an opening flower 'tis like;
Look then, Malvolio, look in my eyes—and strike!

MALVOLIO

[*Drops dagger.*] Fool! I am still the fool that earned
   your laughter
That day in the garden. See my yellow stockings,
If you have eyes. And garters—yes, cross-garters,
Not on my legs, but in my burning brain,
My cracked and burning brain! O, fool! fool! fool!
                    [*Buries his face in his hands over the table.*

OLIVIA

Nay, you are wise as you are cruel. I go.
We have both lost our senses in this darkness.

MALVOLIO

[*Recovering*] Lady, you are free to go. You leave this
   house
Unchanged in soul and body.

OLIVIA

Not in soul.

MALVOLIO

I will not touch your beauty with my hands,
Nor with this useless dagger.

OLIVIA

I could have wished
For one fate or the other; better, both:
I could have wished your hands had given me life,

And, after, death; death as a swift release
From that transcendent and divine unrest
Makes life too strong for life. Both you denied me;
I have gained nor love nor death. The jest is over.
Farewell. May God have pity on your heart—
And on mine, too.   [*Exit.*

MALVOLIO

God will do as God wills.
[MALVOLIO *stands for a moment looking after her.
    Then he sits at the table, opens a great book,
    and stares in front of him. Voices are heard
    outside and the shutting of a door. Then the*
    CLOWN'S *voice as he passes down the street
    escorting* OLIVIA *and* MARIA.

CLOWN

What is love? 'Tis not hereafter;
Present mirth hath present laughter;
        What's to come is still unsure:
In delay there lies no plenty;
Then come kiss me, sweet and twenty,
        Youth's a stuff will not endure.

CURTAIN

THE MAN WHO THOUGHT FOR HIMSELF

by

NEIL GRANT

CHARACTERS

THE JUDGE
THE PRISONER
THE PROSECUTOR
THE POLICE OFFICER
THE MEDICAL WITNESS
THE REPORTER
THE GADFLY

The PUBLIC, *and* JURY, *and the* ATTENDANTS
are invisible.

THE MAN WHO THOUGHT
FOR HIMSELF

*The scene is a Court of Justice. One door, one window.
Emblems and signs abound. They can be or not be swastikas.
Centre is the* JUDGE'S *seat. Beside it on a table, conspicuous,
is a telephone. The dock is* L. *Below the raised seat or dais
of the* JUDGE *is accommodation for* COUNSEL. *The door is
extreme* R. *In the centre is the reporters' table. Again there is
conspicuous on it a telephone.*

JUDGE [*wearing wig and robes*]. Bring in the prisoner.

POLICEMAN [*on* JUDGE'S *right, salutes*]. Very good,
my lord. [*Exit* R.

[*Telephone bell beside* JUDGE'S *table rings.*

JUDGE [*at receiver*]. Hullo. [*Rises most respectfully,
bows.* PROSECUTOR, REPORTER, *and everybody else rise too.*]
Yes, Excellency. The trial is about to begin. I shall
find him guilty and sentence him to death. [*Pause.*]
As expeditiously as I can. [*Salute.*

[*He sits down, so do the others. Telephone on
reporters' desk goes.*

REPORTER [*to* JUDGE]. May I, my lord?

[REPORTER *is middle-aged.*

JUDGE. You may.

REPORTER [*at receiver*]. Hullo, yes. Ready? From
our special crime expert. The great trial is about to
begin. The Judge, one of the most experienced,
erudite, and loyal of our exalted bench will find the
prisoner guilty and will sentence him to death. Justice
must be done. [*Rings off.*

POLICEMAN [*re-enters*]. My lord, the prisoner is here.

JUDGE. A moment. Is he guarded?

POLICEMAN. Yes, my lord. The police are specially
reinforced. Machine-guns are posted on the roof and
all the walls.

JUDGE. Is he handcuffed?

POLICEMAN. Yes, my lord. Only——

JUDGE. Yes?

POLICEMAN. Beg pardon, my lord. He is heavily handcuffed and chained, but his chains have a trick of coming off.

JUDGE. If you are not more careful your head will have a trick of coming off.

[*Sycophantic roars of laughter from everybody present, and* REPORTER *writes frantically as he chuckles.*

PROSECUTOR [*youngish man in wig and robes*]. What wit. What elegance.

JUDGE [*to* REPORTER]. Did you mention my little pleasantry?

REPORTER. Yes, my lord.

JUDGE. See that you get it properly.

REPORTER. Yes, my lord, and I have added that the Court was convulsed. [*More convulsions.*

JUDGE [*severely*]. Silence. This is a Court of Justice, not a place of entertainment. There must be no unseemly mirth even at my pleasantries. This is a solemn, a terrible moment. A dreadful responsibility weighs upon all of us. [*Severely to* POLICEMAN] Now. [*The* POLICEMAN *leads in the* PRISONER. *He is a harmless-looking man about forty years of age, simply, almost poorly dressed, with at times a half-apologetic smile on his face. He may or may not be a gentleman.*] One moment. Has he been searched?

POLICEMAN. Yes, my lord.

JUDGE. When was the last time?

POLICEMAN. He is searched every hour, my lord.

JUDGE. And no lethal weapons found?

POLICEMAN. None, my lord. He himself says that he carries his weapons in his head.

JUDGE. Silence, officer. What the prisoner says about himself is not evidence. Put him in the dock.

[*The* POLICEMAN *escorts the* PRISONER *to the dock. He stands unruffled and occasionally smiles.* POLICEMAN *stands beside him, watching him carefully.*

REPORTER [*at telephone*]. It is a dramatic moment. The monster is in the witness-box. I can almost touch him. He is about the same distance away from the Judge. Yet his lordship, the embodiment of legal dignity, the stern guardian of the sacred rights of the State, is unmoved. He sits there as if danger were a thousand miles away. It is an inspiring sight.

JUDGE [*to* PROSECUTOR]. Prosecutor, proceed.

PROSECUTOR [*rises in the usual way, and addresses Court*]. My lord, you are doubtless aware of the crime, the ghastly, abominable, terrifying crime with which this man is charged. He is accused of thinking for himself.

REPORTER [*at telephone, while the* JUDGE *leans back in his chair, overcome*]. The Public Prosecutor has dispelled all doubts. The unbelievable has occurred. This wretch is accused of thinking for himself. As the dread indictment was read out three women fainted, and I notice that the guards are examining afresh their machine-guns. The Judge sits, a statue, but a statue alive with indignation, horror, and majesty. [*Rings off.*

JUDGE [*in low voice to* PROSECUTOR]. When [*gulping the words*] does he think for himself?

PROSECUTOR. All the time, my lord. In his home, in his college, when he is reading his newspaper, when he is listening-in, even—pardon me, my lord, I am slightly faint—a glass of water, officer, please——

[POLICEMAN *hands him glass. With shaking hand he drinks.*

JUDGE [*sympathetically*]. Shall I adjourn the Court for five minutes?

PROSECUTOR. I'm obliged to your lordship, but I think I can go on. [*Sternly*] He thinks for himself even when our beloved, divine leaders are addressing the nation.

REPORTER [*at telephone*]. Details of the charge are unprintable. The revelations are appalling. The prosecutor can scarcely continue. But he and his lordship have their duty to do, and they are an example to all of us. [*Rings off.*

JUDGE [*with sober eloquence, addressing invisible* JURY *on his right*]. Members of the Jury, citizens of the State, you have heard what the Public Prosecutor has said. Mark you, he is no disseminator of tales, no high priest of gossip. He is a lawyer of repute, who carefully chooses his words, and who never indulges in rhodomontade. But here in this Court he deliberately tells us that even when our leaders are addressing the people, their people, this man dares to think for himself. Gentlemen, are we back in the Dark Ages? Are we reverting to savagery? Here in this enlightened era every citizen, the man at his desk, the woman at her sink, has placed at his or her disposal the words of counsel and wisdom from our beloved leaders. He or she has at their service an admirably regulated Press. Our State-controlled wireless directs him or her from the cradle to the grave. A highly disciplined civil service lifts every burden from their shoulders, only asking in return the signing of various forms which need never take more than four hours a day. Teachers and preachers drill them with the efficiency of a first-class sergeant-major, they need never have a lonely moment, and yet [*raising his voice*] and yet this fiend, this debased wretch, dares, if you please, to think for himself. [*In a voice of thunder*] Prisoner at the bar, do you plead guilty or not guilty to this terrible charge?

PRISONER [*in a simple voice, with no desire to tell anything except the truth*]. Guilty.

JUDGE. Of this treasonable crime?

PRISONER. Of thinking for myself, yes.

PROSECUTOR. Despite all that the State has done for you?

PRISONER. Because of all that the State has done for me.

PROSECUTOR. You know you are breaking the law?

PRISONER. What law?

PROSECUTOR. Our law of high treason.

PRISONER. Yes.

JUDGE. You despise that law?

PRISONER. I think a good deal of it is rather tosh.

PROSECUTOR [*sneering*]. You disagree with it?

PRISONER. I disagree with everything at first. Doubt is the key to liberty. I doubt, therefore I am free.

JUDGE. Aren't you ashamed of yourself?

PRISONER. I am. I am afraid I'm a dreadful nuisance not only to myself but to my family and my friends and the State.

PROSECUTOR. Cannot you control this doubting process?

PRISONER. No.

JUDGE. Some outside influence?

PROSECUTOR [*sneering*]. An angel perhaps?

PRISONER [*gravely*]. Yes, at first I thought it was an angel.

JUDGE. And now?

PRISONER. Now I'm inclined to think it is an imp.

JUDGE. Imp?

PRISONER. Yes, a mischievous, restless, ubiquitous imp who never leaves me alone. When I'm inclined to accept ermine for wisdom, a uniform [*looking round each of them*] for authority, an attorney's wig as the emblem of those who search for truth, or the pen of the reporter, the slave of the moment, as the instrument that writes the book of the eternal facts, then the imp, this gadfly fellow, gives me a prod and then we laugh. Laughter is the sun which disperses humbug.

JUDGE. Have you actually seen this imp as you call him?

PRISONER. No, but he is all over the place. I'm not sure he isn't in Court now.

> [*The* IMP *appears, stalking through the door. He is small, and can be played by an agile boy or girl. He is dressed in fairy fashion, with green cap and doublet, and he is inclined to make music as he goes with bells.*

IMP [*perching near* PRISONER]. Yes, here we are, Nunky.

JUDGE [*severely*]. Silence in Court.

POLICEMAN [*even more severely*]. Silence in Court.

PRISONER. It's no good, my lord. You can't silence him. I've tried.

JUDGE. If I hear any more interruptions I shall have the Court cleared.

IMP. Much good that will do.

JUDGE. Silence.

POLICEMAN. Silence.

REPORTER [*at telephone*]. Flash. The fifth column is in Court.   [*Puts down receiver and scribbles furiously.*

> [IMP *squats beside the* PRISONER, *who looks more cheerful.*

JUDGE [*glaring round*]. The enemies of the State are indefatigable, but we are vigilant. Let them beware.

PRISONER [*cheerfully*]. I don't think he'll trouble you much. He easily gets bored, particularly in a Court of Law. It's extraordinary how boring most human institutions are.

JUDGE [*overwhelmed at this remark*]. Mr Prosecutor, will the Court hear any evidence concerning the prisoner's mental state?

PROSECUTOR. Yes, my lord. We have with us the learned Dean of the State Faculty of Medicine. He will testify in accordance with his instructions that the prisoner is a most dangerous lunatic.

JUDGE. A criminal lunatic, of course.

PROSECUTOR. Certainly, my lord.

JUDGE. Don't forget the criminal. It is most important. Very well, we shall hear the Dean. [*Telephone on* JUDGE'S *desk goes. He takes up receiver, respectfully*] Yes, Excellency. [*They all rise.*] No, but we are making good progress. No, he isn't dead yet. Yes, I shall certainly hurry things up, Excellency. Yes, Excellency. Certainly, Excellency. Salute. [*They all sit down again.* JUDGE *looks round Court and his eyes rest on the* PROSECUTOR.] This trial has been far too long-drawn-out. It could have been finished minutes ago. After all, it is a very simple case. The guilt of the prisoner was apparent from the beginning. Indeed, he pleaded guilty.

PROSECUTOR. As your lordship pleases. I am sorry, my lord, but we have so many enemies.

JUDGE. Well, then, the only thing to do is to get rid of them and as expeditiously as possible. We shall make a start with the prisoner before me. [*Severely to* PRISONER] It was my intention to recapitulate the crimes of treason which you have committed against the State, your insolent intellectual pretensions, your audacity in daring to think for yourself, you admitted trafficking with the so-called Divine Power which was officially abolished in January of last year. This recapitulation consisting of some four thousand words I shall have copied when you are dead, and I shall have it transmitted to your wife and family as a warning to them and a justification of these proceedings. It is just on the lunch hour and a suitable time to have the execution. Officer, do your duty. Remove the prisoner and hang him forthwith.

POLICEMAN. Very good, my lord.

[*And he taps the* PRISONER.

REPORTER [*at phone*]. The solemn proceedings are ending. The last impressive words have been said by the grave and dignified judge. The doomed man is leaving the dock. It is a human tragedy, yes, but also a judicial triumph. [*In ordinary tones*] Private to subs. Half a column of sob stuff to follow later. [*Sits down.*

PROSECUTOR [*rising just as* PRISONER *is following* POLICEMAN *out of dock. He stops*]. My lord, it is a small point, but your lordship was good enough to mention a few moments ago the question of medical evidence.

JUDGE. Oh yes, but is there any need to hear it now?

PROSECUTOR. As your lordship pleases.

JUDGE. The mere fact that a man is dead does not preclude us from inquiring into the state of his mind.

PROSECUTOR. None at all, my lord.

JUDGE. After all, what is history but an inquest into dead men's sayings and doings. [*The* PROSECUTOR *bows and smiles. The* JUDGE *smiles in return. The* REPORTER *claps his hands. The* JUDGE *turns to* PRISONER.] Have you nothing to say, no expression of contrition or regret for what you have done?

PRISONER. Yes, I have quite a lot to say. Most thinkers have. But I shall be seeing you later.

IMP. That's the stuff, Nunky.

JUDGE. Silence.

POLICEMAN. Silence.

REPORTER [*at phone*]. The fifth column is at it again. A state of siege may be proclaimed in the city to-night.

JUDGE [*to* PRISONER]. What do you mean by saying you will see me later on. Do you expect me to attend your execution? Certainly not. It would be most undignified.

PRISONER. No; but, only, I'm difficult to kill.

JUDGE. Take him away. Flippant in this solemn hour. Do you consider you have liberty to jest because you have no longer permission to pray? Away with him.

[*There are howls of* "Away with him!" *The* POLICEMAN *hurries the* PRISONER *to the door.*

IMP [*cheerily*]. See you shortly, Nunky.

JUDGE. Where is this interrupter?

[*They all look round, but the* IMP *grins and capers round the room.*

PRISONER [*at door*]. My lord?

JUDGE. Well?

PRISONER. Cruelty is waste.

[*And he goes out, followed by* POLICEMAN. *The* JUDGE *is upset. He sits silent, brooding.*

PROSECUTOR [*apologetically*]. My lord, your lordship was good enough to say just now that you would hear the medical evidence.

JUDGE [*rousing himself*]. Yes, yes. I shall hear the Dean now.

DEAN [*an elderly man with long white beard, stands before* JUDGE]. Shall I take the oath, my lord?

JUDGE [*testily*]. Don't be silly. You took an oath like everybody else to do exactly what the Government told you to do?

DEAN. Yes, my lord.

JUDGE. Anybody would think you owed allegiance to somebody else.

DEAN. Heaven forbid! I beg pardon. There's no such place.

JUDGE. You had better be careful.

DEAN. Yes, my lord.

PROSECUTOR. Do you consider that this dead man was, when he was alive, sane or insane?

DEAN. Most definitely insane.

JUDGE. Was his brain affected?

DEAN. Yes.

PROSECUTOR. By a disease?

DEAN. By a germ.

JUDGE. Can you prove it?

DEAN. Yes, my lord, medical science can prove anything. I shall be brief.

JUDGE. You had better.

DEAN. This germ from which the deceased was suffering is no new thing. Indeed, it was more common in the ancient world than it is to-day. It flourished, for example, in ancient Athens, and at one time was rampant in Palestine. It has, however, been more or less dormant in the modern cities of Europe and America.

PROSECUTOR. Do those who suffer from it ever recover?

DEAN. Never.

PROSECUTOR. What are the symptoms?

DEAN. Brightness of the eye, restlessness of the body, simplicity of life, freedom from fear, want, hunger, and desire.

PROSECUTOR. Were these symptoms marked in the deceased?

DEAN. His was one of the worst cases on record.

JUDGE. Then it is greatly to the advantage of the nation that this wretch is dead?

DEAN. Most certainly, my lord.

[*The* POLICEMAN *enters in a state of agitation.*

JUDGE. Yes? Is the prisoner dead?

POLICEMAN [*shaking*]. No, my lord.

JUDGE. Didn't I tell you that he had to be despatched at once?

POLICEMAN. Yes, my lord, but he refuses to die.

JUDGE. Refuses to die. This is gross contempt of Court.

REPORTER [*at phone*]. Flash. Terrific sensation. Prisoner refuses to die. Judge calls his refusal contempt of Court. Please submit to censor.

JUDGE. Doesn't the executioner know his job?

POLICEMAN. Yes, my lord, he is one of the most experienced men in the force. He has executed thousands without any trouble at all.

JUDGE. If he isn't dead in three minutes you'll take his place. [*Terrified*] I'll be disgraced. Don't you dare report that?

REPORTER [*terrified*]. Certainly not, my lord.

JUDGE [*rising in his terror*]. Get rid of him.

PROSECUTOR. Crucify him.

JUDGE. Strangle him.

DEAN. Poison him.

REPORTER. Batter him to pieces. The Press demands it.

> [*Howls from everybody:* "Kill him! Batter him to pieces! Trample on him! Riddle him with bullets! Knives, poison, axe, rope!" *The* POLICEMAN *hurries out. It is some time before the Court recovers. They are all gasping and out of breath.*]

> [*When calm is gradually restored:*

DEAN [*humbly*]. Will that be all, my lord?

JUDGE. Yes. [DEAN *is about to retire.*] Stay. [*Tensely*] Is this disease infectious?

IMP [*who has now closely approached* DEAN]. Ah, this is my business. [*He gets up close to the* DEAN, *egging him on to speak what he wishes him to say, prodding him, whispering into his ear.*] Out with it, old time-server. Tell him the truth, d'ye hear?

DEAN. Highly infectious, my lord. [*Clearing his throat*] In ancient Athens the disease was most infectious, and even the world of to-day hasn't got over the amount of original thinking that went on under the shadow of the Acropolis. In Palestine too the plague was at one time rampant. In our time the great cities of Europe and America have been more or less immune, thanks to powerful antitoxins made in our mass propaganda laboratories.

JUDGE. Yes, but come to the point, Mr Dean. Is it possible that this man is or was a carrier of the disease?

IMP. Say yes, old 'un.

DEAN. Yes.

PROSECUTOR. When he was alive?

DEAN. Yes, and when he was dead. Indeed, the thoughts and ideas of such a man are often more powerful and have a wider sphere of influence when he is dead than when he was alive.

IMP. Good. That's the stuff to give them.

JUDGE. But are there no counter-measures available?

DEAN. Well, you have just tried obliteration, my lord.

IMP [*jumping about delightedly*]. That's got him.

JUDGE [*angrily*]. You are behaving very strangely, Mr Dean.

DEAN. I know I am. I'm trying to tell the truth.

IMP. Hooray.

DEAN. In fact, my lord, I'm sorry to say that I believe I have fallen a victim to the disease myself.

[*There is a sensation in Court.*

IMP. Now you're for it, old friend.

JUDGE [*bangs at bell*]. Where is the police officer?

PROSECUTOR [*rushes to door, calls out*]. Policeman, quick.

REPORTER [*at phone*]. Another sensation in this amazing trial. The Dean of the Faculty of Medicine has confessed that he is in league with the prisoner. Anything may happen at any moment. Keep back the country edition for five minutes.

POLICEMAN [*enters very slowly*]. Yes, my lord?

JUDGE. Arrest the Dean. [*Points to* DEAN.

POLICEMAN. Sorry, my lord, I can't.

IMP [*delighted as he capers round* POLICEMAN]. This is a show-down.

JUDGE [*horrified*]. Do you mean to tell me that your brain is affected too?

POLICEMAN. No, my lord, for I haven't any brain to get affected.

IMP. Hooray!

POLICEMAN. But me legs won't work any more.

IMP. It's the uniform, son. It paralyses you sooner or later.

JUDGE [*sternly*]. Prosecutor.

IMP [*jumps to side of* PROSECUTOR]. Now it's your turn, go-getter, pushing jack, careerist Charlie. You can't escape. You must speak out or burst.

JUDGE [*repeating*]. Prosecutor.

> [PROSECUTOR *is convulsed with agitation; he struggles painfully to his feet, while the* POLICEMAN *watches him amazed and the* DEAN *is immersed in thought.*

PROSECUTOR. My lord. I'm not well.

JUDGE. Then leave the Court.

PROSECUTOR. Not until I have spoken.

IMP [*prodding him*]. You have still a chance. Not much of one, but make the most of it.

JUDGE [*furious*]. Are we all going mad?

DEAN. No, unfortunately we are going sane.

PROSECUTOR. My lord, this trial is a farce. I am a self-seeker, the policeman is an automaton, the reporter is a hack, and you, my lord, are a mountebank.

JUDGE [*rising in his rage*]. Arrest him. Kill him. He's a traitor.

PROSECUTOR. They say I'm a rising man. Don't believe it. I'm a falling star. I have forfeited my dignity as a man. I have sold my birthright. The very law that I've studied day and night has gone sour.

JUDGE. You are giving us all away. Villain.

IMP. Stay.

JUDGE. Who said stay? Only I dare say stay.

> [*And he falls back into his chair. The* PROSE- CUTOR *has also sat down and has buried his head in his hands. The* REPORTER *goes to phone.*

IMP [*goes up to* REPORTER, *sternly*]. Take from my dictation.

REPORTER [*repeating as if from dictation*]. Kill everything I've sent. It's all rubbish. Lies, lies in banner headlines. There's only one just man here and he was the man in the dock. There's only one free man here and that's the man who was in chains. The others of us are criminals and we know it.

[*He puts down receiver and collapses, overcome.*

JUDGE [*rises from his semi-stupor, sees motionless* POLICE-MAN]. What are you standing there for? Can't you do something? Is the prisoner dead?

POLICEMAN. He has escaped, my lord.

JUDGE. Escaped. And alive?

POLICEMAN. My lord, I'm the average man and I cannot tell the living from the dead.

IMP [*who has strolled on to the bench and whispers into* JUDGE's *ear*]. Can you, my lord Judge? Can you tell dead law from living law? Don't you all smell of corruption here?

JUDGE [*primly, to Court*]. I am constantly receiving anonymous communications. I shall take no notice of them, and if I catch those who send them I shall deal most severely with them.

IMP [*mischievously to* JUDGE]. Are you beginning to use your brains, my lord? Is there a wasps' nest of cerebral torment buzzing inside that wig at last?

JUDGE [*beginning to tremble*]. Mr Dean, do you think we—er—should put the Court into quarantine?

DEAN. Too late.

JUDGE. This disease may be catching. I'm sorry, but I'm afraid that I may have to adjourn indefinitely. Mr Dean, have you no tablet, no purge that can save me? Pay no attention to the prosecutor. He is but a climbing attorney. But I sit in the seats of the mighty. I may yet reach the highest seat in the judiciary. I have powerful friends. I have had a hint that if this trial goes well great preferment may be at hand. Am I to be stricken down at this critical moment in my career? I have an ambitious wife. My sons, my daughters egg me on. If I become a leper in our modern society, a man suffering from a most un-popular, unseemly disease—if, in a word, I think for myself, like this wretched common creature who was in the dock just now, they will all turn on me and call me fool, fool.

DEAN [*mournfully*]. Physician, cure thyself.

IMP. Judge, you are judging yourself. You are beyond medical help.

JUDGE [*rises in agony*]. Oyez, oyez—hear all of you. I hereby declare this Court dissolved. It serves not the law of mercy and reason, but the rule of violence. It is guilty of murder. Its hands are stained with innocent blood, your hands and mine. We are the real criminals, and the first are last and the last first. [*The telephone bell at the* JUDGE'S *side rings furiously. They all start and are frightened. The* PROSECUTOR *and the* REPORTER *leap from their chairs. The* DEAN *clings to the side of the dock.* POLICEMAN *leans against the wall. Trembling,* JUDGE *takes up receiver. In an awed whisper he says:*] His Excellency. [*He listens at phone, while they all look at him intently. Then he says to them:*] He has heard all. [*Then, at receiver*] Excellency, the Court has been through an emotional crisis, due, I am informed on high medical authority, to the pollution of the atmosphere by the germ of a disease of which the late prisoner was a carrier. But we are better now, your Excellency. In fact, fully recovered. [*A pause.*] Excellency, listen, have pity, Excellency.

PROSECUTOR [*terrified, and pleading to* JUDGE *with outstretched hands*]. My lord, tell him I had planned out a splendid career when I was a stripling at college. I have sacrificed everything to please the powers. Not now surely am I to fall?

JUDGE [*in awed voice*]. His Excellency is angry. His voice was like thunder. Lightning may strike us.

DEAN [*pitifully*]. My lord, I have rivals in the Faculty. I have enemies among my colleagues. Tell him I am myself again. Tell him I can destroy whatever he pleases.

I

JUDGE. We are in danger.

REPORTER. My lord, I have been a good journalist all my days. I have never written a line which was really my own. Only now, when I was one over the eight. I have been drinking beer all the morning. My lord, I have a wife and three kids and not a bean in the world.

JUDGE. We may be arrested any moment. All of us.

POLICEMAN. My lord, I am poor stuff compared with you, my lord, but I'm nearing the pension age. I entered the force for the sake of the pension. I've done my duty all my life and have never questioned it. My lord, will you put in a good word for me?

[*The others repeat:* And for me.

JUDGE [*hysterically*]. We must go, we must hide.

PROSECUTOR. Where?

JUDGE [*as he moves towards door*]. Each for himself. Don't any of you dare follow me! [*And as he rushes out*] And I might have been head of the judiciary. [*Exit.*

PROSECUTOR. Judge, Judge, wait for me. After all, we lawyers must stick together. [*Exit.*

POLICEMAN [*running out*]. My pension.

REPORTER [*following him*]. My job.

DEAN [*stumbling after them*]. Because a physician cannot cure a disease is that any reason why he should be inflicted with it? [*Calling out*] Wait, wait!

IMP [*playfully sits astride on judicial bench*]. An empty, silent Court. How very refreshing, how very stimulating. Why, I could think here. Better still, I could sleep. Shall I have a nap? [*Jumping up*] Ah no, I forgot. Good old Nunky. [*And he goes to door, skipping along and calls out*] Nunky. No shamming now. You're alive, old boy. [PRISONER, *looking wan and tired, enters, but smiles towards* IMP.] Had a bad time?

PRISONER. Not too pleasant. Violent folk are always so excessive.

IMP. What was it like?

PRISONER. I can't exactly remember. I felt very dull. It isn't easy to be bright and original when you've a halter round your neck.

IMP. You chose the wrong planet to live in.

PRISONER [*as he sits on judicial seat which* IMP *has forsaken for him*]. Yes, and in the present lamentable stage of scientific development you cannot change it for another. [*Looking round*] Where's everybody?

IMP [*laughing*]. The Court has adjourned.

PRISONER. Why?

IMP. You've given them your disease.

PRISONER. Poor devils.

IMP. Don't worry, they'll soon be cured and for good. Hush.

> [*The* JUDGE, *the* PROSECUTOR, *the* POLICE-MAN, *the* DEAN *re-enter. But this time they have the grey appearance of ghosts; they act as puppets, as men moving in a dream.* PRISONER *moves aside* R. *and watches them. So does the* IMP, *going* L. *and with sardonic smile on face. The* JUDGE *and all of them take up their respective positions. They go through highly exaggerated pantomime of their previous actions, each playing his rôle silently, though their lips move. The* PROSECUTOR *harangues, the* REPORTER *writes and then telephones, the* POLICEMAN *makes rigid movements and salutes, the* DEAN *wipes his spectacles and reads from his paper. The* JUDGE *takes up receiver. They all rise. The* JUDGE *listens and bows obsequiously. Then they all salute as he takes his place again. They then begin to repeat the same antics.*

PRISONER [*to* IMP]. What's the matter with them?

IMP. Can't you see?

PRISONER. They're moving, but there's no life in them.

IMP. Of course there isn't.

PRISONER [*horrified*]. Laddie, they're not [*pause*] dead.

IMP. Dead for a ducat.

PRISONER. But they'll be found out.

IMP. By the living. Maybe. But then the dead have the majority in Parliament.

PRISONER. But how long can this go on?

IMP. Oh, for ages. [*The pantomime is still proceeding.*] Marvellous how tough are the dead.

PRISONER. But many of them are young.

IMP. Of course. Many are born dead. They are never alive, though the obituary notices forget to chronicle the fact. Many are stillborn, their brand new systems, their new revolutionary doctrines are still-born. There's no life or health in them or their creeds. Fear has frozen them into routine.

> [*They begin to move out again, the* JUDGE *with mock dignity, the* PROSECUTOR *waving his brief, the* DEAN *looking at his note, and the* REPORTER *looking backward at the phone, terrified he may be late with his news. The* POLICEMAN *salutes in the direction of the* IMP, *to his great delight, and hurries out last.*

PRISONER. How horrible.

IMP. How ordinary.

PRISONER. And how long will they go on?

IMP. Until they are shelved. There's always plenty of dead men to take their places.

PRISONER. Tragic.

IMP [*patting him on the back*]. Not a bit of it. Why, Nunky, you're alive.

PRISONER [*looking round*]. Yes, but alone.

CURTAIN

THE ADVANTAGES OF PATERNITY

by

HORTON GIDDY

CHARACTERS

GENERAL YAGUNIN (*a relic of the boulevardier school, with a rich, humorous voice. Age 55–60*)
COLONEL ILYITCH (*a thin, nervous, precise man, who wears pince-nez. Throughout the play he is suffering acutely from nerves. Age 40*)
ORDERLY (*a young oaf*)
BRUNOV (*a pleasant, earnest young man. Age 16. As a soldier in the Red Army, he looks older than he is*)

Applications regarding amateur performances of this play should be addressed to the League of Dramatists, 80 Drayton Gardens, London, S.W.10.

THE ADVANTAGES OF PATERNITY

Scene: The winter of 1921: *a Divisional H.Q. in the White Army lines. It is a small wooden hut, containing a stove, a bare table with two chairs and a bench, a wooden chest, and a field-telephone set. A samovar and some glasses are by the stove, an empty chocolate-box on the table, a pile of cut logs in a corner. A fur cap, sword, and belt hang on a nail in the wall.*

YAGUNIN *sits relaxed in a chair at the table, smoking a cigarette.* ILYITCH *is pacing the floor restlessly. The* ORDERLY *crouches by the stove, picking his teeth. All three are wearing their overcoats slung like cloaks on their shoulders.*

YAGUNIN. You never even went there? My dear Ilyitch, you seem to have led an extraordinarily dull life.

ILYITCH. Your excellency may think so.

YAGUNIN. What on earth did you do with yourself all the time?

ILYITCH. I lived on my estates with my wife and family.

YAGUNIN. A wife and family. Those are blessings which I have successfully avoided.

ILYITCH. Your excellency never married?

YAGUNIN. No. Mind you, I was pretty near it sometimes, but I always escaped. His Imperial Majesty the Tsar more than once urged me to marry—he was a very domestic man, you know—but I made my excuses. That didn't help my career at Court. Yet I've been happy. In fact, Ilyitch, I'm afraid I've led a rather scandalous life.

ILYITCH. Indeed.

YAGUNIN. And I'm afraid you disapprove. But surely, in the War—you were on the Galician front, I think?

ILYITCH. Yes.

YAGUNIN. Surely you had some—ah—adventures? Didn't your eyes wander to those lovely Hungarian girls?

ILYITCH. No.

YAGUNIN. Not just once?

ILYITCH. No. . . . Excellency, forgive me, but we've had no news for . . . it must be ten minutes. Shall I ring Brigade?

YAGUNIN. There's no hurry.

ILYITCH. Excellency, I . . . we must know what's happening.

YAGUNIN. Sit down, man, sit down. We can do nothing to help. The last reserves are in the line. If they want us they'll ring us up.

ILYITCH [*sitting down*]. But as your chief of staff——

YAGUNIN. You're a very good chief of staff, Ilyitch. Indeed, if we have any army left by the end of the month I hope to get you promoted. . . . Tell me, what does your family comprise?

ILYITCH. Two boys and a girl.

YAGUNIN. And where are they now?

ILYITCH. My wife and the two younger ones wait for me in Constantinople. The elder boy is in the Cadet Guards.

YAGUNIN. Yes. . . . Yes. I sometimes almost wish I had married. I begin to suspect I'm getting too old for *la vie scandaleuse*: and what is there then? Eh, Ilyitch, what is left?

ILYITCH. What? . . . I beg your Excellency's pardon. . . .

YAGUNIN. You weren't listening.

ILYITCH. Yes, yes, indeed I was. But I can't help it, Excellency—this waiting for news. . . .

YAGUNIN. Calm yourself. You're like a cat on hot bricks. Have a cigarette.

ILYITCH. I've none left.

YAGUNIN. Well, nor have I. . . . Orderly.

ORDERLY [*a yokel*]. Excellency.

YAGUNIN. A cigarette for Colonel Ilyitch.

ORDERLY. There aren't any left, Excellency.

YAGUNIN. Go back to the town and buy some.

ILYITCH. If he goes we shall be without an orderly.

YAGUNIN. There's Sergeant Blick.

ILYITCH. The swine deserted this morning.

YAGUNIN. So my staff has dwindled to you, and this oaf.

ILYITCH. I would remind your Excellency that you yourself sent Captain Veranov and six orderlies to the front last night.

YAGUNIN. They'll be more use there than here.

ILYITCH. And you sent your servant to the town to buy chocolates.

YAGUNIN. Masha—so I did. The old villain. He could have bought all the chocolates in the town by now.

ILYITCH. I've no doubt at all he's deserted.

YAGUNIN. I'd have you know Masha has been with me for twenty years. I expect he's got drunk. He's always doing it. . . . I wish I had those chocolates.

[*Pause.*

ILYITCH. Shall I ring up Brigade now?

YAGUNIN. No. . . . Orderly, make some tea.

ORDERLY. At once, Excellency.

YAGUNIN. It's annoying being without chocolates or cigarettes. Do you like chocolates, Ilyitch?

ILYITCH. No, Excellency.

YAGUNIN. I got the taste for them from a little French girl. She was singing at that gipsy place on the Neva. Ever go there?

ILYITCH. No.

YAGUNIN. Ah, you should have. The finest girls in Russia. This child, Claudine: she was dark, you know, a plump little partridge——

ILYITCH. Bah !

YAGUNIN [*sternly*]. Colonel Ilyitch!

ILYITCH. I beg your Excellency's pardon. My nerves . . . it's this suspense.

YAGUNIN. Tea will do you good. Is it ready, Orderly?

ORDERLY. All ready, Excellency.

YAGUNIN. If only we had some cigarettes. . . . Orderly!

ORDERLY. Excellency.

YAGUNIN. What is that behind your ear.

ORDERLY. A—a cigarette, Excellency.

YAGUNIN. And you told me there were none left.

ORDERLY. Your nobleness, it's only mahorka. Peasants' tobacco. Not fit for officers. And I rolled it myself in a piece of newspaper.

YAGUNIN. Give it to Colonel Ilyitch.

ILYITCH. Thank you, no. Not when it's been behind his ear.

YAGUNIN. Then give it to me.

ORDERLY. At once, Excellency.

YAGUNIN. Ha. . . . [*He lights up.*] A cigarette . . . and tea. Very pleasant. Where should we be without the samovar? It makes even this hut tolerable. . . . Really this tobacco isn't bad—it has a bite. Try some, Ilyitch.

ILYITCH [*sulkily*]. Orderly, have you any more tobacco?

ORDERLY. A little, Excellency.

ILYITCH. Give it to me.

ORDERLY. It must be rolled in paper for cigarettes.

YAGUNIN. Well, roll it, boy. Don't be so helpless.

ILYITCH. Thank you, no. He will not have washed his teeth to-day.

YAGUNIN. Why does that matter?

ILYITCH. To make cigarettes he must lick the paper.

YAGUNIN. You're very finicky, Ilyitch. You'll have to make them yourself.

ILYITCH. I don't know how to.

YAGUNIN. The boy will show you. Orderly, show Colonel Ilyitch how to roll them.

ILYITCH. Well, really . . .

[*The General begins to hum an old operetta: he comes to a phrase he doesn't remember and stumbles at it.*

ILYITCH [*to the* ORDERLY, *irritably*]. Is that right?

ORDERLY. Now you lick along here.

ILYITCH. So?

ORDERLY. Your Excellency has used too much spittle.

ILYITCH [*angrily*]. Go on: what do I do now.

ORDERLY. You fold over and press. . . . Now pinch off the ends. So.

YAGUNIN. They look rather funny.

ILYITCH. I am not accustomed to roll my own cigarettes. Orderly, a match.

ORDERLY. At once, Excellency. [*A match is struck.*

[*The* GENERAL *hums the same tune, boggles at the same note.*

YAGUNIN [*dreamily*]. If only I had some chocolates.

[YAGUNIN *begins to sing, softly, a traditional Cossack song. After a while* ILYITCH, *half unwillingly, joins in. They sing the verse through and then sit silent for a few seconds. Pause.*

ILYITCH [*jumping up and upsetting his chair*]. This is preposterous. . . . Anything may be happening in the front line. Anything. Nistitsky said they were facing a frontal attack. Excellency, I implore you to let me ring the Brigade.

YAGUNIN. If it will ease your mind, my dear Ilyitch. . . .

ILYITCH [*moves a few steps*]. Yes, yes. . . . [*At the telephone*] Hullo. Hullo, Brigade. . . . Hullo. Hullo. . . . Hullo, hullo, hullo, hullo, hullo. . . . Is that

Brigade, damn it: hullo, hullo. [*Joggling the receiver*]
Hullo. Hullo. Hullo——

YAGUNIN. Stop. You make my head buzz.

ILYITCH [*in a voice of tragedy*]. The line is dead.

YAGUNIN. Dear me.

ILYITCH. Hullo. Hullo. Hullo. Hullo——

YAGUNIN [*loudly*]. Ilyitch! . . . If the line is dead
you won't bring it to life by shouting at it.

ILYITCH. Excellency, you see what it means. They've
broken through. Overrun Brigade. Probably wiped
out every one at H.Q.

YAGUNIN. Oh, I don't know. Telephones are always
going wrong.

ILYITCH. But—but——

YAGUNIN. Come and sit down and have some more
tea.

ILYITCH. Tea? Tea? We must *do* something.

YAGUNIN. What do you suggest?

ILYITCH. We—we must. . . . Oh, I don't know.

YAGUNIN. Exactly. We must wait. Some one is sure
to repair the line soon.

ILYITCH. Some one? If they're all dead? What then?

YAGUNIN. I suppose the Bolsheviki would repair it.

ILYITCH. Bah!

YAGUNIN. Ilyitch.

ILYITCH. I'm sorry, Excellency. I'm ashamed of
myself. My nerves . . . And you sit there, and smoke
that filthy tobacco, and nothing is done.

YAGUNIN. There is nothing to be done.

ILYITCH. If they've broken through, there are no
reserves. Not a soldier between them and the sea.
Excellency, this is the end.

YAGUNIN. Well, perhaps. We can't avoid it.

ILYITCH. We should make sure of escape.

YAGUNIN. The staff-car is outside.

ILYITCH. Yes, but it's freezing hard. It was ten
degrees below zero this morning.

YAGUNIN. What a good thing we've plenty of wood for the stove.

ILYITCH. The radiator of the car may have frozen.

YAGUNIN. You meet trouble before it comes, Ilyitch. It's a tendency of yours.

ILYITCH. I'm your staff colonel. It is my duty to be prepared for eventualities.

YAGUNIN [*petulantly*]. And you're very argumentative.

ILYITCH. Excellency, I have the honour to submit that the car be tested to see if it is in running-order.

YAGUNIN. Very well.

ILYITCH. Orderly.

ORDERLY. Excellency.

ILYITCH. Go outside and start up the car. Keep it running until it is warm. See that the radiator is well covered with rugs.

ORDERLY. At once, Excellency.

> [*He marches to the door, opens it. A high wind is moaning outside.*

ILYITCH [*shouting*]. Shut the door, you fool.

> [*The door slams to.*

YAGUNIN. The wind's got up.

ILYITCH. Yes . . . [*Goes to telephone.*] I'll try the line again. Hullo. Hullo. Hullo. [*Clicking receiver*] Hullo. Hullo.

YAGUNIN. That'll do.

ILYITCH. Hullo. Hullo. Hullo. . . . [*Turning towards* YAGUNIN] Dead as mutton. [*The car starts up outside. It is revved up.*] Well, thank God the car's all right.

YAGUNIN. You know, it's a wonderful thing, a peasant like that boy being able to drive a car. I never understood the things.

ILYITCH. Give me a horse every time. [*The car revs fall and rise again and then it suddenly starts off—the engine note and the sound of the gears make it obvious it is under way.*]

Hullo, what's that fool doing. . . . [*Shouts.*] Hey, you, Orderly! [*Runs to the door and flings it open, letting in the wind.*] Hey, stop, you fool. . . . [*He runs out, his voice receding.*] Hey, stop. . . . Stop, you idiot. . . .

YAGUNIN. Well, well. . . .

> [*He starts again to hum the operetta, meets the same difficulty, tries it a second time.*

>> [ILYITCH's *voice is heard coming back.*

ILYITCH. Excellency. . . . Excellency . . . he's gone. [ILYITCH *enters. His overcoat is snow-powdered.*] He's stolen the car. Deserted.

YAGUNIN. Yes: well, shut the door. I don't want to catch pneumonia.

ILYITCH [*banging the door*]. The villain. The cowardly villain. You see what it means, Excellency. Now we shall have to walk ten miles to the town. If they have cavalry they'll catch us up before we get there.

YAGUNIN. I'm afraid I can't walk—my gout, you know.

ILYITCH. You must. It's our only hope.

YAGUNIN. Our? You can always go alone, Ilyitch.

ILYITCH [*after a very slight pause: stiffly*]. That is out of the question.

YAGUNIN. Why not. I freely give you permission.

ILYITCH. Even to suggest it is insulting, Excellency.

YAGUNIN. Well, there you are. I'm sorry I can't walk. I haven't walked a mile in ten years.

ILYITCH. But now—when it's a matter of life and death.

YAGUNIN. You go ahead too fast. There's no need to panic.

ILYITCH. Panic was not in my mind.

YAGUNIN. Of course not, Ilyitch. I know that. But the telephone line may have broken through quite ordinary natural causes. They do, you know. Some one will mend it.

ILYITCH. Do you believe that?

YAGUNIN. It's quite possible.

ILYITCH. Do you really believe it?

YAGUNIN [*after a pause*]. Well, I don't know that I do.

ILYITCH. Then we must get away.

YAGUNIN. It's no good, Ilyitch. Nothing will make me walk ten miles. But you go.

ILYITCH. If only we had horses.

YAGUNIN. Well, why haven't we? As my staff officer, you surely should have seen to that. You've just said your duty is to be prepared for all eventualities.

ILYITCH [*exasperated*]. Yesterday we had a dozen horses. You sent them all up to the front with Captain Veranov.

YAGUNIN. So I did. I thought they would be more useful at the front.

ILYITCH. And now we're stuck here like rats in a trap.

YAGUNIN. Not you, Ilyitch. You're a youngish man who has apparently led an abnormally healthy and virtuous life. Ten miles should be nothing to you.

ILYITCH. I stay.

YAGUNIN. Then I must order you to go.

ILYITCH. It is the one order I must disobey.

YAGUNIN. Oh, dear . . . then oblige me by putting more wood in the stove. We may as well be comfortable.

ILYITCH [*after putting a log into the stove*]. I think I will try the line again.

YAGUNIN. As you please.

ILYITCH [*rattling the receiver hook*]. Hullo. Hullo. Hullo. Hullo. Hullo. . . .

YAGUNIN. Quite dead?

ILYITCH. Yes. . . .

[*He begins to push the heavy chest against the door.*

YAGUNIN. What are you doing now?

ILYITCH. I propose to barricade the door and window. We may as well sell our lives dearly.

YAGUNIN. I never cared for that phrase. No, Ilyitch, this hut is hardly a satisfactory fortress. Leave it as it is.

ILYITCH. Are we to give in without a struggle?

YAGUNIN. If they come, a struggle will be useless. So why struggle?

ILYITCH. But—but we must——

YAGUNIN. Because it's customary? No, leave things as they are. After all, we're not sure they've broken through.

ILYITCH. I know they have.

YAGUNIN. How?

ILYITCH. I . . . feel it.

YAGUNIN. In your bones?

ILYITCH. Well . . . yes. I feel in a trap here . . . as if they are creeping up . . . as if at any minute they'll burst in the door. I'm afraid it's nerves. If we could meet them in the open. . . .

YAGUNIN. My dear Ilyitch, I don't want you to stay. I've already ordered you to make your escape.

ILYITCH. I refuse.

YAGUNIN. Very insubordinate of you. Really, you must go. There's nothing to keep you. You can't defend me from an army.

ILYITCH [not so definitely]. Your Excellency must see it's impossible.

YAGUNIN. But I don't. It's a mere matter of obeying orders.

ILYITCH. No. . . . No, I can't.

YAGUNIN [sighs]. Well, we must pass the time as best we can. There are no more cigarettes?

ILYITCH. No.

YAGUNIN. What shall we talk about?

ILYITCH. Anything.

YAGUNIN. Women?

ILYITCH. Anything.   [Moves over to window.

YAGUNIN. It's a good, interminable subject. You know, Ilyitch, sitting here and waiting for something to happen is stimulating to the mind. I find myself remembering things vividly which happened many years ago. It's rather like the panorama of life which a drowning man is supposed to see. And, curiously enough, I don't find it depressing: on the whole my life in retrospect looks very pleasantly scandalous: it's a procession of delightful young women. But that is not to say I didn't experience suffering. One must suffer to enjoy love. Don't you agree?

ILYITCH. Eh? I'm afraid I didn't. . . .

YAGUNIN. You're not listening.

ILYITCH. Indeed I am.

YAGUNIN. Suffering, yes: I've had that. Some of them treated me abominably—the darlings. But I always did them well, always, however cruel they were to me. I like to think now that none of them can bear a grudge against me: at least, I hope not, I profoundly hope not. I don't expect I broke any hearts, though mine was constantly being broken. Fortunately it has remarkable powers of recuperation. . . . Give me a cigarette, Ilyitch. [*No answer.*] Ilyitch.

ILYITCH [*at the window*]. Yes, Excellency.

YAGUNIN [*testily*]. What are you doing there? There's nothing to see. And you're not listening.

ILYITCH. I thought I heard. . . . But indeed I am listening. Please go on.

YAGUNIN. I asked you for a cigarette.

ILYITCH. There are none left. I told you so just now.

YAGUNIN. No cigarettes, no chocolates. It's very annoying. Bad staff work, I'm afraid, Ilyitch. . . . Where was I?

ILYITCH [*gloomily*]. Women.

YAGUNIN. Of course, but. . . . Never mind. Shall I tell you the story of a certain little brunette from Kazan—it's really a very romantic story?

ILYITCH [*vaguely*]. Oh, yes, yes.

YAGUNIN. It was during the Japanese War. I'd been

K

slightly wounded—just a flesh affair—and they sent me to the hospital where Irina was a nurse—the Velshinsky—and by George, didn't she look charming in her nurse's outfit. But let's start at the beginning. When I first arrived they put me in a ward, with a dozen other officers. . . . [*As* YAGUNIN *continues* ILYITCH, *by the window, hears something outside in the distance, glances swiftly at* YAGUNIN, *whose back is turned, then tiptoes to the pegs on the wall by the door, takes down his fur cap, buttons his overcoat, and gently opens the door, slips out, and the door closes behind him.* YAGUNIN *does not notice him go, and continues dreamily with his story.*] Irina used to come into the ward sometimes, though she was really looking after a fellow in a private room who had had both legs off. Well, almost at once we were attracted to each other—you know how it is—and after a week or two of delicious strategy I got myself moved into the private room. The fellow who had it died, I think, and that's how the opportunity arose. Now, this was the point: the private room was in a wing, at the end of a corridor, and couldn't have been better arranged for our . . . little affair. . . . Ah, what a charming little kitten she was. I assure you, my dear Ilyitch [*turning round*], I do assure you . . . [*slowly*] my dear Ilyitch. . . . Hullo, where are you? [*He gets up and, after looking round the hut, goes to the door.*] Ilyitch. Where have you got to, my dear fellow? . . . [*Opens door.*] Ilyitch! [*The wind blows a little snow in, and he shivers.*] Brrr! . . . [*Shuts door.*] So. . . . [*He chuckles. Then in the distance there is the sound of firing.*] Oho!

> [*He goes to the window and looks out; he sees something and turns away quickly, goes to the hooks on the wall by the door, takes down his sword and sword belt, and buckles them on. Then he goes back to the window and watches somebody approach. Pause. A rider approaches*

outside: faint jingle of harness. YAGUNIN
*draws his sword. The door opens violently
and* BRUNOV *comes in: he is roughly dressed
in leather jacket, high boots, and sheepskin cap.
He carries a rifle.*

BRUNOV [*fiercely*]. Anyone here? [YAGUNIN, *by the
window, says nothing, but* BRUNOV *sees him and wheels
round, raising his rifle.*] Move an inch and I'll fire.
[YAGUNIN *hesitates, shrugs his shoulders, takes off belt and
offers it and sword to* BRUNOV.] Drop 'em on the floor.
[YAGUNIN *does so.*] Now, stick your hands up.

YAGUNIN. Oh, but why? I'm not armed.

BRUNOV. You're a White Officer. And you're my
prisoner.

YAGUNIN. That may be. But at my age, to hold my
arms above my head——

BRUNOV. Then I shoot.

YAGUNIN. Is that necessary? You can see I'm not
armed.

BRUNOV [*undecided*]. Well . . . sit down in that
chair where I can watch you.

YAGUNIN. Are we going to stay here?

BRUNOV. We're going to wait for the others. I've
ridden ahead.

YAGUNIN [*sitting*]. That's more comfortable, certainly. Will you join me in a glass of tea, Commissar?

BRUNOV. I'm not a commissar.

YAGUNIN. Never mind. Have some tea.

BRUNOV [*excited*]. Why, those epaulettes—you're a
general, aren't you?

YAGUNIN. I must admit it.

BRUNOV. A pretty high up one.

YAGUNIN. Yes, pretty high up.

BRUNOV [*pleased*]. By George! what a bit of luck.
You'll be very useful. I ought to get promoted for this.

YAGUNIN. Splendid.

BRUNOV. Did you say you had some tea?

YAGUNIN. Yes, there's the samovar. I'll see if——

BRUNOV [*quickly*]. You stay there, where I can see you. I'll get the tea.

YAGUNIN. Just as you like.

BRUNOV [*moves to the samovar*]. Hot tea. That's fine.

YAGUNIN. I wonder if you happen to have a cigarette.

BRUNOV [*cheerfully*]. Certainly, comrade General. Here you are: help yourself. [*Throws packet on table.*

YAGUNIN. I'm exceedingly grateful. And a match?

BRUNOV. Here, catch.

[*Throws box.* YAGUNIN *lights cigarette.*

YAGUNIN [*sighs*]. That's good. Better than mahorka.

BRUNOV. Do generals smoke mahorka?

YAGUNIN. Not with any pleasure.

BRUNOV. Muck, isn't it? . . . Here's your tea.

YAGUNIN. Thank you. One other thing: it's very cold. Need we have the door open?

BRUNOV. All right. . . . [*Suspiciously*] No funny tricks?

YAGUNIN. *Parole d'honneur.*

BRUNOV. What's that? French? . . . [*He bangs the door.*] They'll see my horse tied up outside.

YAGUNIN. When will 'they' arrive?

BRUNOV. Not long now. Though I got a good way ahead of them. . . . Look here, what are you doing in this place alone? Damn it, I never thought of that. What's a general doing here alone? Are there any more of you about?

YAGUNIN. I am quite alone.

BRUNOV. I suppose your chaps deserted you. That's a poor sort of trick. You're telling the truth?

YAGUNIN. *Parole d'honneur.* Which means, on the word of a gentleman.

BRUNOV. We don't accept that, you know.

YAGUNIN. You can.

BRUNOV. All right. But, you know . . . [*hesitating*].

YAGUNIN. What?

BRUNOV. When the others arrive . . . They'll probably shoot you, I'm afraid. It's not as if you were an ordinary officer. My lot generally shoots generals.

YAGUNIN [*calmly*]. Evidently your lot doesn't practise its principles. Aren't you supposed to believe in equality?

BRUNOV [*laughs*]. I suppose so. . . . You're a queer old bird. Who'd have thought I'd sit drinking tea with an old capitalist general. What's your name?

YAGUNIN. Yagunin.

BRUNOV [*violently*]. What!

YAGUNIN. Yagunin. Ivan Ivanich Yagunin, major-general.

BRUNOV [*slowly*]. Ivan Ivanich Yagunin.

YAGUNIN. Well? I'm nothing extraordinary.

BRUNOV. Good lord! . . . . Do you know who I am?

YAGUNIN [*testily*]. My dear boy, how should I?

BRUNOV. My name is Ivan Ivanich Brunov.

YAGUNIN [*after a pause*]. Well?

BRUNOV. That means nothing to you?

YAGUNIN. No. . . . No, I'm afraid it doesn't. Ought I to know you?

BRUNOV. My mother's name was Irina Brunova.

YAGUNIN. Irina Brunova. . . . [*Embarrassed*] . . . Er. . . . Brunova? I don't think I . . . young man, have I met your mother?

BRUNOV. Oh, yes, you've met her.

YAGUNIN. I don't seem to . . . Irina, yes, I remember the name, more than once in fact. But Brunova?

BRUNOV. The Velshinsky Hospital during the Japanese War.

YAGUNIN. Huh? . . . Good gracious me, yes. Irina. Dear little—— [*Coughs.*] Yes, yes, I do remember your mother. I remember her very well. A very charming little—a charming woman. . . . Er, she's quite well?

BRUNOV. Yes.

YAGUNIN. Good. Splendid. So you're her son. I suppose she got married after . . .

BRUNOV. She's never married.

YAGUNIN. What? But . . . I don't understand. You . . . [*Very seriously*] What did you say your name and patronymic——

BRUNOV. Ivan Ivanich.

YAGUNIN. My names . . . And you are how old?

BRUNOV. Sixteen.

YAGUNIN. The Velshinsky was in . . . Good God!

BRUNOV. Yes.

YAGUNIN. Well, I'm—taken rather aback, Ivan Ivanich.

BRUNOV. I ought to shoot you . . . for deserting my mother.

YAGUNIN. I suppose you ought. Though I certainly didn't know——

BRUNOV. No. She always told me that. She . . . speaks quite well of you.

YAGUNIN. I'm extremely glad to hear it. I was . . . very, very fond of your mother, Ivan. If it hadn't been for the exigencies of wartime . . .

BRUNOV. Bosh.

YAGUNIN. I beg your pardon?

BRUNOV. Mother said you weren't the marrying sort.

YAGUNIN. Well, no. That's true.

BRUNOV. She used to say that if you'd asked her, she wouldn't have agreed. She didn't want to be a drag on your career.

YAGUNIN. Dear little—— [*Coughs.*] That was very generous of her.

BRUNOV. Yes. But I don't feel that way at all.

YAGUNIN. What do you mean?

BRUNOV. I've always sworn that if I met you I would offer you the choice of death or marrying my mother.

YAGUNIN. God bless my soul, did you?

BRUNOV. Yes.

YAGUNIN. And now we have met.

BRUNOV. Yes. It's odd, I don't feel like killing you. After all, we are related.

YAGUNIN. Fairly closely.

BRUNOV. But it looks as if you'll get shot anyway.

YAGUNIN. It does. What a pity you can't offer the other alternative.

BRUNOV. Meaning you'd marry my mother just to save your life?

YAGUNIN. No, no, not at all. But what you have told me has, I confess, rather changed my outlook. At your age you won't understand, but at mine it is very pleasant to know that a lady still remembers. . . .

BRUNOV [*eagerly*]. Tell me, er—comrade General——

YAGUNIN. Father.

BRUNOV. It doesn't seem natural.

YAGUNIN. As you like.

BRUNOV. What I want to know is, did you love my mother?

YAGUNIN. Of course I did. I remember her very tenderly.

BRUNOV. Well, then, I have a plan. On condition you marry my mother, I will release you.

YAGUNIN. Thank you, my boy. Thank you very much. It's a handsome offer. But . . . does it get me much further? I mean, here I am—and your friends may arrive at any moment.

BRUNOV. Yes. But they mustn't find you. We must get away at once.

YAGUNIN. I can't walk. I can't walk for anybody, not even for your dear mother. I am a martyr to gout.

BRUNOV. All you old generals are the same.

YAGUNIN. Really, my boy——

BRUNOV [*interrupting*]. You can ride pillion on my horse. I'll smuggle you behind our lines, and then you must go straight to Kazan.

YAGUNIN. Kazan?

BRUNOV. That's where we live. It's a fine town.

YAGUNIN. Kazan . . . rather typically provincial. Oh, dear, I shan't like Kazan.

BRUNOV. Better than being shot.

YAGUNIN. I suppose so. Oh, yes, I suppose so . . .

BRUNOV. Mother has two rooms in a house. We're very lucky.

YAGUNIN. Two rooms?

BRUNOV. Yes. Quite a good size, only one hasn't a window.

YAGUNIN. No window . . .

BRUNOV. Mother uses that room for the washing. She takes in washing now, you know. She says it's better than going out to work, because she's getting too stout to do much walking.

YAGUNIN. Huh? . . . What did you say . . . too stout?

BRUNOV. She's put on a good bit lately.

YAGUNIN. But—but I remember her as such a delicate little thing, like a piece of porcelain.

BRUNOV [*laughing heartily*]. Porcelain! Mother! She'll laugh when you try that one on her.

YAGUNIN. Tell me, my boy . . . just how stout is your mother?

BRUNOV. Well . . . [*He fumbles in a pocket.*] Here, I've got a photo. I always carry it with me.

[*Hands over a photograph.* YAGUNIN *examines it, and a look of horror comes over his face.*

YAGUNIN. Good heavens!

BRUNOV. She is putting on weight, isn't she?

YAGUNIN. She's enormous . . . or do you think it's partly the way she's been taken—see what I mean, sitting rather . . . [*points it out*].

BRUNOV. Oh, no. As a matter of fact, that was taken some time ago.

YAGUNIN. You mean . . . she's . . . stouter now?

BRUNOV. Oh, yes.

YAGUNIN. Good God!

BRUNOV. What?

YAGUNIN. Nothing, nothing . . .

BRUNOV [*briskly*]. Come on, we mustn't waste time. *He takes off his overcoat.*] Here, put this on instead of ours. You can't wear that uniform now. . . . Come on, we must hurry.

YAGUNIN [*not moving—he is still looking dazedly at the photograph*]. It is almost incredible. . . . Such a size. . . .

BRUNOV. Please hurry.

YAGUNIN. Yes, yes . . .

BRUNOV. Look here, are you coming, or aren't you?

YAGUNIN [*looking up*]. I . . . the point is. . . .

BRUNOV. If you hang about much longer it'll be too late.

YAGUNIN [*looking at the photograph*]. Perhaps that would be for the best.

BRUNOV. What on earth do you mean?

YAGUNIN [*speaking more decisively*]. My boy, I have been thinking. I feel . . . I should stay and face my destiny.

BRUNOV. You'll face a firing squad.

YAGUNIN. Yes . . . yes. But there are . . . worse things than death.

BRUNOV. Have you gone mad? What are you talking about?

YAGUNIN [*looking at the photograph once more and then laying it face upward on the table*]. You see . . . It's like this. I cannot desert my post.

BRUNOV. But you Whites always desert your posts. [YAGUNIN *shrugs.*] Well, I can't be found here. . . . [*Angrily*] I'm damned if I understand you!

YAGUNIN. You must go. I think I hear your friends coming.

[BRUNOV *stares at him for a minute, then flings away impatiently and struggles into his overcoat.*

BRUNOV. I've given you your chance! If you won'
take it, you won't. I think you're mad.

YAGUNIN [*with becoming nobility*]. My boy, you're ɑ
soldier. You must understand—it is a matter o
honour.

BRUNOV [*now in his overcoat, at the door. He speak
soberly after a pause*]. Yes. I understand.

YAGUNIN. Good-bye, my son.

BRUNOV. Good-bye . . . Father.

> [*He hesitates a moment, then turns and goes ou
> quickly, shutting the door behind him.* YAGUNIN
> *looks after him, retaining his expression o
> heroism. Then he relaxes, looks down an
> sees the photograph face upward on the table
> He turns it over, shrugs humorously, then sits uɲ
> and pulls his tunic straight, takes out a pocke
> mirror and comb, and lightly combs his bearɗ
> and moustache. Then he turns his chair anɗ
> faces the door resolutely. A confused noise oɟ
> shouting and chattering soldiers approaches
> YAGUNIN rises and stands to attention as thɇ
> door is battered open.*

CURTAIN

MOGGY THE CAT-BURGLAR

by

ERIC COPLANS

CHARACTERS

MOGGY
CONSTABLE
JENNINGS
SISTER AGATHA
MRS BROWN
SERGEANT TIMMS

Moggy the Cat-burglar is based on the B.B.C. play *The Plans of Men*, broadcast in 1946, with Dame Lilian Braithwaite in the part of Sister Agatha.

MOGGY THE CAT-BURGLAR

SCENE I

The scene is in Hyde Park on a cold November night. The only light comes from a public standard lamp, near which is a park seat. (The lamp need not be seen and the seat could be illuminated with a moonlight-blue spot-light.)

MOGGY, *a perk cockney, is seen huddled in one corner of the seat, hands in his overcoat pocket, muffler round his neck, and cap well over his eyes. Presently he blows into his hands to warm them, and finally rises and starts to pace to and fro, occasionally flapping his arms.*

By his furtive glances, he is obviously waiting for some one —but not for the CONSTABLE *who suddenly looms out of the darkness.*

MOGGY *retreats a pace or two into the gloom, but his face is illuminated by the* CONSTABLE's *lamp.*

MOGGY [*quickly recovering, and with forced calm*]. Well— and so wot? D'yer fink yer a blinking light-'ouse?

CONSTABLE [*slowly and deliberately*]. So what—so what it is. I think we've met before master—Moggy.

MOGGY. Perhaps we 'ave, perhaps we 'aven't. I reckon one way and anover I met all the blinkin' rozzers in the tahn.

CONSTABLE [*shaking his head*]. But not for some time, Moggy. Let me see now—how long have you been— ahem—on holiday?

MOGGY [*bitterly*]. That's right. Chuck it in me face. Five years it is, if you want to know.

CONSTABLE. Ah—five years. I remember now, and what might you be doing hanging round here. Hyde Park hardly seems the place for our famous little cat-burglar. [*Thumbs in belt, he looks upward.*] There's no joolery up them trees, Moggy.

MOGGY [*indignantly*]. And for why shouldn't I be in this blinkin' park? It's a free country—ain't it? Wherever I go it's the same blinkin' fing. Up pops a rozzer and says, "Wot you doin', Moggy—where you goin', Moggy—look aht Moggy or you'll be FUR it [*with a great show of indignation*]. Ain't I done my time? Ain't I paid for wot I done? Ain't it bad enough I 'ave to show my ticket every munf at the rozzers' club 'ouse, wiv'out *you* 'unting me?

CONSTABLE. Oh, you poor innocent man—you've been badly put on. [*Altering his tone*] Come on—what's the game?

MOGGY [*with raised and indignant tones*]. I'll tell yer wot the gime is. Soon as it's dark I'm goin' to nip dahn to Buckingham Palace and pinch the blinkin' crahn. That's wot the gime is. Till I'm ready, I'm goin' to sit dahn 'ere and 'ave a fag, see. [*Sits on seat.*

CONSTABLE. Yes, I see. Well, look out for yourself. If you get up to anything funny on my ground, you'll take another holiday—a longer one this time.

MOGGY. Come off it, mate. I'm finished wiv all that, got a fruit barrer dahn in Vauxhall. Now 'owd you like me to save you a nice juicy marrer—under the cahnter like—enough for you and the missus and all the little rozzers?

CONSTABLE. That's quite enough of that—you cheeky devil [*with admonitory finger*], look out for yourself, that's what I'm telling you.

[*Exit.*

[MOGGY *rises and resumes his pacing for a moment, turns and stops extreme* L. *to see* JENNINGS *enter* R.: *a man of about thirty, well groomed and poised, wearing a trilby hat, and carrying a walking-cane with leather thong.*

He strolls slowly to the seat, and, sitting at one end, takes out his case and lights a cigarette. He holds the lighted match for a moment, before

> *his face.* MOGGY, *who has been watching the*
> *newcomer intently, steals behind* JENNINGS *and*
> *whispers :*

MOGGY. 'Ullo, Guv—got a light?

JENNINGS [*with a start*]. Moggy! Why—you made me jump.

MOGGY [*coming round and sitting beside* JENNINGS]. Jump? Wotcher nerves got bad since you left the Moor?

JENNINGS. Cut that out—I'm trying my best to forget it.

MOGGY [*abjectly*]. Sorry, Guv. More shame to me to bring it up. When did they let *you* aht?

JENNINGS [*ducking his head*]. Oh my God, *must* you?

MOGGY. Sorry, Guv. It keeps cropping up like. Cut me froat if I mention it again. When did you say it was?

JENNINGS [*wearily*]. Oh—about two months after you. I've had the devil of a time to locate you.

MOGGY. Well, Guv—I got your letter all right, but it beats me 'ow you fahnd aht my abode of residence.

JENNINGS. I wrote to the Prisoners' Aid Society. Said I'd got a job for you.

MOGGY. A job did you say? That's a good 'un.

JENNINGS. Well—I meant it anyway, and it's right up your alley.

MOGGY. My alley!

JENNINGS [*looking round furtively*]. I mean it's in your line—ahem—climbing. Are you game?

MOGGY. Game—me game? Cut it aht, Guvnor. If you want me, I'm game enough, but it's got to be somefink cast iron. If they pinches me this time it's seven years if it's a day.

JENNINGS. It *is* cast iron—and it's money for jam.

MOGGY. Give us the book o' words, Guvnor.

JENNINGS. I wonder . . . if I can trust you.

MOGGY [*indignantly*]. Trust me! Arsk anyone in the gime, an' they'll tell you all abaht that. I been a fool to meself, may be, but I never let a pal dahn in all me born natural. No, not yours trewly. If you're goin' to come *that*, I'll 'op it, see?

JENNINGS [*hastily*]. No—no! Don't get upset. I'm sorry . . . but this is a big thing . . . the biggest thing you ever struck. You remember I told you I used to be a cashier in a bank?

MOGGY. Yus—and you was pinched for milking the till.

JENNINGS [*irritably*]. Shut up, you fool!

MOGGY. There I goes again. Can't say anyfink right.

JENNINGS. Listen. In that bank we had a very queer client—er—customer.

MOGGY. Yus.

JENNINGS. Well, this woman—we all knew her as Sister Agatha—used to be a nursing sister at St Botolph's Hospital—she was there for donkeys' years. Suddenly a relation died and she was left a packet of money, and my bank was named as trustee. That meant that her shares were lodged with the bank and we paid her the interest every quarter. Got that?

MOGGY. Yus.

JENNINGS. Now listen carefully. It came, one way and another, to over two thousand pounds a year. Well over that.

MOGGY. Blimey—that's money if you like, tho' not I says money can't buy 'appiness, but it can let you be un'appy in comfort.

JENNINGS. Stop playing the fool—listen. She used to take away five hundred pounds every quarter, and all in pound notes.

MOGGY. Didn't she put it in the bank?

JENNINGS [*dramatically*]. That's the whole point. Under no circumstances would she have a banking account.

MOGGY. What was the big ideer? Did she fink they'd nark 'er blinking dough . . . like you did?

JENNINGS [*throwing up his hands*]. God—you're hopeless! Yes—she *did* think that. There *are* people who prefer to hoard their money, rather than put it in a bank.

MOGGY. P'raps she was spending it on charity or such like.

JENNINGS. No, no, nothing of the kind.

MOGGY. 'Ow do *you* know wot she done wiv it?

JENNINGS. I'll tell you. She'd been going on like this for years, and one day she dropped a hint to the manager that she was saving something like two thousand a year.

MOGGY [*incredulously*]. You mean—you mean she's got somefink like ten farsand pahnds packed away?

JENNINGS. That's what it amounts to. In the end the bank got a bit worried and sent me down to interview her at her house in the country. You see, they thought I might be able to persuade her to put all this money on deposit. I went down to her place; it's in the heart of Kent, about three hours from London. I had to walk a couple of miles from the station. There wasn't even a taxi. I found her living in a fair-sized house standing back from the road in it's own grounds. The garden was overgrown and neglected, and there were cats all over the place.

MOGGY. Cats—did you say? Blimey!—there'll be one more when I get there—I'm a blinking cat meself —when no one's looking.

JENNINGS. Yes—cats. I counted about a score—all shapes and sizes. God—you never saw such a sight. They evidently belonged to the house, for there was a row of saucers all along the lawn. Well, I called on the old lady, the bank had written and she was expecting me. She took me into her sitting-room, and, my hat, you never saw such a sight!—it was too darn funny. Pictures of cats all round the wall and on the piano. She was nursing a monster of a cat—one of those Siamese.

MOGGY. Cut it aht, Guvnor. What about the dough?

JENNINGS. I'm coming to that. Don't you see I'm giving you all this detail to give you the correct atmosphere?

MOGGY [*sniffing*]. I'll bet there was one, too.

JENNINGS [*laughing*]. Well, I told her what the bank thought about her keeping all that money in the house and, as I was instructed, tried to persuade her to have it deposited with us. I might have been talking to a brick wall. She wouldn't hear of it. [*Imitating* SISTER AGATHA'S *austere voice*] "Mr Jennings. I don't trust banks." I saw it was useless to go on, so I asked her if she'd got a safe.

MOGGY. Now you're *talking*, Guvnor.

JENNINGS. Well—would you believe it, she said [*imitates* SISTER AGATHA], "I don't trust safes, young man, they attract burglars."

MOGGY. And she wasn't far out—neither.

JENNINGS. Well—then she said, as I was going [*again imitates*], "I don't trust men."

MOGGY. 'Garn—ain't she a caution?

JENNINGS. But that's not all. As she let me out of the door she said [*imitates*] "I trust cats."

[*They both burst out laughing.*

MOGGY. Well—if it don't beat the band. And the old geyser was sitting dahn there—on top of ten farsand parnds.

JENNINGS. Yes.

[JENNINGS *throws away his cigarette, takes out a pipe and pouch. Bends down and knocks out pipe, which he refills as* MOGGY *is speaking.*

MOGGY. Arf a mo, Guvnor. It was free year ago since you seen this 'ere Sister Aggyther?

JENNINGS [*calmly and between puffs*]. Yes.

MOGGY. 'Ow do you know she ain't dead or gorn away or somefink?

JENNINGS. Because—my dear college chum—as soon

as I came back from Da—Devonshire, I made it my business to go down there and find out. I drove down there.

MOGGY. You got a car, eh?

JENNINGS. Yes—a little two-seater.

MOGGY. An' you found it all Sir Garnet?

JENNINGS. Yes. She is still there. Everything is just the same. Cats and all. [*Throws back his head and chuckles*.] Gosh! you should have seen those cats.

MOGGY. Ain't she got no servants?

JENNINGS. There's just a woman comes in by the day.

MOGGY. Anyone else in the 'ouse?

JENNINGS. Not a soul.

MOGGY. Any telephone?

JENNINGS. None. I looked for that.

MOGGY. Pound notes you said.

JENNINGS. Yes—pound notes.

MOGGY. Can you tell me anyfink about the 'ouse?

JENNINGS. Well, there's a big porch with pillars and it's got a flat top, a sort of balcony, you know. A french window leads on to it. The lower windows are all barred.

MOGGY. Can you see it from the road?

JENNINGS. No. The whole outfit is hidden by trees and shrubs.

MOGGY. It sounds a bit of orlright to me.

JENNINGS. It certainly is.

MOGGY. No dogs?

JENNINGS. Of course not—the place is packed with her blessed cats, I tell you.

MOGGY. What about the old geyser—I mean—what shape is she?

JENNINGS. Well, I don't mind telling you she'll be a handful. I should say she's absolutely without fear.

MOGGY. I'll put the fear of Gawd in 'er.

JENNINGS. I say, look here, no weapons.

MOGGY. Never carried 'em—don't believe in 'em—

see? Leave all that to me. Now look 'ere, Guv, I know the game—you don't—see?

JENNINGS. That's true enough.

MOGGY. Now you'll do wot I tell you?

JENNINGS. Yes.

MOGGY. Wait a bit—didn't I 'ear you say you got a car?

JENNINGS. Yes.

MOGGY. What a Gawd-send. Nah listen. Wot you gotta do is to push that car somewhere up a side-road where it can't be seen, and you gotta keep watch opposite the 'ouse. There's bahnd to be a field—ain't there?

JENNINGS. Yes, there is.

MOGGY. Well, that's your part of the job, you gotta do sentry-go, and see we come away clean, see?

JENNINGS. So I don't come in the house?

MOGGY. That you do not. *And* if you don't trust me the job's off. No 'arm done and we part friends, see?

JENNINGS [*hastily*]. Don't talk rot, of course I trust you. I agree; the sooner we get on the job the better.

MOGGY. We gotter look at an Old Moore and see a date when there ain't no moon.

JENNINGS. By jove—that's a great notion.

MOGGY. And it's fifty-fifty.

JENNINGS. Rather.

MOGGY. Ten farsand—all in pahnd notes you said.

JENNINGS. It'll be more now.

MOGGY. I 'adn't fought of that. Gawd, it's a cinch. Sounds like somefink out of Egyptian Nights. Listen, Guv, we'll 'ave to go down and do a bit of scouting. Get the lie of the land, as you might say.

JENNINGS. I think it's a grand idea; we'll go to-morrow. Are you game?

MOGGY. Not 'arf. [*Swiftly*] Look aht—'ere comes 'is nibs!

[*Suddenly the* CONSTABLE *emerges from the gloom. He strolls slowly by, and, turning, gives a suspicious look at the two men before disappearing into the darkness again, on the opposite side of the stage.* JENNINGS *and* MOGGY *have sat stock still, only turning after the* CONSTABLE *has passed from view, to peer after him.*

[*It is a dramatic moment for them.*

JENNINGS [*in an undertone*]. Do you think he heard anything?

MOGGY. Wot—'im! Not on yer blinkin' life; 'e's dead from the neck up.

JENNINGS. Well—he looked pretty suspicious.

MOGGY. Fergit 'im, Guvnor. . . . Fergit 'im. 'E's an ole pal o' mine . . . calls me Moggy.

JENNINGS. Well—I hope you're right. [*Rises.*] To-morrow night, then!

MOGGY. That's right, Guv—to-morrow night at nine.

JENNINGS. Right! Good night, Moggy.

MOGGY. Pleasant dreams, Guv—an' be careful 'ow you go up them apples an' pears.

[*And* JENNINGS *has gone, leaving* MOGGY *lighting a cigarette. Just as he is about to go, the* CONSTABLE *reappears and eyes* MOGGY. *There is a long silence, broken at last by the* CONSTABLE *growling* "Good night . . . Moggy."

MOGGY. 'Night—Sergeant!

[*And he disappears into the darkness, leaving the* CONSTABLE *flashing his lamp about for possible clues, and the curtain gradually falls.*

SCENE II

A fortnight later. The curtain rises on SISTER AGATHA'S *sitting-room. It is cluttered up in true Victorian style, with knick-knacks on the mantelpiece, and there are pictures of cats on the walls. To the L. is a large couch with an occasional table beside it. Behind the couch is a screen to keep off the draught from a door leading out to the kitchen. On the R. of the room is another door leading to the outside. The ornate fireplace is in the right wall, and beside it is an easy-chair. At the back of the room, near the door [R.], is a window, and at the moment its venetian blind is down.*

The room is dark save for a red glow from the fire; all is quiet. Suddenly from outside comes the piercing yowl of an enraged cat, followed by a crash of falling masonry.

Then a door opens and a light appears behind the screen. It is SISTER AGATHA, *who peers into the room, and finally emerges clad in a dressing-gown, and carrying an oil lamp. She comes into the middle of the room and looks round; then, placing the lamp on the occasional table, she strides over and opens the door* R. *Loud groans are heard coming from outside.*

MOGGY'S VOICE [*from outside*]. My Gawd! Knocked aht by a blinkin' cat!

SISTER AGATHA [*her voice is austere, dominant, penetrating*]. What are you doing here?

JENNINGS [*appears at door*]. Sister Agatha—my friend. I'm afraid he's badly hurt.

SISTER AGATHA. I know you. . . . You're Mr Jennings—from the bank.

JENNINGS. Yes.

SISTER AGATHA. They told me—years ago—that you had left. What is the meaning of this?

JENNINGS. I'll explain it all after. My friend has fallen. . . .

SISTER AGATHA. Fallen . . . indeed he *has* fallen—from my porch. He was attempting to break into my house. A burglar!

JENNINGS. Yes—but Sister . . .

SISTER AGATHA [*peremptorily*]. Stand on one side, please. [*She brushes past* JENNINGS, *and is out of view. Her voice is heard.*] Yes—he has hurt his leg. We must get him into the house.

JENNINGS. Sister—I . . .

SISTER AGATHA. I don't want any explanations from you—Mr Jennings. You must help me to get this wretched man on to a couch.

JENNINGS. Yes, Sister—come on, Moggy—get your arm round my shoulder.

> [*There are more groans from* MOGGY.

SISTER AGATHA. That's right; put all your weight on the good leg. That's right . . . now then . . . take your time.

> [*They enter the room.* MOGGY, *with an arm round each of their shoulders, hops on one leg, slowly and painfully across the room. He is laid on the couch.* SISTER *bends over him and examines his leg.* MOGGY *groans in pain.*

SISTER AGATHA. Yes . . . he's torn the muscle— but I don't think it's a fracture.

> [*She speaks more to herself than to* JENNINGS.

JENNINGS. Hadn't I better get a doctor?

SISTER AGATHA. Why?

JENNINGS. You said . . .

SISTER AGATHA. My dear good man, for twenty years I have at my hospital taught generations of medical students their fracture work—and you talk about sending for a doctor!

JENNINGS. I'm sorry.

SISTER AGATHA. You may well be. A pretty fine specimen you seem to be—a bank clerk turned burglar.

JENNINGS [*miserably*]. What are you going to do?

SISTER AGATHA. I suppose what I *should* do is to send for the police; but it seems that this poor wretch has suffered enough . . . and as for *you* . . .

JENNINGS [*falteringly*]. Yes?

SISTER AGATHA. You didn't bolt. Most men would have done it in your shoes. You'd better go.

MOGGY [*who meantime has raised himself on his elbow and is listening intently*]. That's right, lady . . . one o' the best 'e is. You clear 'im aht and 'enceforth he'll lead a new life. Strike me pink 'e will. Sunday School and 'imns an' all that. I wouldn't be surprised if they don't turn 'im into a rozzer—s'elp me bob.

JENNINGS [*remorsefully*]. How can I leave you like this, Moggy?

MOGGY. It's a case of can't help ourselves, chum. I couldn't walk a step wiv this blinkin' leg—it 'urts like 'ell. 'Sides, ain't the kind lady said she won't let the cops git 'er little Moggy? [*Ingratiatingly*] Did'n'cher, lady?

SISTER AGATHA. Moggy!—Moggy! Is *that* your name?

MOGGY. Yus, that's your 'umble's moniker. You see, Moggy's a cat.

SISTER AGATHA [*clasping her hands, moves towards a cat picture and gazes at it*]. Yes, yes, I know . . . it's a cat's name.

MOGGY. Well, I'm what they call a cat-burglar, see. I climbs walls and things like all Moggys, see. [*Points here and there to the cat pictures.*] Like them Moggys there, see. . . .   [*He falls back exhausted and sighs.*

SISTER AGATHA [*confronts* JENNINGS *drawn to her full height and rigid. For a moment there is a silence. Then she points to the door and speaks in a half-strangled voice*]. You had better go.

> [JENNINGS *makes an involuntary step towards* MOGGY. *Then with a despondent gesture he walks slowly out of the house.*
>
> [SISTER AGATHA *walks to a cabinet and brings out some lint, bandages, and scissors and places them on a chair by side of couch. She bends over* MOGGY.

SISTER AGATHA [*tenderly*]. Moggy.

MOGGY [*in a tired voice*]. Yes, Nurse.

SISTER AGATHA. I'm going to put a cold bandage on your poor leg—it will make the pain better.

MOGGY. Thank you, Nurse. It do 'urt a bit.

SISTER AGATHA [*goes and returns quickly with a bowl of water and an eiderdown. There is an air of professional dexterity as she wrings out the lint and wraps and bandages the ankle*]. There, now, is that more comfortable, Moggy? [*Then she throws the eiderdown over him.*

MOGGY. It's lovely, ma'am. Good—you are. The Guv told me you was a nurse in the 'orspital.

SISTER AGATHA. The Guv?

MOGGY [*awkwardly*]. Well, you know . . . 'im as was wiv me . . . 'im as was in the bank.

SISTER AGATHA [*as she tucks him up*]. Oh, yes—I know. He stayed and helped me to get you down on the couch.

MOGGY. There's not many as 'ud do that.

SISTER AGATHA. It earned him his liberty. [*Gazes at picture.*] Besides, he was only an instrument of fate.

MOGGY. Instrument? I don't git that.

SISTER AGATHA. He brought *you* here, Moggy—it was ordained.

MOGGY. Yus—a nice blinkin' fing. 'Ere's me a cat-burglar, and the Guv brings me to a crib crawling wiv cats. No sooner 'as I nipped up your porch when a blinkin' great cat, which was more like a lion, flies at me and sends me ruddy well flying; the cops won't 'arf 'ave the laugh on me.

SISTER AGATHA. There won't be any cops—as you call them. I wouldn't dream of giving you up—you poor dear. [*Strokes his head.*

MOGGY. Blimey . . . "poor dear." It's funny you bein' so good to me, considerin' wot I am.

SISTER AGATHA. It's because you are what you are that I'm helping you—you see . . . I love cats.

MOGGY. Cats!

SISTER AGATHA. Yes . . . you are a kind of cat, you know.

MOGGY. Well—if that don't beat the band! Could I 'ave a drink, Nurse?

SISTER AGATHA. Yes . . . here's some lovely milk.

MOGGY. Couldn't I 'ave a cup o' tea?

SISTER AGATHA. No, it isn't good for your hair.

MOGGY. That's a good 'un, 'ere's luck.

SISTER AGATHA. Moggy—you came here for money, didn't you?

MOGGY. Yes, ma'am—in a manner of speaking.

SISTER AGATHA. I suppose that man Jennings told you there was money in the house.

MOGGY [*awkwardly*]. 'Scuse me, ma'am, but Mr Jennings is a friend of mine.

SISTER AGATHA. Oh, you're loyal—very loyal. Would you like to play with some money?

MOGGY. Play?

SISTER AGATHA. Yes—play. I've got an awful lot, and if it amuses you . . . why not. Look . . . you've been lying over it all the time. [*A trunk is dragged from under the sofa. The lid is thrown back.*] Look, there's some money. Play with it, darling.

MOGGY. *Play* wiv it?

SISTER AGATHA. Yes—play with it. You like money, don't you?

> [*She heaps up bundles of notes on the bed.* MOGGY *fumbles them between his hands. He bends over and stares into the open trunk.*

MOGGY. Wot, *me* like money? I reckon I'm goin' mad. There's 'undreds and farsands.

SISTER AGATHA. Play with it, darling.

MOGGY [*hysterically*]. I never seen such a fing in all me natural.

SISTER AGATHA. Play with it, darling.

MOGGY. There's 'undreds—there's farsands.

SISTER AGATHA. It's all yours. You can have as much as you like.

MOGGY. You mean—you mean—to take wiv me?

SISTER AGATHA. Yes—to take with you. When you
go away you can have as much as you want. I have
saved it for you for years. I would not give it to a man.
I don't trust men.

MOGGY [*wildly*]. You wouldn't give it to . . . 'ere
. . . arf a mo. You're 'aving a fine lark wiv me,
aincher?

SISTER AGATHA. I don't understand you. I said I
wouldn't give it to a man. You're getting excited and
feverish. [*Lays hands on forehead.*] Why—you're burning
hot, you must sleep. [*Crosses to cupboard and pours out a
draught.*] Drink this—you must sleep, you poor darling.
. . . You poor darling. You must sleep.

> [*Presently there comes the sound of very soft music
> (Brahms' "Cradle Song"). SISTER AGATHA
> tiptoes over to the lamp and puts it out.*
>
> [*MOGGY is heard muttering in a delirious manner.
> (He should be bathed in a blue spotlight.)*

MOGGY. My 'ead's all rummy. Some one's bashed
me. [*In a flat, loud voice*] Is that you, Ern? Where's
Perce? 'Ullo, me old china. I never see such a fing.
Betcher a quid. There's farsands and farsands of quid
notes. They've all got cats' 'eads on them. Cats' 'eads.
[*A wild burst of laughter.*] Cats' 'eads on quid notes keep
goin' rahnd and rahnd in my 'ead. Oh, my poor 'ead.
My leg do 'urt.

SISTER AGATHA [*stroking his forehead*]. Sleep, Moggy—
sleep.

MOGGY. 'Ere, let's 'ave a tune. Come on, Perce, me
ole china. Come on, Emma. Wot abaht *Daisy*?

> [*A tinkling piano, at first faint and distant but
> gathering in volume, plays opening chords.
> A chorus suggestive of delirium joins in.
> This could be done with a radio-gramophone
> having a double turn-table.*

VOICES SINGING.
  Daisy, Daisy, give me your answer do,

I'm 'arf crazy—all for the love of you.
It won't be a stylish marriage . . .

[*Chorus fades.*

MOGGY. Come on—come on—all join in. [*Sings with chorus.*] Daisy—Daisy.

[*Silence.*

A VOICE [*stern and judicial* (*A microphone could be used for this effect.*)]. You appear to be quite incapable of reform. Rather against my inclination I am going to be lenient with you, but if you appear before me again . . .

[*Faint chorus of "Daisy."*

SISTER AGATHA. Poor thing. He's worn out.

MOGGY. There's farsands and farsands of quid cats.

VOICE OF JENNINGS [*also over microphone*]. Under no circumstances would she open a banking account.

[MOGGY *sleeps. The music* (*Brahms' "Cradle Song"*) *swells, and after a time the blue spot-light fades, and* SISTER AGATHA *goes over to the window and pulls up the venetian blind and sunlight streams into the room.*

SISTER AGATHA. Well, and how are you feeling this morning?

MOGGY. I feel a bit better, ma'am, but my 'ead's a bit muzzy. I ain't 'arf been dreaming.

SISTER AGATHA. Yes, you were rather restless in the night.

MOGGY. Wot—did you come in?

SISTER AGATHA. Yes, I sat by your bed for quite a while.

MOGGY. You must be tired.

SISTER AGATHA. Oh, no; I'm used to night duty . . . besides, it was for *you.*

MOGGY. Why is it you're so good to me, ma'am?

SISTER AGATHA. Because I know who you are.

MOGGY. Who do you fink I am?

SISTER AGATHA. You are Balaster—the god of cats

eturned to life in the shape of a man. For many years
have awaited you.

MOGGY. Blimey . . . you ain't 'arf kiddin'.

SISTER AGATHA. I am not . . . kidding. It is the
ruth. You are the cat god and I am your disciple.

MOGGY. I never 'card such a thing. Excuse me,
na'am, wot's 'appened to that there cat that knocked
ne aht?

SISTER AGATHA. He dared to hurt you . . . he
hould have known. He has paid the penalty.

MOGGY. Penalty!

SISTER AGATHA. Yes. I have put him to sleep.

MOGGY. Sleep?

SISTER AGATHA. Yes, I have chloroformed him—it
vas quite painless.

MOGGY. I'm sorry you done that, ma'am, the poor fing
vas only doing its job. It don't seem right to me at all.

SISTER AGATHA. It was justice.

MOGGY. I'm thirsty. Could I 'ave a drink, ma'am?

SISTER AGATHA. Here—I've got it all ready for you
. . some lovely bread and milk.

MOGGY. Bread and milk?

SISTER AGATHA. Yes . . . it's good for you.

MOGGY. You bet it is. [*A doorbell rings.*] 'Ullo, 'oo's
hat?

SISTER AGATHA. It'll be my daily woman, Mrs Brown.

MOGGY. Excuse me, ma'am . . . but won't she talk?

SISTER AGATHA. Don't worry. I'll put her off. She's
terrible gossip.

> [*She fetches the screen and places it round the couch
> so that it cannot be seen from the door, but
> can still be seen by the audience.*]

MOGGY. So she chloroformed the poor little blighter.
don't feel 'appy. All this cat business is *gitting me
ahn.* [*Whimpers.*] I wish Jennings was 'ere—'e's a pal,
e is; *me* a cat . . . she's got bats in the belfry—that's
vhat it is.

MRS BROWN [*at door*]. Good morning, ma'am.

SISTER AGATHA. Good morning, Mrs Brown. I don't think I shall be wanting you to-day.

MRS BROWN [*edging her way in so that she can look round*]. Not want me?

SISTER AGATHA [*trying to force her out*]. No—you can take a holiday. I have some important business to attend to.

MRS BROWN. Just as you like, ma'am, but I wasn't wanting no 'oliday. And excuse me, ma'am, whatever's happened to the porch?

SISTER AGATHA. Porch?

MRS BROWN [*goes back to porch*]. Yes—look! The railing at the top's all broke . . . and look [*stoops and picks up a kit of tools, comes in, and hands them to* SISTER AGATHA], here's a bag of tools. [*Agitatedly*] Sister— you ain't 'ad burglars, 'ave you?

SISTER AGATHA [*sharply*]. Burglars? What nonsense. [*Taking the bag and looking round furtively to try and find somewhere to put it*] These tools are mine. Be so good as to say nothing about this to anybody—if you do, you needn't come here any more.

MRS BROWN [*rattling away*]. Just as you wish, ma'am, but I've always said it was sheer arsking for trouble— you being 'ere all alone. I was only saying to my 'usband the other day, It's fair arsking for it, I says, not that any one in the village would 'arm a 'air of your 'ead the way you look after them when they're sick. And you will excuse me, ma'am, but some one else 'as been 'ere and seen all this before me.

SISTER AGATHA. Some one else—what do you mean?

MRS BROWN. What about the milkman? Didn't I see 'im down the lane talking to the police sergeant; and my name's Jack Robinson if the sergeant don't come nosing around before you can say knife. So don't go putting anything against *me*, Sister Agatha.

SISTER AGATHA. I wouldn't dream of it, Mrs Brown; you've been coming to me many years.

MRS BROWN [*vehemently*]. That I have, Sister, and well I know, and all the village knows, and with good cause, you got a heart of gold and always one to help the fallen [*points downward*] . . . and when I says the fallen, I *mean* the fallen. Well, you know your own business best [*and she goes off in a huff*].

> [SISTER AGATHA *returns. She is nervous and agitated.* MOGGY *is sitting up fumbling a bundle of notes aimlessly. He is brooding. He turns and stares at a cat's picture. With an impatient gesture he hurls the packet of notes at the picture, other notes he throws pell-mell to the floor and buries his head in the cushion.*

SISTER AGATHA [*crossing to him*]. Don't worry, Moggy darling—they shan't take you from me.

> [*The doorbell rings again and there is a persistent knocking.* SISTER AGATHA *turns and glares across the room. Then she crosses and opens the door.*

SERGEANT TIMMS. Good morning, Sister Agatha.

SISTER AGATHA. Good morning, Sergeant. What can do for you?

SERGEANT TIMMS [*forcing his way in*]. You will excuse me, ma'am, but can I have a word with you?

SISTER AGATHA [*standing between him and the screen*]. It's a rather early call, isn't it—er—anything the matter?

SERGEANT TIMMS. It *is* an early call, ma'am, and there *is* something the matter.

SISTER AGATHA. Well—what is it? I'm afraid I can't ask you in—it's not convenient.

SERGEANT TIMMS. Not convenient!

SISTER AGATHA [*firmly*]. No—I haven't even dressed. If you have anything to say tell me here and now.

SERGEANT TIMMS [*truculently*]. You're not helping me, ma'am.

SISTER AGATHA. What do you mean—not helping you ?

SERGEANT TIMMS. I mean *this*, ma'am. You've seen your porch this morning?

SISTER AGATHA. Well—what of it ! If the wind blows down a few bricks it doesn't become a matter for the police.

SERGEANT TIMMS. Bricks—come now, Sister Agatha, that won't do at all—you are making things very hard for me. When the milkman called this morning there was something more than bricks. Point of fact—there was a bag of tools.

SISTER AGATHA. Tools?

SERGEANT TIMMS. That's what I said, ma'am. Tools —and this—who's cap is this?

SISTER AGATHA. Cap? How should I know?

SERGEANT TIMMS. A broken porch—a cap—tools. All these betoken a *man*. I have every reason to believe, ma'am, that there was an attempt to break into your house last night.

SISTER AGATHA. Really—you surprise me.

SERGEANT TIMMS [*he goes to the fireplace and looks round the mantelpiece and peers in the grate*]. You will excuse me, ma'am, but I will go so far as to say you aren't a bit surprised.

SISTER AGATHA. No?

SERGEANT TIMMS [*stoops and picks a piece of paper out of the grate*]. That's what I said, ma'am, you aren't surprised. [*Rising*] Your porch is broken down, and there is every evidence that a man has fallen to the ground while attempting to enter your house.

SISTER AGATHA. I know nothing at all about it.

SERGEANT TIMMS. Nothing?

SISTER AGATHA. Nothing whatever.

SERGEANT TIMMS [*bearing down on* SISTER AGATHA *and forcing her towards the screen*]. Very well—and now I must ask you to deliver to me, madam, a bag of burglar's tools.

SISTER AGATHA. Burglar's tools!

SERGEANT TIMMS. Yes—you took them from Mrs Brown's hands this morning.

SISTER AGATHA. You are making a stupid mistake. They are the tools I use in the house for little odd jobs.

SERGEANT TIMMS. I see; and might I examine these . . . house tools?

SISTER AGATHA. Certainly not. It's outrageous you should come and question me in my own house in this way. I haven't broken the law.

SERGEANT TIMMS. It is my duty to warn you that being an accessory after the fact is unlawful. Moreover, concealing or harbouring a criminal is unlawful. Come, come, madam: in your own interests I must ask you to allow me to see this kit of tools.

SISTER AGATHA [*with her back to the screen*]. I refuse— absolutely.

SERGEANT TIMMS. In that case, ma'am, you leave me no alternative but to apply to Sir John Crew for a search warrant.

SISTER AGATHA. A search warrant! It's disgraceful!

SERGEANT TIMMS. Furthermore, madam, I'm leaving my man on duty outside. Any attempt to remove these tools is not only useless, but will land you into the most serious consequences. I bid you good-morning.

[*Exit* SERGEANT.

[SISTER AGATHA, *in a state of deep distress,*
removes the screen again. MOGGY, *who during*
the preceding conversation has hidden his head
under the eiderdown, now sits up on one arm.

MOGGY. Excuse me, ma'am, I been finking.

SISTER AGATHA. Yes?

MOGGY. I been finking I ought to go to the 'orspital.

SISTER AGATHA. Why?

MOGGY. No offence, ma'am, but I fink you got me wrong.

SISTER AGATHA. What do you mean?

M

MOGGY. No offence, lady—but you got it on your mind as I'm a cat.

SISTER AGATHA. Yes . . . yes . . . a god of cats.

MOGGY. Strewth—'ark at her! Now, listen, lady— I ain't a cat at all—nor a gawd eiver—see?

SISTER AGATHA. You do not know what you are saying—it's blasphemy.

MOGGY. I know full well what I'm saying—I'm a man, see. Really and truly I'm a man.

SISTER AGATHA. If they take you away—you will be sent to prison. You will lose everything—the light, the air, the sun—they will break your heart—they will kill you slowly.

MOGGY. I don't care—I can take what's coming to me.

SISTER AGATHA. No . . . no . . . it must not be. I won't permit it. Better that you should die painlessly, you poor darling. [*Goes to cupboard.*

MOGGY [*raises his voice*]. Die painlessly! Wotcher talking abaht? Wot you got in that bottle?

SISTER AGATHA. You poor darling.

MOGGY [*shouting*]. Don't 'poor darling' me—I'm sick and tired of it, I tell you! I'm a man . . . a man . . . A MAN.

SISTER AGATHA. You poor darling—there will be no pain.

MOGGY. Git away . . . 'ere, you're choking me . . . 'ere, git away. . . . My Gawd . . . it's chloroform. Wotcher doin', you're choking me. . . . Git away . . . oh—oh! [*And* MOGGY's *voice gradually becomes confused. The sunlight fades and the room grows dark again except for the blue spotlight on* MOGGY.] Perce—is that you, Perce? Come on, me ole china—come on blokes—let's 'ave *Daisy*. . . .

[*And once again come the strains of "Daisy"; and as the chorus swells the curtain slowly falls.*

WE WERE STRANGERS

by

FRANCIS DURBRIDGE

CHARACTERS

NICHOLAS FORBES
GAIL BLAKE
HOBSON

Scene: *A small jeweller's shop in New Bond Street*
Time: *The present, Saturday morning*

WE WERE STRANGERS

*The scene is the interior of a small jeweller's shop in New
Bond Street. A door leading to the street is up* C., *and another
door leading to a private office is down* R. *Above the door is a
small counter, on which there are numerous glass trays containing watches, statuettes, rings, etc. Behind this counter, and
right of the entrance, are green curtains concealing a long, low
window. Two chairs are facing the counter.*

When curtain rises HOBSON *is discovered behind the
counter, carefully examining a tray of rings. He is a spruce
little man of about forty-five.*

NICHOLAS FORBES *enters from the street. He is tall and
good-looking.*

HOBSON. Good morning, sir!

NICHOLAS. Good morning. I want to see Mr Stanford, please.

HOBSON. I'm rather afraid Mr Stanford is out at the
moment, sir. Anything I can do for you?

NICHOLAS. Well, I don't see why not. I should like
to see some engagement rings.

HOBSON. Yes, of course, sir.

[*He places a tray of rings on a small black cloth.*

NICHOLAS [*examining a ring*]. I rather like this one.

HOBSON. That's a lovely little ring, sir, and a genuine
bargain. Thirty-six guineas.

NICHOLAS [*smiling*]. Oh, I see. Well, as a matter of
fact, I want something rather more expensive.

HOBSON. Rather more expensive? [*Taking a ring
from another tray*] Well, how does this strike you, sir?

NICHOLAS. No. No, I'm afraid I don't care for that
sort of thing.

HOBSON. A little too ostentatious, eh, sir?

NICHOLAS. Yes, a little too—er—ostentatious. [*Examining a third ring*] This is rather charming.

HOBSON. A hundred and seven guineas, sir.

NICHOLAS. A hundred and seven? Rather a big jump from thirty-six.

HOBSON. Yes, sir. But the stone in this ring, apart from being larger is definitely of——

NICHOLAS [*thoughtfully*]. Mm—I can't say I'm really keen on it. Have you anything a little more—er—exclusive?

HOBSON. Exclusive? About what price have you in mind, sir?

NICHOLAS. Oh. Two-fifty. Three hundred.

HOBSON. Oh, I see. [*Dubious*] I—don't—think—we have, sir. [*Suddenly*] But I'm expecting Mr Stanford back at any moment, and I rather think he may have something that might——

NICHOLAS. About how long do you think Mr Stanford will be?

HOBSON. At the very most ten minutes, sir.

NICHOLAS. Then, if you don't mind, I'll wait.

HOBSON [*pleased*]. Certainly, sir.

[NICHOLAS *sits.*

NICHOLAS [*making conversation*]. Are you busy?

HOBSON. Fairly busy, sir. We have our off moments like every one else.

NICHOLAS. I see. [*Pause.*

HOBSON. Excuse my asking, sir. But aren't you Mr Forbes—Mr Nicholas Forbes, the explorer?

NICHOLAS. Yes.

HOBSON [*rather thrilled*]. I thought I recognized you.

NICHOLAS [*politely*]. Have we met before, then?

HOBSON. Oh, no, sir. But I saw your film *Heroes of the Jungle*.

NICHOLAS [*rather bored*]. Oh.

HOBSON. A very fine film if I may say so, sir.

NICHOLAS. Thank you.

HOBSON. I took my little boy to see it and he was very thrilled—very thrilled indeed.

NICHOLAS. That's most gratifying.

HOBSON [*very interested*]. Personally, I could never understand how you managed to escape from that lion, sir. The one that entered your tent.

NICHOLAS. It was a very old lion, Mr—?

HOBSON. Hobson.

NICHOLAS. Mr Hobson.

HOBSON. Oh. [*Puzzled*] Oh, I see.

> [GAIL BLAKE *enters. She is a very lovely-looking woman of about thirty-five. Exquisitely dressed. At the moment she is the victim of a violent, and rather embarrassing, attack of hiccups.*
> [NICHOLAS *rises.*

GAIL. Good—*hic*—morning.

HOBSON. Good morning, madam.

> [GAIL *produces a small oval-shaped box, obviously containing a ring.*

GAIL. About two days ago my fiancé purchased this engagement ring, and . . .

HOBSON. Oh, yes, of course. I remember, madam. In fact, I believe I attended to the gentleman personally.

GAIL. He said that if I didn't care for it you'd be quite willing to—*hic*—to *hic* exchange it?

HOBSON. Why, yes, of course, madam.

GAIL [*sweetly*]. Well, I'm afraid I don't—er—care for it.

HOBSON. I see. Then we'll exchange it, by all means. Have you the receipt?

GAIL [*searching in her handbag*]. Yes, it's—*hic*—it's—*hic*—*hic*. [*Irritably*] Really, I beg your pardon, but I've had these confounded hiccups all the morning.

HOBSON. Can I get you a glass of water, madam?

GAIL. I'm afraid it—*hic*—*hic*—it wouldn't be any use, you see——

NICHOLAS [*very calmly*]. Hold your breath and count sixteen.

GAIL [*rather indignant*]. I beg your—*hic*—pardon?

NICHOLAS. I said: Hold your breath and count sixteen.

GAIL [*coldly*]. I've already held my breath and counted thirty-nine. I fail to see——

NICHOLAS [*excessively polite*]. Sixteen makes all the difference.

HOBSON [*apologetically*]. This is—is Mr Forbes, madam. The—er—famous explorer.

GAIL. Really. Do explorers suffer from hiccups?

NICHOLAS. Not for any length of time, they always——

GAIL. Hold their breath and count sixteen, I suppose?

NICHOLAS. Precisely.

GAIL [*after tiny pause*]. Very well. [*She holds her breath. Long pause.*] Ah!

NICHOLAS. Well?

GAIL [*coldly*]. It doesn't seem to have made the slightest difference.

HOBSON [*tactfully*]. About the—er—receipt, madam?

GAIL. Oh, yes—the receipt. Where did I . . . Oh, here we are! [*She takes a slip of paper from her handbag.*

HOBSON. Thank you, madam. Now will you excuse me, please? I'm afraid I shall have to check the number in our books. Mr Stanford always insists on this. It shouldn't take very long.

GAIL. That's quite all right.

[HOBSON *goes into the private office.*
[*Pause.*

NICHOLAS. Do you often suffer from hiccups?

GAIL. I've never had them in my life before.

NICHOLAS. Oh. [*Pause.*] I once knew a man who had hiccups for three days.

GAIL. Really.

NICHOLAS. Yes. [*Tiny pause.*] On the third day he took a cold bath. It cured him completely.

GAIL. I'm so glad.

NICHOLAS. It was a great relief.

GAIL. I'm sure it must have been.

NICHOLAS [*as an afterthought*]. Unfortunately he caught a chill and died of pneumonia.

GAIL. Oh.

[*Pause.*

NICHOLAS. Do you know, I feel quite sure that we've met before somewhere.

GAIL. I feel quite sure that we haven't.

NICHOLAS. I never forget a face.

GAIL. Neither do I.

NICHOLAS [*attempting to pursue the conversation*]. Tell me, do you find it an advantage or a disadvantage?

GAIL [*puzzled*]. What?

NICHOLAS. Never being able to forget faces?

GAIL [*curtly*]. I've never thought about it.

[*Pause.*

NICHOLAS [*suddenly bright*]. I once knew a man who could never forget feet.

GAIL. You seem to have a large circle of rather unique acquaintances.

NICHOLAS [*magnanimously*]. Really, you know, in exploration one meets so many people. It's rather inevitable.

GAIL. I seem to remember reading something about you in *The Tatler*. Didn't you go to the North Pole or somewhere?

NICHOLAS. It was the North Pole.

GAIL [*sweetly*]. I hope you enjoyed it.

NICHOLAS. Thank you. It was very pleasant.

GAIL [*puzzled*]. I've often wondered. Why do people go to the North Pole?

NICHOLAS [*after pause—equally puzzled*]. I haven't the faintest idea.

GAIL. Exploring always seems to me rather a mug's game. I can see very little point in dashing from one place to another when it's far more comfortable staying where you are.

NICHOLAS. I can see you've given the subject a great deal of thought.

GAIL. Didn't you once make a film—*Heroes of the Jungle*?

NICHOLAS. Yes.

GAIL. I saw it at Brighton about two years ago. I loved the part where you were chased by that decrepit old lion.

NICHOLAS. Thank you.

GAIL. Did you ever see it?

NICHOLAS. Once. Now I come to think about it— that's why I went to the North Pole.

GAIL [*amused*]. Oh, I see.

NICHOLAS [*seriously*]. When you smile like that—I can't help thinking you remind me of some one. Are you sure we haven't met before?

GAIL. Quite sure.

NICHOLAS. It's rather odd that . . .

GAIL. Did you ever see a play at the Lyric called *Captain Denby's Excuse*? It ran for almost a year.

NICHOLAS. *Captain Denby's Excuse*? Why, yes. [*Suddenly*] Good Lord, of course! I remember—you played the excuse. You're—you're Gail Blake. Gail Blake, the actress.

GAIL [*quietly amused*]. Yes. Yes, that's right.

NICHOLAS [*after tiny pause*]. You were—awfully good.

GAIL. Did you really think so?

NICHOLAS [*slowly*]. Terribly—good. [*Slight pause.*] I say, I hope you don't mind my saying so?

GAIL [*inwardly delighted*]. No. No, of course not.

NICHOLAS. I saw the play four times.

GAIL. Really?

NICHOLAS. I shall never forget that last act. You wore a blue dress. Blue sequins, wasn't it?

GAIL. How perfectly sweet of you to remember! [*Tiny pause.*] I got awfully good notices.

NICHOLAS. I'm sure you did.

GAIL. James Agate said the sweetest things—all in French, too. Much more intriguing, don't you think?

NICHOLAS. Much more intriguing.

GAIL [*quite friendly*]. Are you very interested in the theatre, Mr——?

NICHOLAS. Forbes. Nicholas Forbes.

GAIL. Oh, yes, of course. Mr Forbes . . .?

NICHOLAS. Very interested.

GAIL. My fiancé's an actor, too. You've probably heard of him—Brian Steele?

NICHOLAS. Brian Steele? Yes, I've heard of him—of course. But didn't he sail for America yesterday?

GAIL. He's gone to Hollywood. I'm joining him in New York at Christmas. We're to be married there.

NICHOLAS. Oh, I see. Congratulations.

GAIL. Thank you. [*After tiny pause*] I'm rather looking forward to it. I've never been to New York.

NICHOLAS. I'm to be married at Christmas, too, oddly enough. I'm joining my fiancée in Scotland.

GAIL. Really? Congratulations.

NICHOLAS. Thank you. [*After tiny pause*] I'm rather looking forward to it. I've never been to Scotland.

GAIL. They say it's charming.

NICHOLAS. Yes.   [*Pause.*

GAIL. Very hilly.

NICHOLAS. Oh, very.   [*Pause.*

GAIL. Have you—known your fiancée very long?

NICHOLAS. About two months. We met at a party. A coming-out party. She was coming out just as I was arriving. We bumped.

GAIL. I see.

NICHOLAS. And—Brian?

GAIL. Brian——? Oh, there's nothing much to tell, really. We first met in rep. about six years ago.

NICHOLAS. Oh. [*Tiny pause.*] Mr Hobson seems to be taking his time. I should sit down if I were you.

[GAIL *sits. Pause.*

GAIL. Please forgive me for my rudeness just now.

NICHOLAS. Rudeness?

GAIL. Yes. I ought to have thanked you for curing my hiccups.

NICHOLAS. Oh, that was nothing.

GAIL. But I was so unnecessarily irritable, please . . .

NICHOLAS. Nonsense! You had every right to be irritable. Besides, there's nothing more aggravating than a gust of hiccups.

GAIL. You're very sweet.

NICHOLAS. Not at all.

GAIL. I must remember that trick about counting sixteen. It's extremely useful.

NICHOLAS. Yes. It only has one disadvantage. It doesn't always work.

GAIL [*amused*]. I see.

[*Slight pause.*

NICHOLAS [*offering cigarette-case*]. Cigarette?

GAIL. No, thank you.

NICHOLAS. You don't mind if I smoke?

GAIL. No. No, of course not.

[NICHOLAS *lights his cigarette.*

NICHOLAS. So you're exchanging your engagement ring?

GAIL. Well, I hope to do so. It isn't very charming, is it? [*She shows him the ring.*] Brian has simply no taste —in jewellery, I mean.

NICHOLAS. It is a little—er—ostentatious, if I may quote Mr Hobson.

GAIL. And you?

NICHOLAS. Me? Well, as a matter of fact, I'm waiting to see Mr Stanford—the proprietor here.

GAIL. Is he a friend of yours?

NICHOLAS. Not really a friend. A sort of acquaintance. We met in Los Angeles about two years ago.

GAIL [*brightly*]. Los Angeles? Oh, isn't that near Hollywood?

NICHOLAS [*amused*]. Yes, quite near, I believe.

[*Pause.*

GAIL. I suppose you'll be spending your honeymoon
i Scotland?

NICHOLAS. More than likely.

CAIL. What part?

NICHOLAS. I don't really know. Maybe the High-
nds. Beatrice seems very keen on the Highlands.

GAIL. Beatrice . . .?

NICHOLAS. Yes.

GAIL. I have a sister called Beatrice.

NICHOLAS. It's not a name I really care for.

GAIL [*a shade embarrassed*]. Well—I rather like Bea.

NICHOLAS [*pensively*]. No one calls her Bea.

GAIL. Oh. [*After a tiny pause*] Is she fair?

NICHOLAS [*quietly, almost mechanically*]. She's tall and
ark, with very beautiful eyes, and every one calls her
eatrice.

GAIL. Oh. [*With a little laugh*] Oh, I see.

NICHOLAS [*quietly*]. I wonder if you do see, Miss——
Suddenly] May I call you Gail?

GAIL. Well——

NICHOLAS [*gently*]. Please?

GAIL. If it will afford you any pleasure—yes. Per-
onally, I derive very little delight from calling com-
arative strangers by their Christian names.

NICHOLAS. So do I. But this is different. Much
ifferent.

GAIL. Is it?

NICHOLAS [*looking at her very intently*]. Yes. You
ee, we're not strangers, Gail. At least, not any
onger.

GAIL. Then what are we?   [*Pause.*

NICHOLAS. We are in love.   [*Tiny pause.*

GAIL [*quietly*]. I beg your pardon?

NICHOLAS. We are in love. Deeply in love.

GAIL [*annoyed*]. Please, don't be silly!

NICHOLAS. I'm not being silly, Gail. Don't thin
that. I'm being sincere—desperately sincere.

GAIL. You're talking complete nonsense!

NICHOLAS. You're not annoyed?

GAIL [*stiffly*]. I have no wish to pursue the subject.

NICHOLAS. From the very first moment when yo
came into this shop—something happened. I don'
know what it was. I don't pretend to know. But dee
down inside of me a devotion stirred—a devotion tha
I have never felt for anyone or anything in my lif
before.

GAIL [*slightly alarmed*]. But—but you know nothing
at all about me.

NICHOLAS. Is that so important? I don't see that it'
going to help me any if I know what you look like a
half-past eight in a morning, or what sort of fac
powder your sister uses.

GAIL [*sharply*]. You're infatuated. Stupidly and
childishly infatuated.

NICHOLAS [*quietly*]. That's a very silly observation
and not worthy of you, my dearest.

GAIL. Please—please go away!

NICHOLAS. Why are you behaving like this? It's no
a bit kind and it's very unintelligent.

GAIL. Unintelligent!

NICHOLAS. Very.

GAIL. Well—perhaps you'll be kind enough to tel
me precisely what you expect of me? Would a girlish
swoon satisfy your apparently modest requirements?

NICHOLAS. While being equally unintelligent, tha
at least would be a far more romantic procedure.

GAIL. I simply don't know how you have the
audacity to stand there and talk such utter nonsense
about being in love. How can you possibly be in love?

NICHOLAS [*gently*]. You're very lovely.

GAIL. And it's no good trying to flatter me, because
I'm quite immune to flattery.

NICHOLAS [*politely*]. I'm sure you are.

GAIL. I think your behaviour is perfectly un-gentlemanly.

NICHOLAS. Ungentlemanly? I'm sorry. [*Taking her by the arm*] Now would you mind terribly if I asked you a question?

GAIL [*after tiny pause*]. Well?

NICHOLAS. Despite this antagonistic attitude of yours —you do believe me, don't you?

GAIL. What do you mean?

NICHOLAS. You do believe that this thing has happened. That we are in love. Deeply in love?

GAIL. I certainly do not.

NICHOLAS [*fervently*]. Then why are your lips trembling, my dear, and your eyes shining with a soft light?

GAIL. If you don't stop talking such nonsense I shall —I shall . . .   [*She falters.*

NICHOLAS [*gently*]. My dear, don't you see—it's no use? This is a moment in a million. An enchanted moment. A moment that means more to both of us than either the past or the future. It won't last. It can't last. But while it does, my sweet, don't let's waste it with hollow little phrases and conventional emotions.

GAIL [*softly*]. Leave go of my arm—please.

[*Slight pause.*

NICHOLAS. All right. All right, if you insist.

[*He lets her arm drop and half turns away.*

GAIL. Thank you.

[*Pause. Suddenly he turns towards her again.*

NICHOLAS. Forgive me if I've annoyed you. If I've seemed just a little mad and impetuous, but——

GAIL [*gently*]. I'm not annoyed.

NICHOLAS. I'm sorry, too, if all this has hurt you a little. The suddenness of it, I mean. But—but we are in love. Aren't we? [*Pause*] Aren't we?

GAIL [*slowly*]. Yes.

NICHOLAS. This isn't just love at first sight. Don't

think that. Please don't think that. It's much more important. Much more enchanting. [*Suddenly*] Why are you smiling?

GAIL [*amused*]. I was just thinking. This moment has its funny points. It really has. I came here to exchange my engagement ring, and you—you came in here to buy one.

NICHOLAS [*laughing*]. Yes.   [*Pause.*

GAIL [*seriously*]. And have you, even once, thought of Beatrice?

NICHOLAS [*vehemently*]. Damn Beatrice!

GAIL. I'm sure that's a little unfair.

NICHOLAS. Yes. I'm sorry.   [*Tiny pause.*

GAIL. What's going to happen?

NICHOLAS. I don't know. [*After tiny pause.*] You said your—your fiancé was in America?

GAIL. Yes.

NICHOLAS. And mine's in Scotland.

GAIL. Yes.

NICHOLAS. I can't quite make up my mind whether that's an advantage or a disadvantage.

GAIL. I'm not sure either.

NICHOLAS. We could write.

GAIL. Yes. [*Slight pause.*] Yes, but we're not going to.

NICHOLAS. Why not?

GAIL. Have you forgotten what you said just now? About us? About this moment? You said: "It won't last. It can't last."

NICHOLAS [*fiercely*]. That's ridiculous. I didn't mean it. It slipped out. It's got to last, Gail! It's got to last!

GAIL. Yes, but it won't. [*Slowly and rather puzzled*] I've never felt like this in my life before, and—I can't understand it. I know the situation's impossible, fantastic, and—and ludicrous. I know that judged from certain standards it's even degrading. But this second nothing seems real beyond the fact that—I love you.

Beyond the fact that I want you always to remember and believe—I love you.

NICHOLAS. Thank you, my dear. [*Pause.*] Gail . . .

GAIL. Yes?

NICHOLAS. I have a small place in Sussex. I was going down there for the week-end. Perhaps if you came we might, together, find a solution of our problem.

GAIL. It's no good us trying to find a solution; because we haven't got a problem. This isn't a problem, my dear—and you know it isn't. It's just a moment. A complete moment of strange enchantment that belongs to both of us. There's nothing certain or real about it, beyond the fact that—it won't last. [*After pause. Softly*] In a very short while you'll be thinking of Scotland and Beatrice again, and I shall be thinking of Brian and New York.

NICHOLAS. No. You know that's not true!

GAIL. And you know, only too well, that it is.

[*Pause.*

NICHOLAS. Well?

GAIL [*softly*]. I'm going. [*She turns towards the door.*

NICHOLAS. Going!

GAIL. Yes. I've no wish to be here when this moment fades—when the enchantment vanishes.

NICHOLAS [*suddenly crossing towards her*]. Gail, please! Listen! Listen before you——

GAIL. No, don't follow me—please don't. Please don't! [*Gently*] Just hold your breath, dearest heart, and count sixteen. [*GAIL goes out.*

[*NICHOLAS goes rather hesitatingly towards the door. He stops.*

[*After a long pause* HOBSON *returns from the private office.*

HOBSON [*apologetically*]. Really, I'm terribly sorry to . . . [*He notices that* GAIL *is no longer present.*] Oh! The lady's gone, sir!

NICHOLAS [*very softly*]. Yes.

N

HOBSON. I thought she wanted to exchange her engagement ring?

[*Slight pause.*

[NICHOLAS *returns to the counter.*

NICHOLAS [*quietly*]. She did. But she changed her mind, instead.

HOBSON [*puzzled*]. Oh. Oh, I see. [*After tiny pause*] Did the young lady say whether she was coming back or not, sir?

NICHOLAS. No. But I'm desperately afraid that she isn't, Mr Hobson.

HOBSON. Oh. [*Pause.*

NICHOLAS. I've decided not to wait for Mr Stanford, I'll——

HOBSON. I'm very sorry, sir. Mr Stanford said he would definitely be back by eleven-thirty.

NICHOLAS. That's all right. As a matter of fact, I've already reached a decision about the ring. [*Taking a ring from one of the glass trays*] I'll take this one.

HOBSON. Thank you, sir. [*Surprised*] Oh! But sir . . .

NICHOLAS [*quietly*]. What's the matter?

HOBSON [*amused*]. Well—this is the first ring I showed you.

NICHOLAS. Yes. Yes, I know.

HOBSON [*bewildered*]. But—but it's only thirty-six guineas, sir!

NICHOLAS [*with a sigh*]. It will do, Mr Hobson. It will do. [*He extracts his wallet.*

THE CURTAIN FALLS

THE CREEL OF TROUT

by

NEIL GRANT

CHARACTERS

THE HON. LORD FINDHORN (*a Scottish judge*)
WILLIAM BRODIE OF ALTON (*a Scottish laird*)
JEAN LOMOND (*a peasant woman*)
COLONEL LIONEL ALLARDYCE
(*County Chief Constable*)

Copyright 1948 by Neil Grant

THE CREEL OF TROUT

The scene of the play is the hall of a small shooting and fishing box, the property of Lord Findhorn, in a lonely valley in the West Highlands. It is sparsely furnished. The atmosphere is one of loneliness bordering on the eerie. There are two doors, one, C., leading direct to the outside and another, L., leading to another room used by the owner as a study. Telephone R. Sideboard on R. with decanter and two glasses.

LORD FINDHORN is seated L. by table in C. He wears a dinner jacket. He is an elderly man, obviously a lawyer, with keen but kindly face. At the other side of the table, not a very large one, is his guest, WILLIAM BRODIE, who can wear either dinner jacket or Highland evening dress. He is a younger man than FINDHORN and belongs to the same class, upper middle, as his host.

As the curtain rises there is the moan of a dying wind.

JUDGE. The wind is dying down.

BRODIE [*rises and goes to window R., peering through curtains*]. Yes. But it doesn't look too good.

JUDGE. No. It seldom does in these parts.

BRODIE [*putting back curtains, slightly shivers*]. No.

JUDGE [*smiles as BRODIE returns to his chair*]. Too eerie for you.

BRODIE [*half apologizing*]. No, no. But we aren't exactly in the Riviera, are we?

JUDGE [*laughs*]. No, indeed. At night this place becomes very isolated despite [*waving his hand*] electric light, telephone, wireless, and so on. I am very seldom honoured by the presence of ladies, and my Edinburgh maids politely refused to come. But I have a special line to my chauffeur down the Glen.

BRODIE. I like the place.

JUDGE [*still smiling*]. Sure?

BRODIE. Honestly.

JUDGE. It isn't everybody's cup of tea, but it is a change from town, and I find I can muse away the days very pleasantly.

BRODIE. And the nights?

JUDGE. On some nights, I confess, I become a fearsome kid again and I hear strange sounds in the Glen.

BRODIE. Many legends?

JUDGE. As plentiful as dandelions on your Selkirk fields. Would you like to hear some of them?

BRODIE. No, thank you very much. [*Both laugh.*] To-morrow, if you like, when I am grown up and sensible. To-night, Judge, I'm a fearsome kid.

JUDGE. Well, I'm seasoned, but I admit that to-night I'm jumpy. It's maybe that very peculiar wind we've had all day, or maybe it's indigestion, or [*more seriously*] the presages of age which are beginning to tease me.

BRODIE. But I take it, Judge, you rather like loneliness.

JUDGE. Good thing for me I do. Any judge is a solitary sort of fellow. You have no idea how lonely a judge feels on the Bench—much more lonely than the lad in the dock opposite him. And, then, I am a bachelor.

BRODIE [*meditatively*]. Yes, bachelors can have quiet.
[*He sighs.*

JUDGE [*smiles*]. Sure you haven't had enough of it? Would you prefer to clear out to-morrow?

BRODIE [*emphatically*]. No, no.

JUDGE [*rises*]. What about a glass of port?

BRODIE. Thank you, Judge.

JUDGE. Nineteen hundred. [*Takes wine from sideboard.*] A good year, and I haven't had a bad bottle in this lot yet. [*He pours out two glasses on* C. *table.*] I have always found old wine a good cure for raw nerves.
[JUDGE *sits down and they toast each other.*

BRODIE. Good luck, Judge. [*As* BRODIE *is about to raise his glass again the centre door is silently opened. There enters very quietly* JEAN LOMOND. *She is a middle-aged woman of peasant appearance. She is dark, stately, stern, with an air of distinction. She wears a kerchief round her head. She shuts door quietly and stands motionless for a second.* BRODIE *has raised his glass to his lips.* JUDGE *doing same when* BRODIE *sees* JEAN. *He jumps.*] Good God !

[*He rises and stares at woman.*

JUDGE. Eh? [*He looks round and also rises, both of them putting down their glasses. She stands* C. *behind the table, motionless.* JUDGE *addresses her.*] Who are you?

JEAN [*reverentially curtseys*]. Lomond, Mistress Jean Lomond is my name, my lord.

[*She speaks slowly and with dignity.*

JUDGE [*gravely*]. How did you get in here?

JEAN. I just came by the door.

JUDGE. Without knocking?

JEAN. Without knocking, my lord.

JUDGE. Unusual behaviour, isn't it?

JEAN [*without budging*]. Unusual it is, my lord. [*A pause.*] You remember me maybe, my lord?

JUDGE. I do.

BRODIE. I remember you, too.

JUDGE. You are the mother of Hector Lomond and you gave evidence at his trial.

JEAN. I am his mother and I gave evidence at his trial.

BRODIE. Where is your son?

JEAN. He left for Canada yesterday, sir.

JUDGE. How did you get here?

JEAN. I walked.

JUDGE. All the way from the Bay?

JEAN. Yes.

JUDGE. You must be tired. Please sit down.

JEAN. Thank you, my lord, I'd just as soon stand.

JUDGE. No, no. [*And he places his chair for her. She sits down with dignity.* JUDGE *stands* R. *facing her*, BRODIE L.] Why have you come here?

JEAN. To thank you, my lord.

JUDGE. For what?

JEAN. For freeing my son from the gallows.

JUDGE. I didn't free him. The jury found him not guilty. And therefore I had no alternative but to set him at liberty.

JEAN. It was you, my lord. As soon as you entered the Court and sat down on your seat of justice, you looked at Hector and I said to myself, "My son is safe."

JUDGE. Mrs Lomond, I ought to point out to you that I make it an inflexible rule never to discuss any cases, particularly criminal cases and above all a trial for murder, with any interested parties. It would be most improper. Allow me, however, to say this. My summing up in the trial of your son was based entirely on the evidence submitted. I had, needless to say, no prejudice one way or the other. He was found not guilty by the jury. I accepted the verdict and discharged him.

JEAN [*quietly*]. You saved my son.

JUDGE [*patiently*]. Very well. And you came all this long way and on such a night to tell me this.

JEAN. Yes. And I am bringing you, my lord, for you and your friend, a creel of sea-trout.

JUDGE [*hurriedly*]. I couldn't possibly accept it.

JEAN. They're not easy to get now, and I caught them myself.

JUDGE. It's very kind of you but——

JEAN [*interrupting*]. I caught them myself.

BRODIE. In the Bay?

JEAN. Yes, sir.

BRODIE. Alone?

JEAN. Alone.

BRODIE. A bit risky this weather.

JEAN. I can manage any boat, sir. I learned it from my husband, and he learned it from his father, and my son learned it from me.

[BRODIE *looks at* JUDGE *as much as to say " Take the poor woman's gift."*

JUDGE. Mrs Lomond, you must be tired. Let me get you some refreshment.

JEAN. No, thank you, my lord. I need neither food nor drink. And I will soon be going.

JUDGE. I'll get my car to take you home.

JEAN. I need no car to take me to my home. I came alone—I go back alone. [*A pause, and then to* JUDGE] My son was worth saving.

JUDGE. I'm afraid I cannot listen to what you are about to say.

JEAN. Yes, my lord, you will listen, you and your friend. [*Something in her tone surprises the two men. They almost seem under a spell. They sit down.*] He was a good son. He would have been a good husband to the right woman. But that woman wasn't right.

[*And she turns fiercely to* BRODIE.

BRODIE. I should say she was a most undesirable baggage.

JEAN. She was out to ruin men, my son Hector and any other lads who came her way. I shouldn't have minded if it was just her wiles. But it went deeper than that. She planned day and night to do evil, she rejoiced in evil. She was ready to see men lose their reason and their lives for her sake, even at the risk of her own life. [*Quietly*] It is good she is dead.

BRODIE. Do you suggest, Mrs Lomond, that this woman plotted to incite your son to violence?

JEAN. Yes, sir. She wanted to see men killing. Killing one another, killing even herself.

JUDGE. And she was killed.

JEAN. She was.

BRODIE. But not by your son?

JEAN. Not by my son.

JUDGE. Why do you wish to go back on this painful story?

JEAN. Because it haunts me, and it haunts you—and [*to* BRODIE] you, sir, and everybody in this place. She plotted to set Hector on the airman and the airman on Hector. She let my son guess she was to meet the airman that night. She hoped for blood. She dressed for the occasion. She flaunted her finery to drive one or the other to bloodshed. Off she went and up on the hillside. She took out her falderals, her paint and her powder, and she beautified herself and looked round on the hills and the loch and the bonnie trees in the wood, and said, "There's none of you so bonnie as me. That's what men think. Aye, and there's none of you so powerful as me. I can do with men what I like." And she lookit round in her pride and went down the hill.

JUDGE. To meet the airman.

BRODIE. To meet her doom.

JUDGE. Down the path called the Path of the Red Deer?

JEAN. So, my lord.

JUDGE [*approaches her*]. Mrs Lomond, I am going to take you home in my car. I shall take no refusal. And I am going to ask you to rest in that room there [*he points* L.], where we shall bring you some food. Please.

JEAN [*rises*]. Did you say rest, my lord? How can I rest? I have lost my son. There's more than the sea that divides us. He still loves that woman. But I thank you [*she curtseys*], my lord, for saving his life.

JUDGE [*goes* L. *and opens door*]. Allow me.
[*He goes out, switches on light off. He returns, holding door.*

JEAN. As you will. I hope you will forgive me for disturbing you, but I had to thank you. [*Fiercely*] I was made to thank you.

JUDGE. I did my duty.

JEAN. Aye, but with mercy and consideration for the broken-hearted. I had to thank you. [*Solemnly*] It was willed I should. [*At the door she hesitates; then pitifully*] My lord?

JUDGE. Something else on your mind?

JEAN. They will leave my son alone?

JUDGE. They?

JEAN. The law.

JUDGE. The law has found him innocent.

JEAN. But supposing the law was to change its mind?

JUDGE. The case is finished.

JEAN. Are you sure of that?

JUDGE. Of course I am.

JEAN. The law said: "You are guilty." It might say the same again.

JUDGE [*gently*]. The law said: "You are under suspicion of the crime of murder. You will be tried in our Court of impartial justice." And we have found him not guilty. [*Emphatically*] And there's an end of it.

JEAN [*rubbing her hands in mental anguish*]. If I was only sure.

JUDGE. You can take my word for it.

JEAN. Yes, my lord. You liked my son. Thank you, my lord. God bless you, my lord.

> [*She curtseys to both men and goes out.* JUDGE, *after closing* L. *door, goes* R.

BRODIE [*resumes seat*]. Poor woman.

JUDGE [*briefly*]. Yes. Very respected family, the Lomonds. Been here for generations.

BRODIE. Not surprising she disapproved of the lady who met such an untimely end.

JUDGE [*after some moments of careful silent deliberation*]. Did you notice a curious admission she made?

BRODIE. No.

JUDGE. About the path up the hill.

BRODIE. Ah. No. But now I see it, I think. You don't miss much, Judge.

JUDGE. I am a lawyer. [*He takes step or two and then goes nearer* BRODIE.] The last person who saw Nellie

Salter alive was the crofter at Dykes Farm. About a hundred yards farther on the road divided at a spot invisible from the farm. One path goes by the side of an arm of the loch, the other, the Path of the Red Deer, goes up the hill and rejoins the loch path about a mile farther west. Nobody knew, and certainly no evidence was given to the Court, to show whether Nellie Salter took the low road or the high road. Her body was found two hundred yards from the west junction of the two paths.

BRODIE. The police, I suppose, made careful inquiries?

JUDGE. Most painstaking.

BRODIE. But nobody could tell?

JUDGE. No.

BRODIE [*after a pause*]. But Mrs Lomond knew.

JUDGE. Apparently.

BRODIE. She didn't say so, however, in Court?

JUDGE. In her evidence she denied all knowledge of Nellie's movements on the day of the crime.

BRODIE. But apparently she was there?

JUDGE. Looks like it.

BRODIE. Now what did she exactly say just now about the path?

JUDGE. I took a mental note of it. Something like this. "Off she went"—that is to say, Nellie Salter— [*emphatically*] "and up on the hillside."

BRODIE. These are the vital words.

JUDGE. Yes. "And up on the hillside she took out her falderals."

BRODIE. "And her paint and her powder."

JUDGE. And then she said something to the effect that the woman beautified herself and looked round on the hills and the loch.

BRODIE. "And the bonnie trees in the wood."

JUDGE [*repeating*]. "And the bonnie trees in the wood."

BRODIE. And then words to the effect that she was bonnier. . . .

JUDGE. And more powerful. . . .

BRODIE. Than the nature around her.

JUDGE. Yes, and I memorized carefully the final words. "I can do with men what I like. And she lookit round in her pride and went down the hillside."

BRODIE. You deduce she was there?

JUDGE. It's a fair deduction.

BRODIE [*rising and moving* L. *and going near the door to be sure they are not overheard*]. . . . And was tracking Nellie?

JUDGE. Possibly.

BRODIE. Her son might have told her, supposing he was the guilty party.

JUDGE. About what the acts and gestures of this woman revealed of her thoughts? No. Her son was a decent, unimaginative sort of chap. No. What Mrs Lomond guessed was in that woman's thoughts came as the result of direct visual observation by another woman.

BRODIE. She might have even heard Nellie mutter something.

JUDGE. Quite possibly.

BRODIE [*looks at door* L. *again, then going up to* JUDGE]. Mrs Lomond murdered Nellie Salter.

JUDGE. That's your conclusion?

BRODIE [*after another look at the door*]. Isn't it yours, Judge?

JUDGE. How can you ask?

BRODIE. Sorry. [*He goes* L. *again and turns to* JUDGE.] Didn't the police suspect her?

JUDGE. Of course. But she had the perfect alibi. The desert. [*He points to window.*] The sands are virtually a desert. Treacherous. Nobody goes near them as a rule. Mrs Lomond says she was there all day and well towards dusk. Who could contradict her?

BRODIE. Why did she tell us all this?

JUDGE. It may have slipped out.

BRODIE. I don't think so. Conscience, maybe, or . . .

JUDGE [*sharply*]. Or what?

BRODIE [*half ashamed*]. I don't know.

[*And he sits down again.*

JUDGE [*goes extreme* R., *then sitting down at table, addresses* BRODIE]. What made me see that woman? I broke the rule of a lifetime, the rule which every sensible judge must follow. I ought to have stopped her as soon as she got on the subject of the murder.

BRODIE. You did stop her.

JUDGE [*excitedly for him*]. Yes, but she forced me to listen.

BRODIE. She forced me.

JUDGE. Yes, but how? Why? [BRODIE *shrugs his shoulders.*] Here to-night this woman made an admission which would give the police a *prima facie* case for questioning her and perhaps detaining her. What am I to do?

BRODIE. Dilemma, isn't it. [*Rising restlessly*] How did this woman get in?

JUDGE [*rising*]. We bolted the door, didn't we? Let's see. [*He is making for the* C. *door, when there is a loud knock.*] Now who can that be? [*He goes out* C.

JUDGE [*off*]. Hullo! [*Alone* BRODIE *looks anxiously at* L. *door. He is about to open door, when he changes his mind and turns to* C. *door as noise of voices can be heard.* JUDGE *returns and brings with him* COLONEL ALLARDYCE, *Chief Constable of district, who can be or not be in uniform.* COLONEL *is soldierly type, about* 45, *and has shrewd, alert, and very matter-of-fact manner.*] You know Brodie—Colonel Allardyce, our Chief Constable.

COLONEL. Of course. [*Shaking hands*] Good evening. Heard you were in these parts.

BRODIE. Yes, been spending a few days with the Judge fishing, or trying to fish.

COLONEL. Nothing doing this weather. Hope there'll soon be a break.

JUDGE. Have a glass of port, Colonel?

COLONEL. Thanks very much, Judge.

JUDGE. Sit down.

[COLONEL *sits* C. *by table, while* JUDGE *pours out glass.* BRODIE, *taking his glass from table, sits* L. JUDGE *stands* R. *They all take a sip, saluting one another.*

COLONEL. Lord Findhorn, you maintain the two great traditions of the Scottish Bench—sound law, sound wine. [JUDGE *bows.*

BRODIE. Two grand things in an unsound world.

COLONEL. I was up the Glen on some poaching business and I thought I'd look in to give you a bit of news.

JUDGE. Delighted to see you.

COLONEL. You remember the Lomond murder case?

JUDGE [*with a brief look at Brodie, who is listening most intently*]. I shall never forget it.

COLONEL [*toying with his glass*]. Yes, an interesting case, though a disappointing one for us. [*Quietly*] Mrs Lomond's body was washed up on the beach early this afternoon.

JUDGE [*amazed*]. Mrs Lomond?

COLONEL. Yes.

BRODIE. The mother of the lad Hector?

[COLONEL *nods. Both men look involuntarily at door* L.

JUDGE. Who told you?

COLONEL. Ordinary police routine. Inspector Soutar telephoned me just before I was leaving for the Glen.

JUDGE. A mistake.

COLONEL. No. Inspector Soutar knew Mrs Lomond well and he himself identified the body.

JUDGE [*quietly*]. Colonel Allardyce, Mrs Lomond is in that room now.

COLONEL [*amazed*]. In that room? [*He turns to door.*

JUDGE [*to* BRODIE]. Will you ask her to come in?

[BRODIE *goes out* L.

COLONEL. I've never known Soutar go wrong before. Are you sure?

BRODIE [*off*]. Mrs Lomond. Mrs Lomond.

JUDGE. Of course I'm sure.

COLONEL [*who has turned* L. *and is listening*]. She isn't there now.

BRODIE [*perturbed, re-enters*]. She's not in the room.

[*Without a word the* JUDGE *crosses and goes out* L. BRODIE *slowly goes* R.

COLONEL. You must have been dreaming, Brodie.

BRODIE. Dreaming?

[*He faces* COLONEL. *Then he looks* L.

JUDGE [*off*]. Mrs Lomond. Mrs Lomond. [COLONEL *smiles discreetly.* JUDGE *slowly re-enters. He looks at the two men.*] She has gone. [*He slowly opens* C. *door, calls.*] Mrs Lomond. [*He returns and heavily sits* L.

COLONEL [*cheerily*]. Let me pass you your glass.

JUDGE. By and by, thank you, Colonel. [*Pause.*] Mistaken identity.

COLONEL. No, sir. Besides the Inspector the body was identified by fishermen, including Mrs Lomond's cousin.

JUDGE [*wearily*]. She was here just now.

BRODIE. She talked to us about the murder. We asked her to go into that room because——

[*He stops short.*

JUDGE. Because she made a strange and significant admission.

COLONEL. Yes, but she wasn't here to-night.

BRODIE [*wildly*]. We were talking to her just before you came. [*Pulling himself together*] I give you my word.

COLONEL [*rises*]. Did she knock at the front door?

JUDGE. No.

COLONEL. Was the front door bolted?

JUDGE. I cannot remember.

BRODIE [*uneasily*]. I think it was bolted.

COLONEL. How did she get in, supposing the door was bolted?

JUDGE. I can't tell you. But she was here definitely. Brodie can corroborate.

BRODIE. Most certainly.

COLONEL. May I have a look at this inside room?

JUDGE. Certainly.

> [*And he opens it.* COLONEL *goes out.*

BRODIE. There can be no doubt, Judge.

JUDGE [*slightly irritated*]. Of course not. You and I are two sensible, sane men. I'm a matter-of-fact, steady old lawyer, now a judge, and you're a solid, stolid Scottish Laird with five years of war to test your nerves. We're not drunk, we're not two old women. Of course there isn't any doubt.

> [*He comes* C. *and again opens* C. *door, shutting it just as* COLONEL *re-enters shutting* L. *door.*

COLONEL. Nobody there, and the shutters are closed. Perhaps she called here earlier in the week.

JUDGE. No, to-night I tell you.

COLONEL [*sits down and sips glass, then quietly*]. It's impossible she could have been here.

BRODIE. She was here. I swear.

> [COLONEL *again smiles.*

JUDGE [*sits down and pulls his chair closer to* COLONEL]. Colonel Allardyce, do you think I'm drunk?

COLONEL. Of course not.

JUDGE. And what about our friend Brodie?

COLONEL. Clean sheet.

BRODIE. As a matter of fact, we each had a cocktail before dinner and we split a bottle of claret.

JUDGE. And as you can see we have scarcely started on the port.

COLONEL. We can rule out wine.

JUDGE. You have known me for some years, Colonel.

o

Have you ever seen in me any signs of mental instability, queerness, any tendency to dabble in the occult?

COLONEL. We have always looked upon you, Lord Findhorn, as one of our best and sanest judges.

JUDGE. Would you describe me as essentially a normal man, inclined both by legal training and temperament to reject the marvellous, the miraculous, and all that sort of thing?

COLONEL. Certainly.

JUDGE. And what about Brodie?

COLONEL. Well, I haven't known Brodie as long as you, but I should say that his war record speaks for itself.

BRODIE. I have seen enough real horrors without having to invent any.

COLONEL. Quite so. Only perhaps you had a brief nap after dinner.

JUDGE. No. I never do have a nap after a meal.

BRODIE. And I was particularly wide awake to-night.

COLONEL. But sometimes queer fancies assail the mind even when one is wide awake, particularly on a night like this when the wind is in a sort of moaning mood.

BRODIE. But both of us, Colonel?

COLONEL. What precisely did this woman do and say? I gather she came into the room without any warning.

JUDGE [*bringing his chair closer still and speaking firmly and quietly*]. Yes. She told us she had come to thank me for saving her son. Nonsense, of course. It was the law which saved him after a fair trial.

COLONEL. Yes, but I know the poor woman was convinced that it was you and you alone who saved her son from swinging. What else?

BRODIE. As evidence of her gratitude she told us she was bringing the Judge a creel of sea-trout.

COLONEL [*laughs*]. Humph. Mrs Lomond, like all her family, knew all about sea-trout fishing, but I doubt if even she could get any fish this weather.

JUDGE. She seemed afraid her son might be re-arrested. I reassured her on that point.

COLONEL. Yes, that was our information too. Indeed, it was common knowledge. Poor soul. You talked about a strange and significant admission?

JUDGE. Yes. We are, of course, speaking in strictest confidence?

COLONEL. Certainly.

JUDGE. You remember that you were unable to state what road Nellie Salter took after she passed Dykes Farm.

COLONEL. True.

JUDGE. She took the Path of the Red Deer, according to Mrs Lomond.

COLONEL. How did Mrs Lomond know?

JUDGE. That's the point.

BRODIE. She made a statement to us, and after she had gone into that room we compared notes. She told us how Nellie went up the hill, took out her paint and powder, gloried, so to speak, in her beauty and power over men, and then went down the path exultant for fresh triumphs and more mischief.

JUDGE. She then gave us the very words which the girl addressed to the trees and other natural objects round her.

COLONEL. In other words, Mrs Lomond was there on the spot.

BRODIE. Tracking Nellie.

COLONEL [*emphatically*]. She wasn't there.

JUDGE. You don't know.

COLONEL. There is practically no evidence in support. The little there is is to the contrary. [*Speaking with solemnity*] But if she was there and knows the path which Nellie Salter took, then there is only one inference to be drawn.

JUDGE. I have nothing to say about that inference.

COLONEL [*turning to* BRODIE]. That Mrs Lomond
fired the shot which killed Nellie Salter.

> [*The telephone bell rings. All three men start.*
> JUDGE *and* COLONEL *rise.*

JUDGE. Excuse me. [*He goes* R. *and takes up receiver.*
Pause.] Yes. This is my lodge. Colonel Allardyce?
Yes, he's here. A moment. [*To* COLONEL] Your
Inspector Soutar to speak to you.

COLONEL. Thank you. Sorry. [*He goes to receiver.*]
Don't go, gentlemen.

> [BRODIE *crosses to* JUDGE *on* L. COLONEL *takes*
> *up receiver.*

COLONEL. Hullo, Soutar. [*Pause.*] Oh, yes. By the
way, there's no doubt about the identification? The
body was Mrs Lomond's? I see. Yes. [*Startled*]
What? A letter? From Mrs Lomond? Addressed to
me? [*Both men are now listening most intently.*] What did
she say? [*A long pause as he nods his head at the end of each
sentence.*] I see. By the Path of the Red Deer. [*A longer
pause.*] She definitely says so. [*Pause.*] I see. Thanks
very much, Soutar. You were quite right to telephone
me. I shall come straight to the office. Good-bye.
[*He puts down receiver. He turns to them.*] That was
Inspector Soutar. There is no doubt, by the way, that
it was Mrs Lomond's body which was washed up.
[*Pause.*] Last night she sent me a letter which Soutar
has just read to me.

JUDGE. Then she drowned herself.

COLONEL. I think so. In the letter she gives an
account of the last movements of Nellie Salter which
[*he speaks in low voice*] largely agrees with what you two
gentlemen have just told me.

BRODIE. Then it was Mrs Lomond who murdered
Nellie Salter.

COLONEL [*takes step towards them, and solemnly*]. She
definitely says so in the letter. [*There is a pause.*] She

seemed to be afraid that suspicion might still be directed towards her son despite his recent acquittal. It was that fear which drove her to write this confession and then to suicide. [*He moves* L., *thinking hard, then turns to* JUDGE.] You are sure she didn't send any letter to you, Judge?

JUDGE. No.

COLONEL. No communication of any kind at any time?

JUDGE. None, except her visit to-night.

COLONEL. Or to you, Brodie?

BRODIE. No.

COLONEL. Strange.

JUDGE [*solemnly*]. It is strange.

BRODIE [*to* COLONEL]. What we told you, Colonel, has been confirmed by the letter?

COLONEL. Yes. [JUDGE *sits down* C., *a prey to anxious thoughts.* COLONEL *speaks more lightly, as if to disabuse his mind of certain fears.*] This is a queer old place, Lord Findhorn. Always was. That was why nobody would take it.

JUDGE [*with wry smile*]. Except a gowk like me.

COLONEL. This old house is as sensitive as a camera plate. In some way it has stretched out and seized for a second or two something connected with this murder. After all, you, sir, presided at the trial, and you, Brodie, attended every sitting of the Court. You were both therefore in a very receptive mood.

JUDGE. To what?

COLONEL. To a sort of hallucination that Mrs Lomond came in person and told you directly what she had written to me.

JUDGE. It was no hallucination.

BRODIE. She was here in person.

COLONEL. Well, gentlemen, there you are. We needn't argue. I admit it's a queer business. After all, we are in the land of that sort of thing. I wouldn't worry about it if I were you, and if I may make a suggestion to an eminent judge I should be inclined to say nothing about it for some time.

JUDGE [*rising*]. It is certainly a matter which I have no desire to discuss. To be quite frank, it has given me a bit of a shake.

COLONEL. I can understand that. [*Cheerily*] But to-morrow you will see it all in another light. I must be going. [*Briskly*] I shall have to ring up the Lord Advocate's people in Edinburgh, and I must also communicate with the Fiscal. Yes.

JUDGE. What about your port?

COLONEL. By Jove, yes, I mustn't forget that. Sorry to dash off such a vintage, Judge. I ought to sip it in leisurely gratitude. That's the worst of being a Chief Constable. No time even to drink a glass of wine. Well, your good health, gentlemen.

> [*And he drains off the glass.*

BRODIE. Your car near, Colonel?

COLONEL. Yes, I parked it just down the road.

BRODIE. Can I come down with you and light your road?

COLONEL. No, no, thanks. I've got a torch. Well, good-bye, Judge.

JUDGE [*shaking hands*]. Good-bye, Colonel. Very kind of you to look in.

COLONEL. Very glad. It has been a most interesting experience. Wouldn't have missed it for anything. Any such story is in itself most unusual, but coming from two such sane, practical men as you two gentlemen gives it quite a special significance. Good-bye, Brodie. [*Shaking hands*] Care to come fishing with me if the weather clears?

BRODIE. Thank you very much, Colonel, but I'm afraid I shall have to be travelling south to-morrow.

JUDGE [*smiling*]. He's had enough.

COLONEL. What about you, Judge?

JUDGE. Oh, I'll stay on for a bit.

COLONEL [*at door, after picking up his attaché-case*]. Pardon me, is it wise? You are all alone.

JUDGE. I don't mind. [*Trying to speak lightly but failing*] Who knows, Mrs Lomond may pay me another visit?

BRODIE. Or perhaps Nellie Salter?

JUDGE [*seriously*]. No, not Nellie Salter. She and I had nothing to say to each other. But between me and Mrs Lomond there was some peculiar affinity which I cannot explain. I am a Judge of the Court of Session and she was a humble peasant woman, and she committed a terrible crime, and I am a law-abiding fellow, but we had something in common which we mortal men cannot explain. These affinities seem to be independent not only of class and social position, but also of time and space. [*Half laughing*] Tut, here I am talking havers when I ought to be drinking port. Stay and finish the bottle, Colonel.

COLONEL. No, no, I must be off, fain though I'd stay. Ta ta.

BRODIE. Let me show you out.

[*Just at the door there is another moan from wind.*

COLONEL. Damn that wind. It gives one the creeps. Never mind, it's a good road and there's a better supper waiting for me [*and to cheer himself up he whistles*]. [*He flashes his torch, and then he exclaims, almost terrified:*] My God!

JUDGE [*standing with* BRODIE *at door*]. Anybody there?

COLONEL [*shaking*]. No—but under the arch. Look! [*He can scarcely get out the words.*] A creel of sea-trout.

CURTAIN

OPERATION 'COLD CURE'

by

JAMES HESKETH

CHARACTERS

ALFRED WELFARE (*aged about* 55)
MAGGIE WELFARE (*his wife, aged about* 50)
ROSIE (*their daughter, aged* 18)
HAROLD (*their son, aged* 20)
DR ANDERSON
AGGIE PATCHAM (*aged about* 50)
FRED PEABODY (*aged about* 55)

Time: *The present*

Applications regarding amateur performances of this play should be addressed to James Hesketh, c/o George G. Harrap and Co., Ltd, 182 High Holborn, London, W.C.1

OPERATION 'COLD CURE'

The scene is a typical bedroom of an average working-class family, in any part of the country. There is an old-fashioned iron bedstead, a wash-stand with jug and wash-basin, a dressing-table near the window on which stands a mirror. On one side of the bed (nearest the audience), is a small chest or cabinet used as a table, on top of which is an array of medicine bottles, a small clock, and a glass; on the other side of the bed is a chair. There is a door leading from the landing (approximately C. back-stage). The walls of the room are covered with several texts, and the usual cheap pictures. The Welfare family should be easily recognizable as one of the components of "this happy breed."

It is about two o'clock in the afternoon, and there is coming from the mound of blankets and eiderdown on the bed a series of loud snorts which finally end in a paroxysm of coughing, spluttering, and violent blowings of the nose. Then a head appears (that of MR ALFRED WELFARE), *followed by a hand which reaches out for the glass on the cabinet at the side of the bed. It is empty, so without more ado* MR WELFARE *lifts up the walking-stick, which he has beside him on the bed, and commences to bang it violently on the floor—using the handle as a knocker.*

The invalid subsides into more coughing, and presently in rushes MRS WELFARE *to see what her husband wants.*

MRS WELFARE [*obviously anxious about her husband*]. What is it, my dear?

MR WELFARE [*croaking, for he has almost lost his voice, but is nevertheless making the most of it*]. Water! [*Points to empty glass.*] Water!

MRS WELFARE [*going over to the wash-stand and filling the glass from the large earthenware jug standing in the basin*]. The jug's nearly empty. I told Rosie to fill it before she went to work this morning. Forgetful hussy—thinks

I'm a centipede. [*Gives her husband the glass of water and then goes over to the door and shouts downstairs* "Rosie!" *several times till at last* ROSIE *shouts back* "Coming!"] She can fill it now, this very instant, since she isn't going back to work this afternoon. I shan't be popular, because she's curling the ends of her hair ready for Ida's wedding. But I can't help that, and it will serve her right if she's late. [*She tidies up the newspaper and magazines which are on the bed and puts them on the chair.*] And why she wanted to be one of Ida Brown's bridesmaids I don't know—the silly child. I told her she was a little idiot spending her savings on a bridesmaid's dress when your Aunt Ethel would have made up my old organdie dress for her. Isn't as if that Ida is a special friend of hers; if you ask me she's an empty-headed little piece —all pictures and dancing and lipstick. A fat lot she'll care about Rosie when she's married. You mark my words.

> [ROSIE *comes in with her bridesmaid dress over one arm and her hair half done; she has obviously heard her mother's last remark.*

ROSIE [*in a loud voice*]. Stow it, Mum! and don't be such a bloomin' spoil-sport. Ida's never done you no harm.

MRS WELFARE. Don't shout so, Rosie! You know your Dad wants a bit of peace and quiet.

ROSIE [*cheerfully*]. Sorry, Dad! What did you call me for, Mum?

MRS WELFARE. To fill that jug with water. I told you about it at breakfast-time.

ROSIE [*exasperated*]. Do you mean to say you've made me trapes up those stairs to fill that rotten old water-jug when you knew I was curling my hair.

MRS WELFARE. Yes, Rosie, I do. It's high time you began to think a bit about other people now and then; and now your Dad's got to stay in bed I think you might have a little thought for *him*—if not for me.

ROSIE [*protesting and throwing her dress on the bed*]. Why can't Harold do it—he's got ten days' leave?

MR WELFARE. Why should he? I would be ashamed of it, Rosie—never a willing finger will you lift in this house.

ROSIE [*defiantly*]. Why *shouldn't* Harold do it! the lazy hulking brute. Look at him! breakfast in bed and a hot bath every morning—and he's been using my bath-salts—the pansy; and he struts about like a bloomin' Field-Marshal.

MRS WELFARE. Rosie! do stop nattering about Harold.

ROSIE [*over at the mirror, preening herself and touching up her 'curls'*]. That's right! protect your darling little blue-eyed boy. King bloomin' Harold can never do any wrong—never a bloomin' arrow in *his* eye.

MR WELFARE [*croaking*]. Rosie! I won't have you talk to your mother like that. [*Coughs.*

ROSIE [*striding over to her father*]. That's right! you take his side as well. I'm just an outsider here.

MRS WELFARE. Rosie, you know that's not true.

ROSIE. Yes, it is. You know it is. It's Harold *this* and Harold *that*—you make me sick. You're worse than old Aggie Patcham slobbering over her Siamese cat.

MRS WELFARE [*perturbed*]. You have no cause to turn round on your Father and me like this. We've always tried to be fair to both of you—you know we have—and this is all we get.

ROSIE [*sulkily—like a spoilt child*]. Well! it's all your fault.

MRS WELFARE. All my fault! I like that!

ROSIE. So it is—all this fuss just because I forgot to fill that beastly old water-jug.

MRS WELFARE. Yes—like you forget everything else. Where do you think you'd be, my fine young miss, if I spent all my time forgetting everything. If you spent a quarter of the time helping me that you do in front of the mirror titivating yourself we might——

MR WELFARE [*trying to intervene*]. Maggie! Rosie! Stop your bickering! [*but he has another bout of coughing*].

MRS WELFARE [*goes round to bed and hands him the glass of water*]. Now look what you've gone and done—upsetting your Father like this just when he wanted a bit of peace [*goes back for the jug*]. Here! take this jug—and mind you *fill* it this time.

ROSIE [*flouncing out in a rage*]. Wish I was Ida—the lucky little devil.

MRS WELFARE [*taking the glass from her husband and then sitting on bottom of bed*]. Can't think what's come over Rosie lately. There's never any peace with children. The older they get, the worse they seem to get. Here's Rosie eighteen next week and behaving like a spoilt child of three. But there! I suppose we've spoilt her all her life. You can't expect a leopard to change its spots. [*Looks at the clock on the table.*] Good gracious! just look at the time—it's past two o'clock, and Dr Anderson will be here in a jiffy. I'd almost forgotten him. I don't know what he'd have said if he'd come in a few minutes ago. Peace and quiet was what you wanted, he said—peace and quiet [*there is a sound of smashing crockery, and* ROSIE *is heard screaming*]. Sufferin' snakes! Rosie's dropped the water-jug down the stairs. [*Rushes to door.* ROSIE *is still screaming.*] Rosie! ROSIE! for goodness' sake control yourself—the neighbours will think this is a lunatic asylum.

ROSIE [*bursting into the room, her dress drenched with water*]. Aggie's blasted Siamese cat came rushing downstairs and tripped me up. Look at me! Soaked!

MR WELFARE [*sitting up and protesting*]. Rosie! I won't have you use such language.

ROSIE. Well! what do you expect me to do! spew over the mangy creature like Ma Patcham does?

MRS WELFARE. Rosie! There's a way to talk.

ROSIE. That's right—now you start again. Nag! nag! nag! nag! that's all I get. This house gives me the willies.

MRS WELFARE [*heatedly*]. Now look here, Rosie! I've had enough. Either control yourself and be reasonable, or you can pack your case and go and live with that Ida creature. I mean that. I won't put up with your high and mighty ways any longer. Just think of it! here's your poor Father ill, and yet you pick on this very moment to give a vulgar display of your tantrums—and in this room—when you know your Father wants to be quiet. I'd be thoroughly ashamed of myself if I were you. Now go and change your dress and finish your hair, or you'll be late for the wedding.

[ROSIE *realizes she has over-stepped the mark and flounces out.*

MRS WELFARE [*calling after her*]. Rosie! you've forgotten your dress—just like you do everything else. [*She holds up a flimsy net of thing, and adds with disgust.*] Five pounds up the spout! All her savings gone for her week at Butlin's—and when the time comes she'll want a 'sub.' A dish-rag I call it—not worth five shillings, let alone five pounds.

[*And while she is still surveying it at arm's length* ROSIE *returns, looking as black as thunder, and, snatching the dress away, strides out again.*

MRS WELFARE. Ah, well! I suppose we all have to pay for our experience—but if you remember, Alf, that week we had at Blackpool when the children were small only cost five pounds. Just think of it! and cream on the table every day, too!

MR WELFARE. Never mind, Maggie!

MRS WELFARE [*who has been running her finger over the dressing-table*]. Just look at the dust! and I gave this room a thorough 'do' yesterday.

MR WELFARE. Leave it, Maggie! nobody'll notice it.

MRS WELFARE. I can't have Dr Anderson coming up

here thinking we live in a pigsty. Just look at every-where! [*and she begins to straighten the bed by shaking the eiderdown, and in so doing sends a few feathers fluttering to the floor*]. I shall have to run the cleaner over the carpet again—what with these loose feathers and the mess Rosie has made.

MR WELFARE [*sitting up and protesting*]. Not the cleaner, Maggie!

MRS WELFARE. It won't take a moment—if Mrs Patcham has brought it back. [*Goes to door and shouts downstairs.*] Rosie! ROSIE! has the cleaner come back from next door?

[ROSIE *shouts back,* "Yes! I'll bring it up."]

MRS WELFARE [*eyeing the room*]. That looks a bit more civilized. [ROSIE *appears clad in her cami-knickers—and pushes the electric cleaner into the room. It should be an old machine that makes a maximum noise when in operation.*] Thank you, Rosie! Have you finished your hair?

ROSIE [*evidently subdued*]. Yes.

MRS WELFARE. Then don't forget to turn the gas out and put the curling-tongs away. [*Looking at clock*] You'll have to put your best foot forward if you don't want to keep Jim waiting when he comes with the taxi.

ROSIE. I shall have to finish off in my bedroom.

MRS WELFARE [*fixing the flex to the mains-plug*]. All right! I'll come and put the finishing touches on when I've just run the cleaner over the room. [*Switching on the cleaner*] Out of the way!

[*And* ROSIE *goes out. Meanwhile* MRS WELFARE *runs the cleaner over the room with great vigour, using far more energy than the makers had ever intended should be used with a machine they had thought was "labour-saving." The noise is at last too much for poor* ALFRED WELFARE, *who, in sheer desperation, suddenly dives under the bed-clothes.* MRS WELFARE *rushes over, leaving the cleaner on, wondering*

*whatever has happened to her husband, and in
the midst of the upheaval* DR ANDERSON
appears at the bedroom door.

DR ANDERSON [*after surveying the scene with a twinkle in
his eye*]. Good morning!

MRS WELFARE [*startled and embarrassed at being caught in
this predicament, and rushing over to switch the cleaner off*].
Oh! Doctor! I didn't see you!

DR ANDERSON. No need to apologize. Nice to see
somebody else busy. How's the invalid to-day?

MRS WELFARE. He seems a bit better.

DR ANDERSON. Good! Now Alfred, let's have a look
at you!

> [*He goes through the normal routine, testing pulse,
> temperature, throat, chest. During this procedure
> MRS WELFARE has slipped out with the cleaner.*

DR ANDERSON. H'm! that's better—almost a human
being again.

MR WELFARE. Yes! I'm all right now, Doctor.

DR ANDERSON. Still a bit husky. [*Picking up one of the
bottles of medicine*] You needn't take any more of this;
I'll give you a prescription for something to clear your
throat up. [*Writes prescription.*] There we are!

MR WELFARE. Thank you, Doctor. [*Pause.*] When
do you think I can get up?

DR ANDERSON. Get up! What's the hurry, man!
You take it easy for a few more days. It's rest and
quiet you want.

> [MRS WELFARE *comes in again.*

MRS WELFARE. How is he, Doctor?

DR ANDERSON. All right! but you'll have to keep him
in bed for a bit. He's had a nasty turn, you know—only
just missed pneumonia.

MRS WELFARE. That's just what I told Rosie. Do
you hear that, Alf?

DR ANDERSON. You needn't give him any more of
the M and B tablets. Just keep him quiet—that's the

chief thing. [*Picking up his bag and going*] I'll look in again the day after to-morrow. [*At the door and talking to* ALFRED] Don't forget the Grand National. [*He looks at his watch.*] It's almost due to start. I've put my shirt on Dick Barton.

MRS WELFARE [*fussing round the bed, tucking him in*]. I'm surprised at Dr Anderson having anything to do with horse-racing. Well! he knows what I think about it. There! now you can have a nice snooze. Mrs Patcham was saying only this morning that she could do with a few days in bed, like you.

MR WELFARE. She would—the old battle-axe!

MRS WELFARE [*laughing*]. Alfred! there's a way to speak of your neighbour—and then we wonder why Rosie is so rude about her. Now I'll go and put the finishing touches on the young lady, and leave you to have forty winks.

> [*But as she starts to go* ROSIE *bursts in, hair over face, her dress undone at the back, a hair-brush in one hand and her "dinkie" hat and small make-up box in the other. She is in a fine old paddy.*

ROSIE [*in a loud voice as she throws her hat on the bed*]. I can't see to dress myself in that poky old mirror in my bedroom. And the dress was too tight to go over my head, and just look at my hair!

MRS WELFARE. Rosie! there's no need to shout. Remember your Father.

ROSIE. But Mum! Jim's outside with the taxi, and look at me! [*Catching sight of herself in the mirror*] LOOK AT ME! I shall have to stay here and finish.

> [*And she begins to brush her hair vigorously.*

MRS WELFARE. Why you couldn't make shift with your own mirror when you knew I was coming to help you, I don't know.

ROSIE. I can't see myself properly in that awful thing —makes me look like a dead cod-fish.

MRS WELFARE. Rosie! don't be so vulgar.

ROSIE [*still trying to get her hair in position*]. Junk, that's all it is; and it's no good you telling me over and over again that you had to put up with it till *your* mother died and left you this one.

MRS WELFARE. I'm ashamed to hear you go on so about your home.

ROSIE. I'm not going on about home—I'm talking about that beastly old mirror [*and she bangs the hair-brush down on the dressing-table and proceeds to use her lipstick*].

MRS WELFARE. So that's it! getting too proud to live at home are we! I always said that Ida Brown was a stuck-up little bit of goods—coming here riding her high horse and sticking her nose in the air. If you're going to copy that little minx you can hop it, and quick, because I won't have a daughter of mine ashamed of her home. It'll be your Father and me next, like as not.

[*The taxi can be heard hooting for* ROSIE.

ROSIE [*her exasperation has almost reduced her to tears. She is struggling to do her dress up*]. Can't you hear the taxi tooting for me! Why can't you help me do these blasted buttons up instead of nagging. That's all I get, and I'm fed up with the whole lot of you.

MRS WELFARE. *You* fed up! I like that!

MR WELFARE [*sitting up and trying to shout*]. For the love of mike, shut up! Talk about forty winks!

[*More tooting from taxi.*

MRS WELFARE [*firmly*]. Now look here, my fine young miss—any more of your sauce and I'll——

[*But her words are drowned in loud singing—one of the latest songs—coming from the landing, and there is a loud bump on the door as in bursts* CORPORAL HAROLD WELFARE, *her son, aged twenty, home on leave from the Army. He is in battle-dress, and is carrying a portable wireless set which he plants down on the eiderdown.*

HAROLD [*sensing the atmosphere*]. Hullo! hullo! hullo!
what's cooking! Rosie jumped off the deep end again?

ROSIE [*shouting*]. You mind your own business,
Corporal Welfare.

HAROLD. Pipe down, beautiful! No need to scream
like a Hottentot just because darling little Ida's getting
spliced. I can't think why Mum doesn't put you across
her knee and give you the woirks. Do you the world of
good, ducky [*and he picks up her hair-brush and gives her a
smart crack on her seat with the back of it*]. Just an old
Spanish custom!

ROSIE. Ow! [*And she tries to smack his face.*] You
ignorant pig!   [*Taxi is tooting again.*

HAROLD. Ignorant, eh! What do you think *you* are,
running around with a Barbary ape like Ida.

ROSIE. You leave Ida alone! it's bad enough when
Mum starts. There's one thing—she wouldn't have
married you if you were the last man on earth.

HAROLD. Listen, sister! I'd rather spend a night in
the Chamber of Horrors than five minutes with that
little nit-wit.

MRS WELFARE [*intervening*]. Come here, Rosie! [*She
clutches hold of her, turns her smartly round, and starts to do
up the offending buttons on the dress.*] Harold! take that
wireless off my eiderdown! Whatever next! This
dress isn't big enough for you—little wonder you
couldn't get it over your head. [*Eyeing her up and down*]
Skimpy thing! fancy wasting all your money on it—
and it doesn't seem decent to go out in such a flimsy
thing.

HAROLD [*who has lifted the wireless off the eiderdown and
pauses to eye his sister*]. Positively diaphanous!

ROSIE. Nobody asked for your opinion.

HAROLD. Well! you've got it, Rose-bud, free, gratis,
and for nothing. Where shall I put the set?

MRS WELFARE [*trying to make the best of ROSIE's dress*].
Oh! anywhere—on the floor. I can't think what you

wanted to bring it up here for—you know your Father
wants a bit of peace.

> [*The taxi redoubles its tootings.* HAROLD *puts the*
> *set on the floor, and starts to clear* ROSIE'S
> *brush, lip-stick, and powder off the dressing-*
> *table with a view to putting the set there.*

ROSIE. Hi! keep your dirty hands off those!

> [*Makes a dart for him, but is restrained by her*
> *Mother.*

MRS WELFARE. Rosie! stand still!

> [*There is more violent tooting from the taxi, and*
> *a voice is heard shouting up the stairs*
> "Rosie."

HAROLD [*dipping* ROSIE'S *powder-pad in her compact and*
dabbing it on her nose]. There you are, Sunshine! one
for the road.

MRS WELFARE. Harold! stop it!

> [*And she wipes* ROSIE'S *face with her handkerchief.*
> [HAROLD *dumps the things in the wash-basin and*
> *lifts up the set on to the place he has cleared.*
> *His eye then lights on the hat* ROSIE *has thrown*
> *on the bed: it is one of those "dinkies"*
> *covered with forget-me-nots, with a series of*
> *tiny woollen knobs hanging round it, so that*
> *they shake like bells.* HAROLD *picks it up,*
> *surveys it at arm's length, and shouts in*
> *derision,* "Attaboy!"
>
> ROSIE *makes a violent attempt to get away from her*
> *mother, who is still busy with a safety-pin*
> *because* ROSIE'S *petticoat will persist in*
> *hanging below her dress.*
>
> HAROLD, *however, rushes round to the other side*
> *of the bed and grabs the walking-stick his*
> *father has been using, and putting* ROSIE'S *hat*
> *on his head at a rakish angle, and pretending*
> *the walking-stick is a guitar, he starts croon-*
> *ing,* "I ain't nobody's darling."

ROSIE *screams and tries to pull it off his head, calling him "a pig" and "a beastly cad," and* MRS WELFARE *in her turn shouts at* ROSIE, *and pulls her away from* HAROLD, *while the voice outside has now apparently reached the top of the stairs and is shouting for* ROSIE *to "buck up"; and the taxi is now keeping up an incessant tooting. In fact, it is bedlam, and poor* MR WELFARE *has once again dived down in the bed.*

At last MRS WELFARE, *hands over her ears, shouts* "Stop it, you children!" *and this has the effect of silencing them. There is a moment's pause and then* ROSIE *makes a sudden dive for her hat, calling* HAROLD *"a beastly rotter," and, clapping it on her head, she rushes out of the room.*

HAROLD [*as she goes*]. So long—Salome!

[ROSIE *bangs the door in answer.*

MRS WELFARE [*sinking down on the bottom of the bed*]. Why did I ever have any children?

HAROLD. Cheer up, Maggie! All in a day's march! Do you know what's the matter with Rosie? Our psychology wallah would say the self-assertive part of her innate or instinctive pattern of behaviour is predominant—or, what you poor ignorant civilians would say: she's getting too big for her shoes. She'll be all right when she realizes nobody will ever want to go to 'the pictures' to see *her*. [*Suddenly remembering his father*] How's the big white chief? [*Goes over to bed, and, after looking round, lifts up the bed-clothes.*] Come on out of your wigwam, Governor—'All Clear's' gone.

MRS WELFARE. Harold! I won't have you bring your Army ways home here; "big white chief" indeed! and it wasn't very nice to call Rosie "Salome."

HAROLD. Why not? dressed in a blinkin' veil wasn't she! Come off it, Mum! you're as bad as she is.

MRS WELFARE. Well! a line's got to be drawn some-where, and you make her a thousand times worse than she would be. I do wish you wouldn't tease her.

HAROLD [*fiddling with the radio*]. That's just what she wants—a bit of chivvying around. You spoil her—you know you do—waiting on her hand and foot, and then expecting her to jump to it. The trouble is she now expects life to be one long hay-ride. What she wants is a bit of the jolly old Army life to knock the nonsense out of her.

MRS WELFARE. Well! it doesn't seem to have knocked much of it out of you. [*A sudden loud noise comes from set.*] Harold! for goodness' sake don't make that noise.

[*She is tidying-up again after ROSIE.*

HAROLD [*still trying to tune-in*]. Old dooh-dah down the road said he'd mended it.

MR WELFARE. How much did he charge you, Harold?

HAROLD. Five bob, and all he seems to have done is blow in it.

MR WELFARE [*anxiously*]. Won't it go?

[*There is another howl of distortion from the set.*

HAROLD. Got the colly-wobbles if you ask me.

MRS WELFARE. Take it downstairs, Harold, there's a duck. You can't make that awful noise here, upsetting your Father just when he wants a bit of peace.

HAROLD. Half a sec'—you know Dad likes a nice cinema organ. Just the thing to soothe him, and there's one on right now. [*After more desperate twiddling he finally tunes in to the organ.*] Here we are!

[*It is a popular, sentimental ballad, and he tunes it in till it is 'blasting.'*

MRS WELFARE. Harold! What are you doing! You'll blast the roof off. Turn it down!

[*He does so till it is, at least, bearable.*

HAROLD. There we are [*pretending he is playing a cinema organ*], Soft Lights and Sweet Music. Now we can leave the Guvnor to sink into oblivion. He can close his peepers and think he's in the one-and-ninepennies at the Regal. [*In a loud, raucous voice with the type of American accent usually associated with travel films*] "And so we say farewell to the surging rollers of the Pacific and leave the sun to sink, a burning, bloody ball, into the mighty ocean."

MRS WELFARE [*shocked*]. Harold!

HAROLD. Come on, Maggie! get down them stairs and put the jolly old kettle on for a nice cup of tea.

MRS WELFARE [*sighing*]. Peace at last!

> [*But there comes a tap on the door.*
> [*The door opens slowly and a voice says,* "It's only me, dearie." *It is* MRS PATCHAM, MRS WELFARE'S *next-door neighbour. She is a real old trollop.*

HAROLD. For crying out loud! Aggie!

MRS PATCHAM. 'Ope I ain't intrudin', dearie, but I thought as 'ow I'd jist pop in an' see 'ow Alf was a'gettin' on, seein' as I saw Dr Anderson 'ad just bin in, and as Rosie 'ad left the front door open, I said to meself, "I'll just pop in an' see 'ow Alf's gettin' on." My! didn't your Rosie look a bit of orl right in 'er dress. Fair took my breath away she did. I said to meself, "She'll be a bride 'erself afore long, 'er in that bit o' gauze." Mark my words, dearie! fine feathers like that don't go about long afore they dazzle somebody's eyes. You'll be 'avin' one o' them gents riding up 'ere one of these fine days in 'is *limesoon*, like as not—then she'll be Lady Rose summat or other. [*The wireless is still on.*

HAROLD. She's Lady Rosie all right, now.

> [HAROLD *turns the wireless off.*

MRS WELFARE. There's no need to run Rosie down in front of Mrs Patcham. I think you'd better go down and put the kettle on. [*He goes out.*

HAROLD. O.K., Mum!

MRS PATCHAM [*over at the bedside*]. An' 'ow's Alf? After all, that's what I come for.

MR WELFARE. Better to-day, Mrs Patcham, thank you.   [*Coughs.*

MRS PATCHAM. I think you look a better colour, dearie, to-day. [*Coming round to* MR WELFARE] I didn't like the look of 'im the other day, did you, Mrs Welfare? 'E 'ad that 'orrible grey look about 'im just like my poor Ernie 'ad 'afore 'e was took. Dreadful 'e was— nearly coughed 'is lungs up, 'e did, and when I 'eard your Alf coughing in the night I said to meself, "That's just like my poor Ernie." 'Ack! 'ack! 'ack! night after night 'e did—just like your Alf did the other night. I said to meself, "If they ain't careful, poor old Alf'll be slipping through their fingers, just like water. 'E's 'ad 'is tickct like as not," I said to meself. But 'e do look better an' no mistake. But you must be careful 'e don't 'ave a relapse. That's what did my poor Ernie in. Went out one day in May without one of his west-kits on.

MR WELFARE [*who has had more of her tongue than he can bear*]. I'm all right, Mrs Patcham—worth twenty dead 'uns. All I want is a bit of peace.

MRS PATCHAM [*who can never take a hint*]. Ah! nothing like a bit o' peace. I allus used to tell my Ernie if only 'c 'ad rested isself 'e would 'ave lasted to be a 'undred. But 'e was allus on the go. Like an ear-wig 'e werc. Still! we must count our blessings—I've got my Siamese cat.

MRS WELFARE [*coming to the rescue*]. Would you like a cup of tea, Mrs Patcham?

MRS PATCHAM [*sitting on bed*]. No dearie, thank you, it binds me dinner up into a ball—like a 'ot ball o' lead it is across my chest—if I 'ave tea after my dinner. An' the pain's something awful. I daresn't 'ardly breathe —like a dagger it is—stuck right through me gizzard. But at breakfast-time I can jist go on swillin' tea and it don't 'urt me nowise. My poor ole Ernie used to say to me, "Aggie, my old cough-drop"—'e allus called me 'is cough-drop—"Aggie," 'e used to say, "if you go on drinkin' tea like wot you do at breakfast you'll drown yourself." 'E liked 'is joke did my poor Ernie. [*Rises.*] Well! I must pop along. I want to 'ear the Grand National on the wireless. Takes yer mind off things, don't it! I've got my little bit on Saucy Sal. I see the picture of 'er jockey—ever such a nice-looking boy 'e is. But there! you don't 'old with 'orse-racing, do you, dearie!

    [HAROLD *rushes in,* "Kettle's boiling, Mum!"

MRS PATCHAM [*continuing*]. It's nice to 'ave 'Arold 'ome on leave, I'm sure. 'Im an' Rosie must be such a comfort to you. [*As she goes out—to* ALF] Good-bye, dearie—'ave a nice snooze.

HAROLD. Good old Aggie! the little ray of sunshine! Wonder she didn't bring a bunch of lilies and a harp.

MRS WELFARE. She means well—the poor old soul.

HAROLD [*turns on wireless again*]. "Poor old soul" my foot! The old haggis! She wants our sergeant-major round her—he'd pull her silly tongue out of her head by its roots and strangle her with it.

MRS WELFARE. Harold! you're worse than Aggie! Now perhaps we can have this cup of tea and leave your Father in peace.

HAROLD. Do you want a cup of tea, Guvnor?

MR WELFARE. No, Harold, thanks—just forty winks.

HAROLD. O.K. [*In a barrack-square voice*] Fall in, Mrs Welfare! Eyes right! Eyes front! Right turn! Quick march!

    [MRS WELFARE *hasn't, of course, obeyed these commands, but has stood watching* HAROLD *with a growing sense of pride. Presently she breaks out into laughter and they leave the room arm-in-arm.*

HAROLD [*as he closes the door*]. Fine soldier you'd make! You'd be up before the colonel for insubordination.

[MR WELFARE *is, at last, left in peace, except for the wireless. It looks as if he will get his forty winks, but presently he sits upright, peers round, and then dives down the bed and brings out a newspaper, which he quickly opens at the racing page and begins a thorough scrutiny of it. While he is engrossed the bedroom door opens very slowly, and a furtive little figure slips in and closes the door very quickly, but with great care lest he should make a noise. He is a lively man of about fifty-five, with a ragged moustache, and is wearing a long, faded overcoat and rather dingy collar and faded tie, and a very green bowler; yet there is something about his mouse-like agility that stamps him at once as 'a character.'*

He is FRED PEABODY, *who has for the past forty-odd years managed to scrape a living in the poorer type of second-hand furniture dealing; but his agile mind, in spite of the early handicap imposed upon it by a system of education once known as 'Elementary,' has ever been on the alert to acquire knowledge, until now he is quite an 'educated' man, with ideas about architecture, books, plays, music—indeed, almost everything, which his shabby exterior quite belies.*

He has one weakness common to our race, rich and poor alike: he likes horse-racing, but, unlike most punters, who scarcely know one end of a horse from the other, FRED PEABODY *loves horses, and, what is more,* understands *them.*

That FRED PEABODY *should be a bosom friend of* ALFRED WELFARE *is not far to seek:* ALF *likes his 'little flutter' too, and so a certain affinity exists between the two men. But whereas* FRED *has the gift of the gab,* ALF *is quiet, and*

               a good listener, and so the perfect foil for
               FRED, who, in our 'advanced' society, finds
               few who will lend him an ear; indeed, he is
               regarded by most of his associates as a bore or
               'a bit touched,' or, as ALF sometimes says, 'an
               anachronism.'

     MRS WELFARE *long ago made up her mind—a*
               typically feminine one—that FRED PEABODY
               is lazy, *and so has always looked askance*
               at her husband's 'conferences,' as she calls
               them, with FRED. *That is why he looked*
               round furtively as he tiptoed into the bedroom
               just now; he knew he would be 'warned off
               the course' by MRS ALFRED WELFARE. *But he*
               also knew that ALF *might want to make a*
               last-minute bet on the Grand National, which
               was due to start in a few minutes, and that he,
               FRED, was the only means by which that bet
               could be laid, because the rest of the Welfare
               family were adamant on the subject of betting,
               MRS WELFARE'S *father having squandered*
               away a prosperous butcher's business through
               acting upon information he had received straight
               from a whole succession of 'horses' mouths.'

FRED PEABODY [*he doesn't remove his bowler*]. Is the coast clear, Alf?

MR WELFARE [*slight coughing*]. Yes. How did you get in without being spotted?

FRED. Aggie Patcham left the front door open—so I risked it. Where are—they?

MR WELFARE. Downstairs having a cup of tea.

FRED. Good—then we're safe for the time being.

MR WELFARE. Yes, but you'll have to watch your step [*coughs*].

FRED [*fumbling in his pocket*]. 'Ere! try one of these—humbugs—better'n all that stuff in them bottles. Shall I turn that row off [*nodding towards the wireless*] and get the other station? We might as well listen to the broadcast of the race.

MR WELFARE. Better leave that organ on for a bit —only turn it right down.

FRED [*turning it right down so that it is only just audible*]. Fancy listening to a cinema organ.

MR WELFARE. I only had it on to please Harold. He's trying to eddicate me to listen to this modern stuff.

FRED [*in disgust*]. An' 'e starts with a cinema organ! When I first saw one o' them illuminated contraptions come up out o' the entrails o' the Regal, murdering one o' Chopin's beautiful nocturnes, I knew that we 'ad taken another step down the slippery slope. Progress they calls it! We're livin' in Tin Pan Alley— music out o' tins like bloomin' sardines. It's all tins to-day. Why, the winners of the Dunmow Flitch 'ave to put up with a *tin* of rashers for their prize nowadays. It's a tinny age. Nobody seems to care about *quality*. Look at the beer! an' look what it costs! Think o' them good old days, Alf, when you could buy a pint o' beer—an' what beer it were—a packet of fags, a nip o' whisky, an ounce of shag, an' a box o' matches, all for a bob—a blinkin' bob! think of it! You'd 'ave to be a bloomin' Rothschild to-day to buy all them at one sittin'—an' they say we're better orf! Ichabod! Ichabod!

MR WELFARE. Come off it, Fred Peabody. There's no time now to settle the affairs of the nation. You're forgetting the race.

FRED. Lor', the race! Where's the paper? We'll follow it with the picture of the course.

MR WELFARE. Here we are! What did you back in the end?

FRED. Sir Galahad. Whatever made *you* fancy an outsider like Cold Cure I don't know. The bookie bloke nearly choked hisself with laughing when I said I wanted two quid each way on Cold Cure. Like chuckin' money down the drain. It's one o' the 'undred to ones.

MR WELFARE. Well! that was my fancy. Call it superstition if you like, but here I am, in bed for the first time for thirty years, and all on account of a cold, and when I twigged Cold Cure I thought it seemed like a good omen.

FRED. You ought to know better at your age, Alfred Welfare, than to deal in omens: they are the food of the ignoramuses. [*Scornfully*] Cold Cure! Why, he'll doubtless fall in Becher's Brook an' die o' pneumonia. Like as not 'e's wither-rung and troubled with the lampas, full o' windgalls, sped with the spavins, swayed in the back, shoulder-shotten, an' like to mose in the chine—just like Petruchio's 'orse when he come to wed that hornet, Katharina.

MR WELFARE. There's no time for your Shakespeare stuff now. Tune in to the course—but keep it low, or they'll hear downstairs.

> [FRED *darts over furtively to the door and peeps out, and, gently closing it again, he goes to the set and tries to find the right station. This proves more difficult than he had anticipated: in fact, he is quite unable to tune in to the Grand National, and he gets down on his knees to manipulate the knobs.*
>
> MR WELFARE *is getting agitated lest they should fail to get the station, but* FRED *perseveres, and chats away at the same time.*

FRED. I remember being at Aintree when that old warrior Sergeant Murphy won the National. Fine, honest old horse he were—thirteen years old. Never knew a horse make fewer mistakes. Seven Nationals he run and got home every time; his last when he were fifteen. But the year he won, 1923, it were, he 'ad a tussle with Shaun Spadah, Conjurer II, and Drifter. I can see 'em coming up the straight now:

the Sergeant leading, with Conjurer II at 'is 'eels, and Shaun Spadah a close third, but the Conjurer couldn't live with Mr Murphy after the last fence, and it were left to Shaun Spadah to issue the final challenge—but the Sergeant got 'ome by three lengths. An' a funny thing 'appened that day at the water-jump: Conjurer II got bumped by Drifter, an' as 'e 'it the ground 'e bit 'is tongue real bad—guts that 'orse 'ad got, swallerin' 'is own blood all the time. An' then there were that Tipperary Tim—an' come to think of it, he won at a 'undred to one—so you *might* pull a chestnut out o' the fire with your Cold Cure.

MR WELFARE [*now getting very agitated*]. Look at the time, Fred—the race is nearly over.

FRED [*taking out his watch*]. You're right, Alf! It's later than I thought.

MR WELFARE [*jumping out of bed*]. Let me have a go!

FRED [*trying to push him back to bed*]. 'Ere! you'll catch yer death o' cold. Then where'll your Cold Cure be!

MR WELFARE [*at the set and twisting the knobs, which causes a good deal of 'howling' from the set*]. Why didn't I do it at first! I might have known you couldn't have tuned a wireless set in. Harold said that new bloke at the bicycle shop round the corner hadn't made much of a job of mending it. [*He gives it a hefty bang.*] Ah! that's bucked its ideas up! Listen! [*and he is just in time to hear the final stages of the race*].

COMMENTATOR [*in an excited voice, over the radio*]. Here they come—over the last fence—Pegasus is still leading, with Golden Boy second—and Cold Cure third—that outsider has hung on like grim death—a plucky little jumper—hasn't put one foot wrong—here they come into the straight, and it's neck and neck now. Cold Cure is coming up—yes—he's a length in front of Golden Boy—he's coming up—Pegasus is still leading —no! it's Cold Cure—Cold Cure is in the lead—it's a titanic struggle—almost neck and neck—Cold Cure has just done it—it's Cold Cure. Cold Cure has won by half a length, with Pegasus second, and Golden Boy three lengths behind.

> [*At this point* MR WELFARE'S *joy knows no bounds: he throws all decorum to the winds and jumps on the bed, commences a kind of Highland fling, and shouts,* "Good old Cold Cure! A hundred to one! Three cheers for Cold Cure!" *The commentary is still going on.*

COMMENTATOR [*continue from above without a break*]. Here comes Uncle Remus, the favourite, without his jockey, and Saucy Sal, followed by two more loose horses—I can't quite see who they are—yes—one is Sir Galahad. Now here comes a whole stream—quite a procession: Black Prince, Dan Chaucer, Dick Barton, Winnie the Pooh . . . [*At this point* FRED PEABODY *has gone to the door to make sure that* MRS WELFARE *is nowhere about, but he suddenly closes it very quickly, rushes over to the wireless and switches it off, and makes a motion to* ALF].

FRED. Quick, Alf! the Missus! 'Op into bed!

> [ALFRED WELFARE *obeys without a word, and as quick as knife* FRED *rushes round and hops into bed with him, bowler hat still on.* MR WELFARE, *realizing what has happened, tries to pull the sheet over his face, and succeeds in covering him over but for the bowler. Both men lie dead still just as* MRS WELFARE *comes in and stands at the door, and, looking round suspiciously, says half to herself:* "That's funny—I could have sworn I heard voices," *and, thinking her husband is having his forty winks, she closes the door very gently lest she should wake him. After a few moments the two men raise themselves into a sitting position, and, after satisfying themselves that the coast is clear again, they turn to each other and shake hands vigorously.*

FRED. Congratulations, Alf! Two 'undred quid! You're a bloated capitalist now!

MR WELFARE. But what about Maggie! How can I break the news to her?

FRED. Money talks, Alf. Do you think there's a female alive what wouldn't be blinded by two 'undred quid? They can't resist it. Money casts a spell over 'em. Like Eve and the apple in the Garden of Eden. They can't keep their fingers off it.

MR WELFARE. But you know what Maggie's like when she's made up her mind about anything.

FRED. But you ain't never 'ad two 'undred quid to bargain with before.

MR WELFARE. That's her sore point—as you well know. She says we should have been well off if her father hadn't ruined his butcher's business backing horses and left her mother penniless.

FRED. You mark my words! with a bit o' diplomacy you can draw rings round your missus. Ask her if she'd like to go for a 'oliday. You'll need a bit of a change yourself after this "do"; and that'll be a good lead-in.

MR WELFARE. But she knows we can't afford a holiday.

FRED. Why, man! don't be such a flap-eared knave! tell 'er you've been putting a bit by on the quiet like, and so grow to a point. Get 'er in the mood—that's half the battle with women. Convince 'er a holiday's in the offing, and she'll drop like a ripe plum in August. You don't think she'll be particular, once she's made up her mind, whether the money comes off a Christmas-tree or a bookmaker. It's easy, Alf! If you can't work a simple oracle like that you don't deserve the two 'undred quid.

MR WELFARE. It *sounds* easy enough.

FRED [*getting out of bed*]. Gird up your loins, man, and wade in!

ALF. When shall I tell her?

FRED. When she comes in again. What you need is a spot o' the ole Dunkirk spirit.

MR WELFARE. Ah! talking of spirit, you might see if you can get a bottle of Johnny Walker, so we can celebrate—and get yourself one, too.

FRED. I think I can get a 'half,' but you've got to pluck the nettle first. Then we'll drink the nectar. [*Pauses and goes to the door and listens.*] Here she comes again. Thank heavens your stairs creak.

MR WELFARE. Quick, man! under the bed this time.

> [FRED *darts under the bed and vanishes only just in time. The door opens very slowly and* HAROLD *peeps in, and is surprised to find his father sitting up.*

HAROLD. Thought you were asleep.

MR WELFARE. Didn't feel like it after all.

HAROLD [*tentatively*]. I've just been listening to the—er—race—round at Aggie's.

MR WELFARE. Oh!

HAROLD. Yes.

MR WELFARE. What won?

HAROLD. Thought perhaps you might have heard like—it was on the Light Programme.

MR WELFARE. As a matter of fact, I did.

HAROLD. Well! what I really came to tell you was this: I've had an extraordinary stroke of luck.

MR WELFARE [*standing his ground*]. Oh!

HAROLD. Yes. [*Pause.*] I backed the winner. Jolly old Cold Cure.

MR WELFARE [*showing no signs of enthusiasm*]. How much?

HAROLD. Ten bob each way.

MR WELFARE. That's fifty pounds.

HAROLD [*warming up, now he has broken the ice*]. Right first time. Fifty of the best.

MR WELFARE. What made you pick an outsider like Cold Cure?

HAROLD. Intuition! I thought to myself, "There's the old Guv. in bed getting over an illness that started as a cold." And it came to me all in a heap—"Cold Cure," and as I'd won a pound in the football pool last week, I thought I'd try my luck again. And here we are with fifty pounds to play with.

MR WELFARE. Does your Mother know?

HAROLD. Yes.

MR WELFARE. What did she say?

HAROLD. You'll see. [*He goes to the door and shouts downstairs for his mother.*] I reckon we've killed that old hoodoo about horse-racing. I've had a flutter now and again since I've been in the Army. But you can't keep a win like fifty pounds to yourself, can you? [MRS WELFARE *comes bustling in, all smiles.*] I've just been spilling the beans.

MRS WELFARE. I ought to be very, very angry.

MR WELFARE. Yes, Maggie, you ought to be!

MRS WELFARE. But I've forgiven him. You see— fifty pounds is a lot of money, isn't it? and Harold has had such a brainwave.

MR WELFARE. Oh!

MRS WELFARE. Yes! he wants you to go down to the seaside for a fortnight to recuperate.

HAROLD. That's right, Dad, Blackpool, Brighton, Margate, where you like—and put the expenses down to the Old Firm.

MR WELFARE. But I couldn't do that!

HAROLD. Why not?

MR WELFARE. What! go away alone?

MRS WELFARE. We thought perhaps you'd like to have a real good fortnight all on your own, doing just what you like.

HAROLD. That's right! Go down on the sands and sit in a deck-chair and pick out all the winners to your heart's content. I'll even buy you a spade and pail.

MR WELFARE. That's very kind of you, Harold, but if I go, we both go.

HAROLD. That's O.K. if that's the way you want it. That was my first suggestion. It was Maggie who thought you'd rather go alone. [*Turning to his mother, puts his arm round her.*] There you are, Mum! You can thank your lucky stars *you* aren't an outsider.

MRS WELFARE. Well! that's very kind of you, Harold. Rosie can go to Aunt Ethel's.

HAROLD. Let her stay with the beautiful Ida and see the ginger-bread with the gilt off.

MRS WELFARE. There's just one small thing, Alf.

MR WELFARE. What's that, Maggie?

MRS WELFARE. I'm sorry old Fred Peabody's got to know all about this.

MR WELFARE. Why?

MRS WELFARE. He'll gloat so!

HAROLD. He needn't know.

MRS WELFARE. But we can't suddenly splash out on a fortnight's holiday without him perking up and wondering where the money's coming from.

MR WELFARE. I can't see that it matters. He's bound to know—sooner or later.

MRS WELFARE. Yes. I suppose you're right. But he does look through you so. He always seems to be weighing me up.

MR WELFARE. Perhaps he does.

HAROLD. He's sure to be round to see you. Tell the old josser then and get it off your chest.

MRS WELFARE. Well! who'd have thought we were in for a day like this. Come along, Harold, we're forgetting what Dr Anderson said your Dad wanted—Peace and Quiet. Perhaps you'll have a cup of tea now, Alf?

MR WELFARE. Yes—on second thoughts, I think I will, Maggie!

MRS WELFARE. That's right! Come along, Harold.

[*At this moment* ROSIE *bursts into the room, out of breath.*

MRS WELFARE [*in tone of surprise*]. Rosie! Whatever's the matter?

ROSIE. I've just come to congratulate Dad.

HAROLD. What's the big idea?

ROSIE. He has won two hundred pounds.

HAROLD. Christopher Columbus!

MRS WELFARE [*flabbergasted*]. Two hundred pounds! How?

ROSIE. He backed Cold Cure.

MRS WELFARE. Alfred!

HAROLD. How'd you find out?

ROSIE. I heard you telling Jim you'd backed it, so I put a half-crown on too. And Jim took me straight round to the bookmaker's after the service to collect my five pounds.

HAROLD. So the bookie told you?

ROSIE. Yes.

MRS WELFARE [*quite overcome*]. Well! they say it never rains but it pours. But when did you back it, Alfred?

[ALF *looks somewhat blank, not quite knowing what to say, but* FRED *comes to his rescue: his head, minus his bowler, pops out from under the bed, and, still on his hands and knees, he says,* "I'm the guilty party. I backed it for him, Mrs Welfare."

MRS WELFARE, ROSIE, *and* HAROLD *are dumbfounded by the turn of events, and stand speechless, while* FRED, *very embarrassed, scrambles to his feet, hugging his bowler on his chest with both hands. He looks a forlorn figure as he stands there waiting for* MRS WELFARE'S *onslaught—which suddenly comes, but not quite in the way* FRED *expects, for she rushes over to him, puts her arms right round him, hugs him vigorously, and gives him a full-blooded kiss, adding:* "You mustn't take any notice of what I said about you, Fred." *She then rushes over to her husband and hugs and kisses him too, leaving the bewildered* FRED *trying to restore his bowler to its original shape.*

HAROLD [*surveying the scene with a broad smile*]. Operation 'Cold-Cure' complete.

CURTAIN

SONG IN THE WIND

by

PATRICIA BEVAN-PARRY

CHARACTERS

MAM
BRANWEN HOWELLS
DILYD HOWELLS
TYDNO HOWELLS
DAI THOMAS
GERWYN MEREDITH

Song in the Wind was a prize-winning play in the British Drama League's Under-twenty One-act Play-writing Competition, 1945.

SONG IN THE WIND

The scene is the living-room of a Welsh house. Spotlessly clean but comfortable. It is a cold evening, with a fierce wind howling down the valley. TYDNO, *a young boy, is curled up in a chair reading. When the curtain rises his sister,* DILYD, *who is a little older, is poking the fire.*

TYDNO. What is Terraghan, Dilyd?

DILYD. And what silly old book is that now?

TYDNO. No silly old book, but somethin' good. There is a woman here talks about the curse of Terraghan. What is that?

DILYD [*teasing*]. Ah! [*Calling off*] Mam, will I tell him about the Terraghan?

MAM [*off*]. Well now, that is a question. Wait for a bit. Branwen is comin' down.

DILYD [*dancing across the room*]. Oh! Watch you now, Tydno. Branwen is comin' down.

> [*Soon* BRANWEN *enters—a lovely young girl, dressed for a special party. To-night there is a strange light in her eyes. She waits, and there is silence.*

DILYD. Oh! There is elegant you are. And the dress so pretty! Who is to guess that——

MAM [*entering*]. Shut up, you! This is a fine dress from the town that cost more than is right to give. [DILYD *laughs—there is a pause.*] Now what is up with you, Branwen?

BRANWEN. I am waitin' for Tydno to judge me.

TYDNO [*considering*]. Good. But you are awful old in that, and it is spoilin' my story not to know Terraghan.

BRANWEN. You and your old story. Never a woman for you if——

MAM. Branwen! None of that to him, now. Wait still while I fix your flower, my gel, and breathe small or your hooks will give away.

249

DILYD. There is such little bows and so many. Is it easy with you at the waist?

BRANWEN. As easy as any.

DILYD [*watching her mother arrange the flower*]. Oh! Where will you put it?

MAM. Wait for a bit while I see.

TYDNO. Never did I see a girl so pretty, mind, but three-quarters of my brain is wonderin' about this Terraghan.

DILYD. There is an obstinate old boy for you—when we are so busy too.

BRANWEN. Well tell him quick and perhaps we shall have some peace.

MAM. Not so quick that you forget to open the door.

[BRANWEN *laughs, but* DILYD *runs to the door.*

TYDNO. Why do you——

MAM. Sh, boy! No talkin'!

[DILYD *opens and closes the door three times, looking out each time. The others are quiet.*

BRANWEN. There is silly we are to be so serious. I do not believe there is any difference whether you open the door three times or stand on your head five times.

MAM. Now be quiet, my gel. That is the way to tempt the devil.

BRANWEN. Gerwyn Meredith, come down from town, says that there is no devil.

[*There is a general reaction of horror.*

DILYD. Oh! That is wicked to say.

MAM. The only answer to that is that Gerwyn Meredith is the devil himself, see.

BRANWEN. Gerwyn Meredith is a fine young gentleman and straight in the leg.

MAM. Close your mouth, and not another word of that kind will I hear from you. That is the talk of nasty girls.

TYDNO. If you would tell me that bit about Terraghan, I could be quiet in my story.

MAM [*to* TYDNO]. Wait a minute, you. Branwen, will Gerwyn Meredith be at this party, is it?

BRANWEN. I do not know—nor do I care.

MAM. Well then, that is an end of it. Now my son, about this old Terraghan. Long ago it was, at the turn of the valley, there lived a young man whose name was Terraghan. He was—what is this book you are readin', anyway?

TYDNO. It is a good book, Mam. *Can y Gwynt.*

[MAM *is not enlightened, and looks at the book.*

MAM. Well, it is a nice picture there is, so perhaps you are right. Dilyd, my gel, do not sit idle when mendin' there is for you. Now, where was I with all these interruptions. A young man Terraghan, who was beautiful from head to toe inside and out. But the girls in the valley was frightened of him because he was so nice to look at, see. Now there is strange it is, but so it was. And—Branwen! How will I do your hair if you will fidget like you was an old flea?

BRANWEN. There is good I will be, Mam. Go on.

MAM. And Terraghan froze inside so that he was not quite so handsome because his face was terrible still, just his eyes was good, and then all them gels followed him, see. But he was not so nice, for after he had talked with them a bit, he would look at them strange like, till they was funny in the head and thought there were things to be heard, when it was only the wind there was.

TYDNO. Oh, Mam! What then?

MAM. Then to his museum under the mountain and never to be seen again.

[TYDNO *considers a moment.*

TYDNO. But why did you open the door three times?

DILYD. Because those who know say that Terraghan is still about, and if you talk of him, he will come with his eyes at a girl. If you look out once he will be there the next minute, and if you look out twice he will come the minute after, but if you look out three times he will get tired of dodgin' back, and he will go, see.

TYDNO. Oh, that is a story for girls to believe in. And anyway, perhaps one night he would not get tired of dodgin' back so there was a waste of good time and energy openin' and shuttin' the door.

BRANWEN. Askin' me, it is a story for no one but old women to believe in.

MAM. Branwen! Unlucky it is to talk like that. Now forget this old Terraghan all of you, and for that story, my boy, I get a hand with the dirty dishes in the back.

TYDNO. Oh, Mam! Wait for a bit till I finish my chapter.

MAM. I will wait till I am ready and not beyond. Branwen, I think we will have a ribbon by here.

BRANWEN. Will it be better, Mam?

DILYD. Lovely it will be, Branwen.

MAM. I will find a bit of my own, laid up for a time like this.

BRANWEN. Oh, Mam! There is good you are to me.

MAM. Not so much talk, gel. Wait you still for a bit.
[*She goes to find the ribbon. There is a moment's silence.*

DILYD. It's not wantin' you are to go to the party, Branwen.

BRANWEN. Oh, Dilyd! So excited I am, I must not talk for fear of Mam.

DILYD. Why now?

BRANWEN [*making signs to indicate that she cannot tell while* TYDNO *is there*]. She will be afraid that I am to forget myself and flirt with the young gentlemen. But it is not me to misbehave myself. Still, I will hold my tongue for now, in case.   [*Enter* MAM.

MAM. I am too old for this, so perhaps you will have it, Branwen, is it?

BRANWEN. Oh, Mam! There is lovely.

MAM. And you are to sew it, Dilyd—here. But careful mind. You have quite a little time before Dai calls —good little stitches to last.

BRANWEN [*unnoticed*]. Only a little time.

DILYD. Yes indeed, Mam.

MAM. Now out in the back with you, Tydno.

TYDNO. Now Mam?

MAM. Now.

[*She goes to the kitchen and* TYDNO *follows*.

DILYD. Hold still, Branwen, if I am not to sew you together.

BRANWEN. Oh, Dilyd! It is lies I was speakin' to Mam just now. Gerwyn Meredith will be at the party and my heart is goin' like an old pump. Oh! How I have waited these last days! Never you tell, mind.

DILYD [*amazed*]. Is it love with you, Branwen?

BRANWEN. I did not say it. [*Pause*.

DILYD. You will not let him kiss you to-night.

BRANWEN. I have let him kiss me, Dilyd.

[*Enter* MAM *carrying food*.

MAM. Come you now and have to eat before you go, gel.

BRANWEN. Oh, Mam, not a thing could I eat should I die for it.

MAM. Well then, a good cup of tea is it, to keep out the cold?

BRANWEN. Thank you, Mam. I will try.

MAM [*as she goes*]. You will not go out on a night like this without somethin'. There is a wind fit to kill.

[*Exit* MAM.

DILYD. How did you let it happen?

BRANWEN. It was after chapel. I was takin' a couple o' plates back to Mrs Lewis and he was there on the bridge, see. Soon we was talkin'.

DILYD. Oh, Branwen! After chapel too. If anyone had seen—— There was awful.

BRANWEN. But then I did not care a button for talk or trouble. He told me I was pretty, Dilyd.

DILYD. Then he is wicked to talk to a girl so—— Treatin' you like a pit woman. Mam was right.

BRANWEN. No, Dilyd. He was truthful in the eye. It was his eyes that done it, for after lookin' at them those minutes, I could see they was askin' for a kiss. He did not say nothin', and his face was still, not a smile, but just his eyes sayin' "Please" stronger and stronger.

DILYD. There is frightened I would have been. Whatever came over you to stay.

BRANWEN. I could——   [*Enter* MAM *with the tea.*

MAM. Let me see what you are doin', Dilyd. [*She looks.*] Nice it is, my beautiful, and wonderful you will look, Branwen . . . but remember to keep your looks to yourself. Dai it is takes you and watches you and brings you back. No nonsense, see.

BRANWEN. You know me, Mam.

MAM. Why else would I say what I do? [*There is a crash off.*] Oh! There is that old boy breakin' every dish I have.   [MAM *bustles out.*

BRANWEN. Do you think she knows anythin', keep comin' in like this?

DILYD. You have been quiet as an old statue, but who can tell?

BRANWEN. Oh, Dilyd, I love him. He does not kiss like you and Mam. There is a—— Oh, Dilyd, what it is to love like you was burning with a flame in the soul, fit to kill you.

DILYD. Sh! Branwen! That is awful talk. If Mam should hear!

BRANWEN. If you will breathe a word to Mam—I will scratch out your eyes.

DILYD. There is a mean old thing you are to be cross for somethin' not done. For Mam's sake I will not tell. Branwen, don't look at him to-night. He is a wicked man it is to kiss you—and if Ceridwen Lewis see you look at him strange like, there will be talk from here to the next valley—and she so jealous of you.

BRANWEN. Oh, I wish I talked lovely like I had elocution. Gerwyn Meredith talks good—strong from the throat, but soft and gentle. . . . Oh, Dilyd! there is slow! Dai will be callin' straight.

DILYD. I am finished now, Branwen. But frightened I am for you.

BRANWEN. There is silly you are, gel. And never a husband for you if you will be an old goose. [*There is a knock.*] Oh, there is Dai. Open the door, Dilyd, while I get my cloak. [DILYD *opens the door.*

DILYD. Hallo, Dai. Early?

DAI. Yes. I'm afraid—I—er . . . [MAM *has entered.*

MAM. Hallo, Dai.

DAI. Good evenin', Mrs Howells. Er—bad news, Branwen. The gale is worse down the bottom, and it's rocked the old bridge sideways, so that hangin' by the skin of its teeth it is, and the water angry to pull it down. No one can cross unless they want to drown, and nothin' can be done till mornin'! Pity it is for none on this side can go to the party, which will be the worse for the evenin' and every one there. And there is beautiful Branwen looks. Sorry I am we cannot go.

BRANWEN [*urgently*]. We can go, Dai. Somehow, we will go. We must——

DILYD }
MAM   } [*together*]. Branwen!
              Don't be silly, gal.

DAI. But Branwen, the bridge is broken. Don't you understand? We can't go.

BRANWEN [*going to* DAI *and putting her arms round his neck—desperately*]. Please, Dai bach. Think of some way. I'll give my soul to go to the party.

DAI. But Branwen, talk sense. There is silly to make so much of one old party. Only one place there is for anyone goin' over the bridge to-night—and that's not a party, look you.

BRANWEN. Yesterday you said you would do anythin' for me. Now I know you are a liar. You was playin' with me—shame to you!

DAI ⎫
MAM ⎬ [*together*].
DILYD ⎭

Branwen——
Branwen, I won't have you talk——
Oh, Branwen!

BRANWEN. All right then, Dai Thomas—if it's scared you are, I know some one who'll be glad to take me. And *very* glad I'll be to go with him.

DAI. Branwen . . . [*pause*]. Who?

BRANWEN. Wanting to know is it? Well, you won't, see—and I have nothin' more to say, Dai Thomas.

DAI [*after a pause*]. All right, Branwen Howells. Good evenin', Dilyd. Good evenin', Mrs Howells.

MAM [*who has been gazing at* BRANWEN *in amazement and displeasure*]. Wait you a minute, Dai. Will you go from here with Branwen in this mind?—tellin' you a lot of nonsense?

DAI. Nothin' more to be said to that last, Mrs Howells—unless somethin' ugly. Better for me to go.

[*He goes without another word, and only* DILYD, *as she closes the door, says* "Good night, Dai," *rather timidly.*

MAM. Well, and aren't you ashamed, my gel. That was a fine exhibition of selfish, stupid bad temper—and rude you were too. Dai givin' you a piece of common sense an' you throwin' it back in his face like you was an old dunce, an' as if parties was all that mattered to you.

DILYD. There is mean you was, Branwen.

BRANWEN. Oh, don't you start on at me, too. Leave me quiet to think.

MAM. I am thinkin' too, gal. And I am wonderin' about these lies you have been tellin' Dai! I suppose I

am to know this person who will be "very glad" to
take you to the party—and over a broken bridge too.
[*Changing her tone*] Sorry I am to hear you talk so,
Branwen—[*there is a knock*]. There is Dai come back.
You go, Dilyd. [*To* BRANWEN] Say you are sorry and
make it up now, gal.

> [DILYD *opens the door and rushes back with a shrill
> scream as a man slumps to the floor on the
> threshold.*

DILYD. Oh, Mam! It isn't Dai.

> [*She runs to her mother—and* TYDNO *runs in.*

MAM [*after a pause while she looks from a safe distance*].
There is silly you are, Dilyd. Screamin' as if you had
seen some monster and it's only a boy in need of help.
[*She has gone over to examine him.*] Breathin' he is, but
somethin' must have hit him hard, for he is like a log.

> [BRANWEN, *who has drawn near with the others, gasps.*

BRANWEN. Oh, Mam! I know him!

MAM [*suspicious at once*]. Oh?

BRANWEN. It is Gerwyn Meredith. Oh, what has
happened to him!

TYDNO. The wind is tearin' down the Valley—
perhaps an old branch blew down and hit him on the
head. . . . But how will he come to the door?

BRANWEN. Oh, never mind how he come. He is here
and nearly dead. Is he livin', Mam?

MAM. As far off dead as I am. Put some water in the
kettle, Tydno, and quick. Now then, you girls, help
me to get him in front of the fire.

DILYD. Heavy he is.

BRANWEN. Oh, Gerwyn, hurtin' with you, is it?

MAM. No good talkin' to him soft, for he can't listen
to you.

BRANWEN. See I am beside you, Gerwyn.

MAM. And how about your new dress, then?

BRANWEN. What do I care for an old dress? Gerwyn,
look at me.

R

DILYD. Branwen!

[MAM *looks at* BRANWEN, *considering*.

MAM [*calls*]. There is slow, Tydno! [*To* DILYD] See whatever he is doin', Dilyd. Branwen, get up from by there and put your dress away. Perhaps I will have something I would give that one if it is to be found in all this old rubbishy place. [MAM *goes out*.

BRANWEN. Oh, Gerwyn. What has happened, my love? Open your eyes and look at me. Gerwyn, you are listening, I know. You can hear me. And I can hear them singin', Gerwyn—or is it only the wind?

[*She listens.* DILYD *enters, followed by* TYDNO.

DILYD. Is he movin' yet?

BRANWEN. No. Leave me, you two.

DILYD. Oh, Branwen, there is wicked you are to your dress!

BRANWEN. Who cares about a dress? Be quiet, will you, and give him some peace. Gerwyn. Look at me. I am callin' you. Will you hear me, is it? Gerwyn! Open your eyes, I am waitin'. I know they are singin' now and ridin' in the wind. There is good to feel the earth slip from under you and only the cold new day to come.

MAM [*who has entered*]. Branwen! Get up at once! *I* have a care for your dress, anyway.

BRANWEN. No, Mam. I am stayin' here. Perhaps for ever. I could not move if you kill me for it. I am with him alone in the light of the morning, and the world is black at our feet. Mam, are his eyes open? They look shut, but I feel as if they was open and gazin' at me and starin' and starin'. There is cold I am. Dilyd—put my cloak round me.

[DILYD *makes a move to go, but her mother stops her.* MAM *has decided that this is serious and she must take action.*

MAM. Tydno! Bed. Quick now!

TYDNO. Am I to leave all the women at the hands of a strange man?

MAM. No. You'll go to bed straight and leave a man in the hands of a lot of strange women, and no back answers. Good night now.

TYDNO. But it's down here I am wanting to—— [MAM *looks at him.*] Good night, Mam.

[TYDNO *goes out.*

MAM. Branwen. Come along, gel. Up a bit.

BRANWEN. Don't touch me, Mam—— We are movin' away, see. He is gazing at me and we are walkin' into the sky. I am sorry. I cannot help it. It's the singin' on the wind and the light. Don't touch me. I will die if you touch me.

DILYD. Mam! It's a spell he has put on her.

MAM. Shut up, you. Branwen, come now. [*She touches* BRANWEN, *who gasps.*] Branwen, you are cold as stone. Get up now and be sensible. Think straight for a bit.

BRANWEN. No good, Mam. I can't get up or move or anythin'—— Just my soul meltin' into his eyes. Creepin' sweet, like honey.

DILYD. Mam, what can we do? It is a spell. Branwen! don't look at him.

MAM. No good shoutin', Dilyd. [*Pause.*] Only one thing there is to do. [*Pause.*] Go you and see that Tydno is in bed. [DILYD *is unwilling.*] Are you deaf, gel, or stupid? Do as I tell you. [DILYD *goes.*] Branwen, look at me and talk sense, my beautiful——

BRANWEN. I love him. I love him. I have lost myself in the light and the singin'.

MAM [*urgently*]. Branwen! Look at me! Think what you might make your Mam to do.

BRANWEN. Never look at anyone again. Only his eyes and the light.

MAM. Then may the Lord understand that this is to save one of his sheep from the devil.

[MAM *stares for a long time, making up her mind and summoning her strength. Then she slowly picks up a knife and with a sudden movement stabs* GERWYN.

BRANWEN [*utters a long indrawn scream*]. Gerwyn! [*She leans forward over him, the body quivers a moment before becoming quite still.*] Murderess! You have killed him. I loved him. You knew. I told you. Then you killed him. You are not my Mam. I hate you! I hate you! I will mark you and your ribbon and my dress and all the house with his blood. Then they will know who done this thing.

DILYD [*coming in*]. What has happened?
[*She is paralysed with horror at the sight of the dead body.*

MAM. Branwen, beautiful, bed now is it?

BRANWEN. Do not speak to me. Listen!

MAM. There is silly talk, my little one. Go you and lie down a minute.

BRANWEN. Listen! Down the valley to the bridge and waitin' in the arms of the wind. Will I go with you now, Gerwyn? Wait for me while I get my cloak. Then I will come, quick too.

[BRANWEN *is speaking dreamily as if to some one far away.*

DILYD [*nearly crying*]. Oh, talk sense, Branwen.

MAM. Branwen, love. To bed now.

BRANWEN. To the party it is. With you, my love. Anywhere then. Up to the light and the wind in the sky. But down to the bridge now. Wait for me, Gerwyn!

MAM. There is nonsense now, Branwen. Listen to me. Outside it's dark, with a wind ready to pluck you away. Suppose you slipped by accident and fell in the water.

BRANWEN. I won't slip by accident. I am not afraid of an old bridge or the old dark or the wind or any old weather. You will not hold me now. He is waitin' to take me. I have to go or I shall die.

MAM [*looking at* BRANWEN *intently*]. You are right, my gal. You have to go. Your eyes are tellin' me plain. It is not for me now to ask you to do anythin'. Not dreaming we are, but livin' with evil beyond our power to stop.

DILYD. What are you sayin', Mam? Oh, Branwen, are you mad?

[DILYD *tries to stop* BRANWEN *as she moves slowly to the door, but* BRANWEN *only laughs gently.*

MAM. Quiet now, Dilyd my love. Come to me. We can do nothin'. It was all in vain. Branwen is gone.

DILYD. Oh, Mam, is it the curse, think you?

BRANWEN. Good-bye, Mam.

MAM. Oh, Branwen—find yourself. Try to come back, my love.

BRANWEN. Good-bye, Dilyd. Say good-bye to Tydno for me, is it?

DILYD. Oh! watch your step by the bridge, Branwen.

BRANWEN. I will watch my step by the bridge, Dilyd.

[BRANWEN *goes out—and the*

CURTAIN FALLS

BICYCLE BELLES
A BURLESQUE OF THE NINETIES

by

LILIAN McCARTHY

CHARACTERS

in order of appearance

HENRY BRACE (*the caretaker*)

ALGY
MONTY } (*Great Minds that think alike*)

COMPETITOR No. 2 (*the gushing one.*) (*Clothes—neat, natty, and quaint*)

MONTY'S MAMA

ALGY'S PAPA

COMPETITOR No. 1 (*Maud.*) (*Short and stocky. Clothes—clumsy and ill-fitting*)

COMPETITOR No. 3 (*the French one.*) (*Clothes—rather outrageous*)

THE PHOTOGRAPHER

COMPETITOR No. 4

PAPA JUNIOR, *and his offspring* THE TWINS (*babies*)

Applications regarding amateur performances of this play should be addressed to the publishers, George G. Harrap and Co., Ltd, 182 High Holborn, London, W.C.1

BICYCLE BELLES

COMPETITOR NO. 2 *is in rational clothes, dark and tailored.*
NO. 1 *is in dark bloomers and blouse, white cap.* NO. 3 *is in
striped light-coloured bloomers, blouse with little basque, and
trimmed hat.* NO. 4 *is in long, wide skirt.* ALGY *and* MONTY
*should be 'as like as two peas'—typical London johnnies with
canes, spats, and bell-toppers.* THE TWINS *are babies in long
clothes.*

*The scene is the enclosure in front of a pavilion in Battersea
Park, London, in* 1896.

As the curtain is drawn HENRY BRACE *is pumping the tyres
of a lady's bicycle and whistling (or singing) "Daisy,
Daisy" in time with a distant band.*

Enter ALGY *and* MONTY *from opposite sides, each carrying
a chair which they endeavour to place in the exact* C. *front of
stage.*

ALGY and MONTY

[*Speaking together*] Ah, here's the place
To view the race !
Were you addressing me, sir?

ALGY

My aged père
Requires this chair.

MONTY

My mater's 'tis to be, sir.
   [ALGY *bows and moves his chair to* R. *front.*]
I thank you !
   [MONTY *and* ALGY *each produce a popular 'gentleman's'
   paper and read.*

BRACE

Hi there ! Number two.
   [NO. 2's *head appears* C. *back.*]
I've fixed your bike. She's good as new.

NO. 2

[*Entering*] You clever man! How simply grand!
Its workings I don't understand.
I only know when I'm awheel,
My joy, I scarcely can conceal.
[NO. 2 *mounts her bicycle, and trills last two lines. Enter* MONTY'S MAMA, L.

MAMA

Well, Montague! So there you are!
I have been searching near and far.
I did expect when I was late,
That you would meet me at the gate.
But no! You just sit there and read,
Regardless of your mother's need.
[MONTAGUE *tries to speak*.]
No, Montague! Don't be absurd.
I will not hear another word.
You're just like your poor dear Papa
He used to argue——

MONTY

[*Breaking in*]   But, Mama!——

MAMA

And try to prove that wrong was right!

ALGY

[*Without looking up*] That black was white!

BRACE

That day was night!
[MAMA *glares at* ALGY, *then at* BRACE.

MAMA

Is this where you have put my chair.
'Twould be much better over there.

[*Looks to* R. *front, then points.* MONTY *brings chair to* L. *front.*

MONTY

There, dear Mama, does that please you?

MAMA

Much better! Thank you, Montague.

BRACE

You find she's running sweet and true?

NO. 2

[*Dismounting*] The tyres are pumped up nicely too.
Oh, dear, I was in such a panic!

BRACE

No need, miss, I'm a good mechanic.

NO. 2

I'm, oh, so grateful, Mr Brace!

BRACE

I'll wheel her to the starting-place.
[*Wheels bicycle to door* L.

NO. 2

[*Following*] Oh, Mr Brace, to start the race
Don't fire a horrid pistol.

BRACE

No, missy, no. They're goin' to blow
A blast upon a whistle.
[ALGY *moves chair from* R. *to* C.
[*Exit* L. *followed by* NO. 2.

PAPA

[*Entering* R.] It's fine, my boy,
To reach the joy,
Of this select enclosure.
The crowds ! The dust !
    [*He catches sight of* NO. 2, *who reappears* L. *and exits*
    C. *back.*]
There's more, I trust,
Such feminine exposure.

ALGY and MONTY

Here Pater [Mater] is the racing-card.
It gives both name and number,
And here's the make of cycle too.

MONTY

Our Maud, see, rides a Humber.

PAPA

That glimpse of limb and ankle trim,
Has made me wish for more, sir.
You may regard that piece of card,
I'm going to watch that door, sir.
        [PAPA, *who has been twisting his head round while*
        seated C., *moves his chair to* R.
        [MAUD *enters* C. *back.*

MAMA

Here comes dear Maud !

ALGY and MONTY

I say !

PAPA

Good Lord !

MAUD

If you're tilting your nose
At my rational clothes
I really don't mind in the slightest.
I can cycle in these
With the greatest of ease
Without fear of the breeze
Exposing my knees
In a manner that's not the politest.
So a fig for the sneers!
The gibes and the jeers!

PAPA

The winks and the leers!

MAMA

Your poor Mama's tears!

MAUD

I refuse to wear skirts as a cyclist.

[*Enter* NO. 2.

NO. 2

Oh, Maud dear, the rest of us haven't a chance.
Number Three has arrived, and she's straight from
    France.
She's strutting around like the Rajah of Bhong.
For *she* won the race at the Bois de Boulonge.

[*Enter* NO. 3 C. *back.*

NO. 3

Attendez à moi, s'il vous plaît!

MAMA

What does that bold young woman say?

PAPA

Egad, my lad, she's pretty gay.

NO. 3

[*Strong French accent.*]   I wish to make ze leetle bet
     That I will win on my bicyclette !
          [*The* PHOTOGRAPHER *enters in a great hurry*

PHOTOGRAPHER

I'm glad the race has not begun.
To make up time, I've had to run.
Pray don't blame me for this delay.
It was my hansom cabriolet.
Allow me, please, one moment's grace
While I, my camera, set in place.
          [*During this speech the* PHOTOGRAPHER *has se*
               up his camera, and now puts his head under
               his black velvet cloth.

NO. 3

Ze photograph is for ze Press?

NO. 2

Oh, surely not !

PHOTOGRAPHER

[*Popping out from under cloth*]   The answer's 'Yes !'

NO. 3

[*To* NOS. 1 *and* 2]   I'll stand in front and you behind.

PHOTOGRAPHER

Now smile, please. Thank you. Very kind !
Who's this appearing at the door?

NO. 4

[*Entering*]   I, if you please, am Number Four.

PHOTOGRAPHER

Then ladies, please, I'll take one more.
Are you the last competitor?

[NO. 4 *nods and takes her place.* ALGY *and*
MONTY *gaze at her, lost in admiration.*

ALGY

Oh, face divine !

MONTY

Oh, face so fair !

PHOTOGRAPHER

Under cloth] Quite still, please ! Some one's moving
there.

ALGY

So blue her eyes !

MONTY

Such wondrous hair !

PAPA

Poking him] Now, Algernon, it's rude to stare.

MONTY

How feminine her garb, how sweet.

ALGY

It rustles gently round her feet.

MAMA

There ! Maud was foolish to desert
The modest, neat, becoming skirt.

MONTY

She's like a flower !

ALGY

An English rose !

MAMA

Poking MONTY *with parasol*] Tell Maud she's
wrinkling up her nose.

PHOTOGRAPHER

And, Ma'mselle, please don't mask her.

ALGY and MONTY

[*Together*] How virginal, how pure is she.
I wonder if she'd marry me?

PAPA

Then why, my boys, not ask her?

MAMA

[*To* MONTY] Pray ascertain first her identity.
She's possibly just some nonentity.
I'd like my daughter-in-law to be
A lady of rank with a pedigree.

PAPA

And a large and flourishing family tree.

MAMA

And yet, would even a peeress do,
If her ways were black as her blood was blue?
The young person here looks good and pure,
[*Pathetically*] But how can a mother be really sure?

PHOTOGRAPHER

There, thank you, ladies! That will do.
I'll see the proofs are sent to you.
Wait Number Four, please do remain.
I'd like to take you once again.

NO. 3

Then, moi aussi. I too will stay.
My photograph you'll need this day.

MAUD

How can she hope
With wheels to cope
In that outmoded garment?

NO. 2

They said these were the only wear.
I thought at first I wouldn't dare,
But surely there's no harm in't.

[*Exit* MAUD *and* NO. 2.

ALGY and MONTY

[*Kneeling*] Oh, sweetest maiden!

ALGY

Aphrodite!

MONTY

Venus!

[*Together*] We ask you, please, to choose between us.
[*They spread appealing arms in a gesture that
unfortunately almost includes* NO. 3.

NO. 3

I thank you, sirs, for your proposal
But I am not at your disposal.
Mon père arranges my betrothal.
[*Still kneeling*, ALGY *and* MONTY *move nearer* NO. 4.]
They speak to her and not to me!
Whatever can the reason be?
They know not of my victory.
Ah! Let them wait and they will see.
'Tis then on me their eyes will be.

[*She struts off.*

S

ALGY and MONTY

We did but see you, Number Four,
And yet we love you ever more.

[*Enter* HENRY BRACE.

BRACE

[*To* NO. 4] The cove is 'ere whose bike you hires.
He says 'is cash he now requires.
　[NO. 4 *hurries off* L.]
Now gents, don't clutter up the place.
Folks want to watch the ladies race.
It's nigh on time it started.　　　　　　　[*Exit.*
　　[ALGY *and* MONTY, *unaware of* NO. 4's *depar-
　　ture, pick up and kiss the edge of* PHOTO-
　　GRAPHER'S *cloth, under the impression that
　　it is the hem of* NO. 4's *skirt.*

ALGY and MONTY

Sweet maiden, gentle, kind, and fair,
Oh, answer, please, our earnest prayer.

PAPA

[*Poking* ALGY]　You'd better look and see who's there.

MONTY and ALGY

Oh, dear, she has departed!
This means, I fear, by jove, you know,
Our love is unrequited.

PAPA

Get up, my lads, don't kneel as though
You're waiting to be knighted.

PHOTOGRAPHER

The whistle is about to blow.

PAPA

By gad, I feel excited!

PHOTOGRAPHER

They're ready now at the starting-place,
Placed in a line by Henry Brace,
Waiting the signal to start the race—
And there's the whistle blowing.

> [*Loud whistle off stage followed by crowd noises
> and cheering.   During the race the five players
> left on the stage look out at the back of the
> auditorium, starting at the* L. *and gradually
> working round and finishing at* R.

PAPA

Yoicks! Tally ho! They're off, I say.
An excellent start with no delay,
For every one is well away.

MONTY and ALGY

How quickly they are going.

ALL

Faster and faster the wheels go round
Their cycles are skimming along the ground.

PHOTOGRAPHER

The French Ma'mselle is leading.
Pedalling along with main and might,
Looking to neither the left nor right,
If only the camera could follow the sight
And photograph them speeding!

PAPA

For Number Four they're far too fast.
You see, she's now the very last.

ALGY and MONTY

Rough sports are not for such as she.
She should be cherished tenderly.
Were she my bride I'd guard her well,
She'd ride no more a bicycle.

PHOTOGRAPHER

Number Three is now far ahead.

PAPA

By gad! She'll win, just as she said.

PHOTOGRAPHER

Two has begun to feel the pace.

MAMA

But Maud goes well in second place.

PAPA

Poor Number Four is very slow.

PHOTOGRAPHER

It's her trailing skirt that makes her so,
Catching the pedals as round they go.

MAMA

I think there's a wind beginning to blow.
It's nice that we're all so sheltered here,
But out on the course it's strong, I fear.

ALGY and MONTY

Look at that great big swirl of dust.

PAPA

Poor Ma'mselle got the worst of the gust.
It's tilted her hat right over her nose,
She can't see at all where it is she goes.

ALL

Her cycle runs still with sweet perfection.
She's going quite fast—in the wrong direction.

PHOTOGRAPHER

But what is happening there in the rear?

ALGY and MONTY

I say, by jove! How frigthfully queer!
Did ever you see such a thing before?

ALL

The wind is helping Number Four!

PHOTOGRAPHER

Her skirt has filled out like a sail in the breeze,
And forward she glides with the greatest of ease.

PAPA

How rapidly now she is bowling along.
She's caught up on Two and is still going strong.

ALL

There, now she has taken the foremost place.
This is a most exciting race.

PHOTOGRAPHER

How quickly she pedals and widens the gap,
With her skirt no longer a handicap.

PAPA

Number Three is back with her hat on straight,
Charging along at a furious rate.

ALGY

She dashes past Two!

MONTY

She overtakes One!

ALL

The final struggle has now begun.

PHOTOGRAPHER

The race is only a few lengths more.

MAMA

I think she's gaining on Number Four.

MONTY and ALGY

She'll catch her, I fear!

PHOTOGRAPHER

Oh, no, she won't!

MAMA

I think she will.

PAPA

Do you? I don't!

ALL

Pushing the pedals with might and main,
Striving an inch of ground to gain.

ALGY and MONTY

They've only a few more yards to go.

[*Distant cheers*

PHOTOGRAPHER

She hasn't caught her, I told you so!

ALL

A wheel ahead at the winning-place,
So cheer Number Four, she's won the race!
      [*They cheer loudly. Enter* PAPA JUNIOR, *carryin*
      THE TWINS.

PAPA JUNIOR

Did you say Number Four had won the race?
Oh, tell me, please, if that is the case.
Your pardon I crave for not raising my hat,
I haven't, dear madam, a hand for that.
My hopes have risen like morning sun,
Oh, please break it gently if she hasn't won.

PAPA

There's no doubt whatever upon that score.

ALL

The race was won by Number Four.

PAPA

Indubitably!

PHOTOGRAPHER

Incontestably!

MONTY

Unquestionably!

ALGY

Indisputably!

ALL

'Twas won by Number Four!

PAPA JUNIOR

My heart is filled with joy and pride
I feel my place is by her side.
Please hold this babe, and you the other,
I must acclaim my wife, their mother.
[*He hands* THE TWINS *to* ALGY *and* MONTY, *claps, then
walks to exit.*]

PAPA JUNIOR

[*Pausing at exit.*] And hold them most carefully, I pray,
You can't get twin babies every day. [*Exit.*

ALGY and MONTY

I say, old chappie, what a blow!
I never thought of this, you know.
I hoped she'd promise you or me,
To love, obey, and honour.
But now, alas, that ne'er can be.
Our virgin's a madonna!

MAMA

I'm horrified! It's a disgrace!
The home is surely a mother's place.
But to enter a public cycle race!
I never heard such a scandalous thing,
She doesn't deserve a wedding ring.

PAPA

He's taking your photograph, my lad.

ALGY

Oh, sir, I beg of you. That's too bad.

MONTY

The act of a cad, I'd say, by jove!

ALGY and MONTY

Making a bally ass of a cove!

PHOTOGRAPHER

I have my living to earn, if you please,
An invalid wife and her doctor's fees,
And *Topical Titbits* will jump at these,
But I'm sorry if you're offended.
I think, perhaps, by the look in your eye,
That you would prefer the plates to buy.
The price will not be unduly high.

PAPA

'Twill be money that's well expended.

ALGY and MONTY

Here comes the winner. What shining eyes!

MAMA

Easy to see who's won the prize.

PHOTOGRAPHER

The others are following close behind,
Each pretending she doesn't mind.

MAMA

Maud's a failure at that, poor dear!

PAPA

Let's give the bevy a hearty cheer.
[*They cheer as* COMPETITORS *and* PAPA JUNIOR
enter.]

NO. 4

[*Taking a* TWIN. PAPA JR. *takes the other.*]
Oh, thank you, so much, for each holding a twin,
The darlings wanted their mother to win.
Just listen a moment—we'll tell you why.
Oh, hush, my precious ones, hush-a-bye!
[PAPA JR. *joins in.*]
When we were free from family care,
We used to cycle everywhere,
But with the advent of this pair,
We ceased to roam at random.
But now my wife that I have has won this prize
Our dearest hopes once more arise,
We'll cycle 'spite of family ties.
For it's a brand new tandem,
And we will take them near and far
In baskets on the handle-bar.

NO. 4

[*Alone*] And I shall buy some rational clothes
With the money that's also awarded.
I've hated wearing this trailing skirt,
But 'twas all that could be afforded.

MAMA

I was almost resigned to losing my son
To gain a modest daughter,
How glad I am she's already won,
She's not at all what I thought her.

PHOTOGRAPHER

Well, time and tide no man awaits,
So I'll hurry away and develop my plates.
Accept, please, this card with my compliments,
Good afternoon, ladies! 'Afternoon, gents!

[*Exit.*

[NO. 2 *comes up to congratulate winner.*

NO. 2

Oh, the darling wee petsy-wets!
I'd like to hold one. Oh, do, please let's!
Oh, she's got such a teeny wee foot,
It's just her own precious wee tootsy-woot.
She's a sweet little girly curly kale. . . .

PAPA JUNIOR

[*Breaking in*] Pardon me, Madam, the child's a male.

[*He takes baby. Exit* NO. 2.

MAUD

[*Congratulating winner*] Forgive, please, the envious
tears in my eyes,
I'd hoped for a different story.
I don't begrudge you the actual prize,
But only the honour and glory! [*Bursts into tears.*

PAPA JUNIOR

Pray take my voluminous handkerchief,
It's large enough to absorb your grief.

MAUD

Thank you so much ! 'Tis a great relief !
There's nothing for tears like a man's 'kerchief.

[*Exit* MAUD.

NO. 3

It was a silly leetle race,
I'd scarce begun to show my pace.
And such a very breezy place,
'Twas that my win prevented.
I'm glad that yours the prize will be.
I also am ze sport you see.
A tandem is no use to me,
So I am quite contented.
To-morrow I leave this Angleterre.
I go to Brussels to join my père.
With the wonderful prize for the race that is there
'Tis certain I will be presented.   [*She swaggers off.*

MAMA

No English girl would travel alone,
Without a sign of chaperon.
I'd not be a bit surprised if she
Was not a whit better than she should be.

PAPA

I've ordered, dear Madam, my carriage and pair,
It should have arrived from my home in Mayfair,
So if you wish to proceed anywhere,
I'd be delighted to drive you there.

MAMA

That's exceedingly kind of you.
I'll see you later, Montague.

PAPA

Good-bye, Algy. Good luck to you [*to* NO. 4].
                    [*Exit* MONTY'S MAMA *and* ALGY'S PAPA.

ALGY and MONTY

What do they think we're going to do !

NO. 4

It's time our babies (let's have one peep)
Were in their cradles rocked to sleep.

PAPA JUNIOR

I fear your tandem here must stay.
We'll call for it some other day.
No doubt, they'll find a place for us
Upon some crowded omnibus.   [*Exit.*

MONTY

Algy !

ALGY

Monty !

MONTY

I'm very sad, aren't you?

ALGY

Not too jaunty.

TOGETHER

What are we going to do?
We can't have her in marriage [*pause*].
Say ! Let's hire them a carriage,
And we'll ride back
From the racing-track
On her bicycle made for two.
        [*Once again the distant band is heard playing "Daisy."*

MONTY

Algy!

ALGY

Monty!

TOGETHER

That's very bright of you!
We're quite jaunty,
Knowing the thing to do!
It seems quite a happy marriage,
So we'll hire for them a carriage,
While we'll look great,
Riding in state,
On her bicycle made for two.
 [*With the band now playing loudly*

THE CURTAIN FALLS